Elizabeth,

Thank you for your lively, important contribution to the life of theatre in Saint John.

Mary Elizabeth Smith

himney Corner,
a playbill
(New Brunswick
Museum)

Gipsy Queen,
a playbill
(Harvard Theatre Collection)

Too Soon the Curtain Fell

A History of Theatre in Saint John 1789 - 1900

Mary Elizabeth Smith

Brunswick Press
Fredericton, N.B.
Printed by Unipress
Fredericton, N.B.

Book design: Karen Timmins

[Cover] *The Academy of Music* (New Brunswick Museum)

ISBN 0-88790-111-5

For Bob

Contents

A view of the City & Harbour of St. John, New Brunswick, N.A. taken from Hills W.S.W. of Fort Howe by Ralph Stennett, engraving.
(Public Archives of Canada)

Introduction

In 1975, a student of mine at the University of New Brunswick in Saint John asked me a question: "Was there any theatre of significance in Saint John?" Since I did not at that time know of the city's rich theatrical heritage, the class and I began our research. Now, five years and many newspapers later, this book is the answer.

My research led to a fascination with the city to which I had come as an adult and to a desire to show her citizens the cultural heritage I had discovered — a heritage in which Canada's oldest incorporated city can well take pride. As well, I wanted to show that heritage to others, and certainly to the students of theatre and cultural history who are assiduously trying to rediscover our past. Because no local theatre history had as yet been written and because of the disparate nature of the audience I wanted to reach, I chose to write a narrative history that would, I hoped, be readable, as complete as space allowed, reliable, and amply documented.

The discipline of Canadian Theatre History is young. Later we shall need a complete calendar of performance and a fuller analysis of the facts, preferably in the context of a greater understanding of New Brunswick and the other Maritime provinces, when more of their theatre history has been uncovered.

Saint John, situated conveniently on the Atlantic seaboard, enjoyed from 1789 one of the oldest and richest theatrical traditions in Canada. In the nineteenth century, its tradition is fuller and more consistent than that of its sister Atlantic city, Halifax, even though the initial performance in Halifax was eleven years earlier, in 1768. The bringing to light of Saint John's theatre history thus lays a significant part of the foundation for the study of theatrical traditions in Canada. Fortunately, a wealth of material survives, primarily in newspapers, but also in theatre programmes, letters, and diaries.

Saint John's position as a port city made it accessible to professional actors as they travelled among London, Boston, New York, Halifax, and later, Montreal and other more westerly Canadian cities, and the city contributed its own share to the international theatre-world in, for example, the person of Margaret Anglin, a girl from a well-known Saint John family who became famous as an actress in the United States and abroad. Again, largely because of its position on the sea, the southern New Brunswick city was the centre of theatrical activity in its own province, although from the 1840's it was in touch with Fredericton and, after the building of the Intercolonial Railway, with Moncton. In the second half of the century, professional actors moved increasingly among the three cities, sometimes visiting also provincial towns such as Sackville, Sussex, Chatham, and Woodstock.

Certain trends are discernible in the period covered by this book. From 1795, when the young Loyalist Gentlemen Amateurs performed *Everyone Has His Fault*, then only two years old, the theatre-goers of Saint John demonstrated a desire to be up to date. Through the whole of the nineteenth century, the fashions in theatrical taste reflected those of Britain and America. In the same pattern as elsewhere, a fondness for the legitimate drama gave way to increasingly scenic spectacles, to society drama, and to farce comedy heavily sprinkled with song-and-dance routines. Yet, though a certain percentage of novelty was expected by the theatre's patrons, a partiality towards the familiar brought many old favourites to the boards time after time — a partiality which operated also for actors and managers. A manager with staying power like J. W. Lanergan won the public's trust and respect (and hence its support), and returning actors whose talents were appreciated were treated like friends coming home. The security found in the familiar may partly explain the tendency to give inadequate patronage to visiting artists of stature. An additional factor may well have been the social structure of the city, for the number of the elite who travelled and read was proportionately small; most paying customers probably gained their knowledge of theatre in their hometown and may not have been sufficiently aware of international reputations, nor were they usually impressed by them.

The tone of reviews generally reflects the education and taste of the class whose money and influence chiefly supported the theatre and who considered itself responsible to mould public taste. The wit and sophistication of the *New Dominion and True Humorist* in the 1860's and 70's, the superior air of *Progress* and the genial pomposity of the *Sun* in the 1880's and 90's, like the *Telegraph, Courier, Morning News*, and other papers, gave approval to entertainment of substance which had to be clean and wholesome, whether scenically novel and skillfully produced or not. There is evidence, however, that, as the theatre changed from a social outlet for the elite in the earliest period to entertainment for a much broader segment of the population, the paying customers at the box-office often delighted in allegedly *risqué* froth.

The fortunes of theatre in Saint John fluctuated. Although both local and world-wide seasons of prosperity and depression inevitably had their effect, economic conditions were seldom reflected immediately in the theatre, either for good or for ill. The opposition of evangelical churchmen and press, moreover, seems to have had little effect.

The availability of a suitable facility was, of course, one of the most important requirements for successful theatre — one that the frequent fires in Saint John helped to frustrate. Yet even more fundamental than this was the large positive factor in the presence of energetic patrons in the community. These included the Loyalist amateurs who were responsible for the earliest performances as well as the vigorous amateur societies which over the years stimulated response to the professional theatre and were in turn stimulated by it, the members of the Micawber Club who in the 1880's engaged artists for the Mechanics' Institute, and assorted merchants, physicians, and lawyers who supported the theatre financially and promoted it in countless other ways. In the 1830's, loans from merchant Thomas Millidge enabled Hopley's Theatre to continue, and in the later part of the century the dogged perseverance, optimism, and financial involvement of other men were responsible for the erection of both the Academy of Music and the Opera House. When to these factors was added in the 1850's the good fortune of a shrewd manager like Lanergan whose annual seasons brought stability, the theatre could indeed flourish.

Whatever the vicissitudes of the theatre, there remained a general attitude of superiority in Saint John — a feeling that Saint John was at least equal to any other city whether in Canada, Britain, or the United States. Of course, this attitude was an effective ally in enabling her citizens to overcome the numerous adversities with which they were faced, even if in the last two decades it began to seem more forced — a general air of romanticism, even of apparent naïveté, inhabits the 1890's talk about 'progress' and the anticipated promise of the future. In marked contrast to our own age is the whole of the period under study. Indeed, the general cynicism that pervades our culture (the fact that Canadian theatre now survives only with government support) prevents us, perhaps, from fully understanding a period and a people who believed in history, in themselves, and in the future.

Many people have helped in the preparation of this book, including Monica Robertson and the staff of the New Brunswick Museum Archives; Constance Acheson, Deborah Carhart, and Barbara Malcolm at the Saint John Regional Library; Heather McCallum of the Metropolitan Toronto Library; the staffs of the Harvard Theatre Collection, the New York Public Library at Lincoln Centre, the Public Archives of Canada, the Rare Book Collection at McGill University, and the Ward Chipman Library at the University of New Brunswick in Saint John. Hazel Hazen asked the question that sparked the research, James Richards gave me access to his personal collection of *Progress*, and Debra Bentley read issues of that newspaper that were available only at the University of New Brunswick in Fredericton. Ann Condon, Edward Mullaly, Constance McCollom, Richard Plant, and Peter Toner read the manuscript and made helpful comments. My mother, Rhoda Holm, read the first draft and assisted in preparation of the Index. Three persons deserve special mention. The first is my publisher, Tom Crowther, whose belief in the project has been encouraging throughout; the second is my research assistant, Elizabeth McKim, who has worked with diligence, care, and devotion; and the third is my husband, without whose practical assistance and loving support the book would not have been possible.

The research was conducted with assistance from the Social Sciences and Humanities Research Council of Canada and the University of New Brunswick Research Fund.

Mary Elizabeth Smith
University of New Brunswick, Saint John
July 1980

i
Loyalist Beginnings

"On Saturday evening last was presented before the most numerous and polite Assembly which has appeared in this Town, The BUSY BODY, with WHO'S THE DUPE? by a company of GENTLEMEN. Mallard's long Room on this occasion was converted into a pretty Theatre. The scenes, decorations, and dresses were entirely new and in a very fine style. . . . Some of the Company displayed comic talents which would have done honor to a British Theatre; and 'tis justice to say that all exceeded the expectations of the most favorable of their friends."[1] The date was February 28, 1789, and the occasion was an important one in the cultural life of Saint John and of all New Brunswick, since it was the "first dramatic exhibition in this province". So significant was the event that Colonel Edward Winslow journeyed to Saint John from his home at Kingsclear, on the St. John river a few miles above Fredericton, specifically to be present. Winslow did not mind the journey in the winter, for travelling was easy when he could use the frozen St. John river as his highway: "One hundred and thirty miles of clear going on the ice",[2] he described it. The "theatrical jaunt" was a quick one; Winslow did not linger in the city, but was off for home the morning after the performance, leaving behind him at the home of his friend the Hon. Ward Chipman, Solicitor General, a bottle of Sassaparilla Cherry that Chipman had meant for comfort on the road, his penknife, razor-case, and shoes.[3]

That the first dramatic performance in New Brunswick was an amateur one does not detract from its significance; rather it demonstrates emphatically the desire of the colonists for a cultural life of the kind they had left behind in New England. As circumstances necessitated that they carve out homes and businesses for themselves

1

from a wilderness, so also they had to promote for themselves whatever entertainments they could to enrich their labour-filled lives.

Theatre came to Saint John, in fact, amazingly early. Only in the autumn of 1783 had the Loyalists begun to erect their first homes in a land previously populated by Indians and a few white settlers. Just four years earlier, in 1785, the towns of Parr and Carleton on the east and west peninsulas of the harbour had been amalgamated and incorporated to form the city of Saint John. In contrast, although the first colonists had arrived in America in the early part of the seventeenth century, the first recorded theatrical production (an amateur one) took place in Virginia only in 1665. Halifax waited nineteen years from its founding in 1749 until its first theatrical performance in 1768 by the professional American Company of Comedians; as far as we know, Haligonians had done nothing earlier to stimulate a culture of their own. In Saint John, the Loyalist settlers were extremely quick to recognize the value of having their own theatre.

The plays chosen for that first night in 1789 were Sarah Centlivre's comedy *The Busy Body* and the farce *Who's the Dupe?* by Hannah Cowley. *Who's the Dupe?* was the newer play, having been performed for the first time at the Drury Lane in London ten years previously. Both were satirical comedies of intrigue in the Restoration manner, each plot concerned with outwitting an insensitive parent or guardian in order that the course of true love might run smoothly. The names of the characters in *The Busy Body* indicate, as was customary, the nature of the complication: Marplot, Sir Francis Gripe, Sir Jealous Traffic, Whisper.

Ward Chipman's hope that the performance would "be a prelude to other exhibitions of the same kind"[4] was not disappointed, for *The Busy Body* was repeated on April 2, this time in combination with *All the World's a Stage*, a popular farce which pokes fun at amateur theatricals and, on this occasion, allowed the gentlemen amateurs to have fun at their own expense.

Somewhat heavier fare concluded the first season of drama, as Edward Moore's tragedy of *The Gamester* was combined with Arthur Murphy's afterpiece *The Upholsterer* on April 20. Allardyce Nicoll describes *The Gamester* as "a truly excellent prose drama with a characteristically moral aim".[5] Its plot follows the misadventures of Beverley, a gambler deceived by the villain Stukely, until, in prison accused of murder, he swallows poison and dies just as news of a handsome inheritance is brought to him. In London, Sarah Siddons played Mrs. Beverley. William Charles Macready, who played opposite her, described her behaviour in the moment following her husband's final anguish:

2

Her glaring eyes were fixed in stony blankness on his face; the powers of life seemed suspended in her; her sister and Lewson gently raised her, and slowly led her unresisting from the body, her gaze never for an instant averted from it; when they reached the prison door she stopped, as if awakened from a trance, uttered a shriek of agony that would have pierced the hardest heart, and rushing from them flung herself . . . on the prostrate form before her.[6]

Actresses for years afterwards copied Mrs. Siddons' gestures, but the imagination boggles in contemplation of the Saint John "company of GENTLEMEN" in imitation of the famous Siddons' style.

Saint John saw no more theatre until the Gentlemen offered a season of five programmes in the winter and spring of 1795. *All the World's a Stage* provided the afterpiece for the first production on January 5 and was repeated twice more in a season devoted to comedy. Its last production, on April 10, is particularly interesting for the local touch inserted when the proscribed setting was rejected in favour of a "New Scene, representing Partridge Island".[7] Significant also was the performance of Elizabeth Inchbald's moral comedy *Everyone Has His Fault* (also on April 10), because it was then only two years old, having received its initial performance at Covent Garden in 1793: Saint John's tastes in theatre were indeed up to date. Other plays given in the 1795 season included Richard Cumberland's sentimental comedy *The Impostors* on January 12, and Arthur Murphy's farce, *The Citizen*, in combination with *The Upholsterer* on February 19 and March 5.[8]

As in 1789, all performances were in Mallard's Tavern (owned by Thomas Mallard, who had been a Lieutenant in the Thirty Seventh Company of Militia), known in the newspaper advertisements as the Theatre, King Street. This was the hall where the Common Council met from 1785 to 1797 and which housed the first meeting of the Legislative Assembly of the province in 1786. Like the Theatre Pontac, where dramatic entertainment had begun in Halifax, the theatre at Mallard's was simply a large room which could be transformed by platforms, benches, and chairs. It had a stage with scenery, behind which no member of the audience could on any account be admitted. Since there were no boxes or gallery, tickets all sold for the single price of three shillings. There seems to have been some attempt to make the sight lines as open as possible, but advertisements note that insufficient height in the room and ladies' hair fashions made this difficult: "The want of sufficient height in the Theatre to allow the back Seats a proper elevation, obliges the Managers to request of the Ladies, that they will come with their heads as low dressed as possible".[9] This and other notices are indicative of the need to control an audience in the makeshift quarters: "It is to be observed that the Seats are all numbered, and the Tickets are not generally for *any* Seat; but *only* for the Seat of the same Number with the Ticket".[10] To minimize confusion at the doors, tickets had to be procured at the Tavern during the day: no money would be taken at the door; nor could a person be admitted without a ticket.

The Loyalists who arrived in Saint John in 1783 were a heterogenous collection of individuals representing every segment of American society, having in common only their preference for the British system of government. The largest and most powerful group was, of course, the Loyalist elite. To it belonged civil and military officers appointed by England, Anglican clergymen dependent on English support, lawyers educated in the English system, and merchants dependent on the trans-Atlantic trade. This group, who became the founding fathers of New Brunswick, had been avid supporters of theatre in the places they had left and, not surprisingly, they were the people who established the theatre in Saint John.

In the very first years of their residence in a new land, Loyalists of all sorts found sufficient occupation in providing for themselves the practical necessities of life — houses, roads, food, means of livelihood. But, by 1788, 1000 houses stood on the east and west peninsulas, affording "striking illustration", Bishop Inglis wrote in his diary, "of what industry is capable of doing".[11] Shipbuilding had already become a major industry, and a fleet of sixty square-rigged vessels had been acquired to cope with the increasing trade with the British West Indies, a trade which since the war had been reserved for the King's subjects, excluding the Americans who had controlled it previously. Commercial houses in the city were growing in number and in wealth. Especially for the young men, sons of the households, more leisure provided both the desire and the opportunity for diversions. These young men were the ones who selected and rehearsed the plays, built the scenes, and re-arranged the hall at Mallard's, confident of the support of their elders, and no doubt encouraged by them.

An epilogue, written for recitation at the opening of the theatre season on January 5, 1795, stresses both the youth and the amateur status of the performers:

You've seen no vet'ran Hero tread this Stage,
. . . .
But humble youths, whose timid steps proclaim
Them, Candidates for Suffrage, not for Fame.

4

Mallard House, Saint John. (New Brunswick Museum)

THEATRE,
KING-STREET.

For Public Charity,
On THURSDAY the 2d of *April*, 1789,
Will be PERFORMED,
The COMEDY of

THE BUSY BODY;

To which will be added,
All the World's a Stage.

THE DOORS TO BE OPENED AT HALF PAST
FIVE,—TO BEGIN PRECISELY AT HALF
PAST SIX O'CLOCK.

☞ TICKETS at *three shillings* each, to
be had at MALLARD'S Tavern.

No MONEY will be received at the door, nor
any perfon admitted without a Ticket.
March 27th, 1789.

*Theatre, King
Street*
(New Brunswick Museum)

Rude nature's Pupils, novices in part,
And self instructed in the comic art.

Two of the actors in the 1789 season were Jonathan and Stephen Sewell, sons of Jonathan Sewell, formerly attorney-general of Massachusetts, who had demonstrated his own practical interest in the drama with his pamphlet play *The American Roused, in a Cure for the Spleen* (1775). Both boys had performed in Addison's *Cato* while students at the Bristol Grammar School, England. Sarah Siddons had seen the production and, impressed with Jonathan's handling of the title role, had written to him in verse:

'Tis rare for boys like thee to play the man —
There are but few in years who nobly can;
But thou, a youth of elegance and ease,
In Cato's person, to perform and please,
Hast common youth and manhood both outdone,
And proved thyself dame nature's chosen son.[13]

Jonathan's roles are unknown in 1789, but Stephen played Mrs. Beverley in *The Gamester*, Isabinda in *The Busy Body*, Miss Doiley in *Who's the Dupe?*, Miss Bridget Pumpkin in *All the World's a Stage*, and Harriet in *The Upholsterer*.[14] Of the 1795 company the only actor whose name is known was Ebenezer Putnam. A young storekeeper, he was a son of James Putnam, Assistant Judge of the New Brunswick Supreme Court.

Presumably the audience of the first seasons included the elder Sewells, the Putnams, and parents of the other boys, as well as young friends of the performers and others of the elite and middle classes. The attendance of Edward Winslow, the hot-headed gentleman who had supervised the settlement of the region between Fredericton and Woodstock, has already been mentioned. His reaction to the performance, expressed in a letter to Ward Chipman, who attended on the second night, has a note of paternal indulgence: "I am gratifyd at hearing that the play went off so well — & feel a little tickled that the prologue is as well received. It convinces me of the truth of an observation I made very seriously to Mr. Grady — That nonsense never fails to please if it is civil".[15]

While the Loyalists' cultural heritage in Britain and America made it natural that they should seek to maintain that heritage in a new place, the occasional prologues to the plays performed reveal the qualities that enabled them to succeed in building a new society. The prologues indicate a belief in the importance of commerce as well as a sense of the importance of attention to duty, and the in-

6

tertwining of these with a love of the arts. The prologue for February 28, 1789, moves from poetry to obligation:

> The scenic Muse in every clime admir'd,
> Has cherish'd genius and her sons inspir'd;
> Has polish'd manners with peculiar art,
> Guided the passions and reform'd the heart:
> Unveil'd the page, from whence ourselves we know,
> And trac'd the sources whence our errors flow.
>
> But these the general uses of the stage,
> Have not been all; in every place and age
> The sisters, guardians of the laugh and sigh,
> Have still gone hand in hand with charity.[16]

In this way, the prologue introduces the fact that proceeds from that night's performance, as indeed those of the entire 1789 and 1795 seasons, would go to charity. The prologue for January 5, 1795, moves from commerce to poetry:

> What rais'd this City on a dreary coast,
> Alternately presenting rocks and frost,
> Where torpid shell-fish hardly found a bed,
> Where scarce a pine durst shew a stunted head?
>
> 'Twas commerce — commerce smooth'd the rugged strand,
> Her streets and buildings overspread the land;
> Her piers the mighty Fundy's tides control,
> And navies ride secure within her mole.
>
> Yet what are these without the muses' aid!
> When swindlers circumvent, or thieves invade:
> Or credit staggers with misfortune's stroke,
> Or brightest speculation ends in smoke;
> When toil on toil, on labor labor pours,
> Or dire impends the task — of vacant hours!
>
> Make then the muses your peculiar care,
> 'Midst loss, midst profit, still to verse repair;
> Verse, which refines the pleasures of success,
> Brings hope, and consolation to success.[17]

The Loyalist elite placed faith in "commerce" as a civilizing force but believed that their own good fortune obliged them to serve their country and its people, even gratuitously where necessary. Thus, when Ward Chipman was denied compensation for his services as Solicitor General, he accepted the decision in terms of good Loyalist rhetoric: "I must acknowledge that I never expected

7

compensation for all these services, aware that in the infancy of the Government, it was the duty of every one to contribute a proportion of services to the public without any other reward than that which is indeed above all others, a consciousness of having done our duty".[18] Thus the amateur thespians believed they should do what they could for the less fortunate, especially if they could enjoy themselves at the same time:

> A humane band of citizens 'tis true,
> Having done much good; but much is yet to do.[19]

In the first years, it would not have been reasonable to expect a professional company to risk failure in New Brunswick. Ten years after the earliest dramatic performance in 1789, however, Mr. and Mrs. Marriott, originally from the Theatre Royal, Edinburgh, and laterly from Boston, New York, Philadelphia, and Halifax, decided to test the theatrical climate. They cannot have met with an enthusiastic response, for their stay in the city lasted only six months.

The Marriotts, in their professional backgrounds and in their abilities, as far as one can judge these, are typical of the calibre of professional entertainer who would visit the Maritime provinces for some years to come. Until well after the Revolution, theatre in America was provided largely by British military officers and by second rate British actors who, having failed to rise to the top of their professions at home, decided to try for recognition on the other side of the Atlantic. It is true that between 1810 and 1821 three actors — George Frederick Cooke, Edmund Kean, and Junius Brutus Booth — came to startle the American theatre into new life, but no native-born American achieved the full bloom of stardom earlier than Edwin Forrest in the middle 1820's, and certainly "the best level of Shakespearean acting in America down to 1810 seems to have been competent but unremarkable".[20]

The Marriotts failed to win encomiums from audiences in America, who saw them only in minor roles. The press was disappointed with their acting abilities, found Mrs. Marriott pleasing to look at if overly nervous, and largely ignored them. Probably they came north to Halifax to try for a more hospitable climate of criticism. They came with the C. S. Powells, formerly from London and lately also unsuccessful in America. Mr. Powell's career in America had begun more auspiciously than Mr. Marriott's, for he was the first manager of two major Boston theatres, the Federal Street Theatre and the Haymarket. He preferred management to acting and so, when misfortune befell him in both managerial positions in Boston, he took his own newly-formed company to Halifax rather than remain as an actor at the Haymarket. From 1798 to 1805 the Hali-

8

fax Theatre performed regularly under his leadership, and with the assistance of officers from the garrison. The Marriotts were with him except for the six months they spent in Saint John in the first half of 1799.

On February 25, 1799, the Marriotts opened in Saint John with a company that consisted of themselves and several ladies and gentlemen of the city, probably including the Mr. Tomlinson and Mrs. Salenki who appear in later notices. For their opening night they chose wisely for an audience no longer restricted to a Loyalist elite but now including a number of powerful Scottish merchants. John Home's tragedy, *Douglas; or the Noble Scotch Shepherd*, was originally performed in Home's home town of Edinburgh on December 14, 1756, twenty-two months after the author had set off for London on horseback with the manuscript in his pocket, only to have his hopes dashed when Garrick failed to see its merits. The Scots were more appreciative. The applause on the occasion of the premier production was enthusiastic, while the tears of the ladies bespoke their approval. "The town", said Dr. Carlyle, "was in an uproar of exaltation, that a Scotsman should write a tragedy of the first rate, and that its merits were first submitted to them".[21] The judgment of our age does not confirm the Scots' enthusiasm, but *Douglas* was repeated again and again in Saint John until well into the 1800's.

The production of *Douglas* in February 1799 marked the first appearance of a woman on the Saint John stage. Lady Randolph, another of Sarah Siddons' tragic roles, was played by "a Lady of this City", while her son, Young Norval, was performed by Mrs. Marriott. Mr. Marriott was Glenalvon, and the parts of Old Norval and Lord Randolph were taken by 'Gentlemen'. For whatever reason, there was a rearrangement of parts for the repeat performance on March 27. This time Mrs. Marriott was Lady Randolph, Mr. Marriott was Young Norval, and the other characters were "properly cast, and fitted for representation".[22]

From February through April the Marriotts used as a theatre the Assembly Room on the second floor of the Exchange Coffee House at the corner of King and Prince William Streets. With judicious arrangement of platforms and benches, the 50 by 25 foot room was turned into an auditorium with boxes and a pit, and with a decorated stage at one end. Admission was by ticket only — 2s.6d. for a box, 1s.3d. for the pit, less than the amateurs had charged. To minimize confusion, which was still a problem, notice was given that all seats would be numbered.

Most of the performances were benefits. The second production of *Douglas*, on March 27, belonged to Mr. Tomlinson, while

Mrs. Marriott took her benefit in George Lillo's domestic tragedy, *The London Merchant*, on April 8. With these tragedies, the first a forerunner of the Gothic play and the second a moral lecture, the company combined comedies such as Congreve's *Love for Love*, pantomimic interludes such as *Jack in Distress*, various spoken prologues, dances, and songs to make lengthy and diversified programmes that lasted for several hours.

For May through July, the Marriotts moved their productions to an amphitheatre in an unknown location "at a small distance from the City".[23] This theatre must have been larger and more elaborate than either Mallard's or the Exchange Coffee House, since its auditorium consisted of boxes, pit, and gallery, to which admittance could be gained for 3s.9d., 2s.6d., and 1s.3d. respectively. Great care was taken to keep persons from entering illegally, for tickets were taken at the first door and checks of admittance were given at a second, or entrance, door.

The new theatre opened with the two act comedy, *The Citizen*, in combination with *The Miller of Mansfield* and an occasional prologue composed by Mr. Marriott about the "late happy preservation of the American ship Sally, in Hampton Roads, by His Majesty's ship Hinde".[24] The titles of only two other programmes are known: Nicholas Rowe's verse tragedy *Jane Shore*, with Mrs. Salenki in the title role and Mrs. Marriott as Alicia, followed by a pantomime called *The Bird Catcher and the British Tar* (May 27) and Garrick's comedy *The Lying Valet* with *The Citizen* (July 31).

A combination of factors contributed to the Marriotts' decision to return to Halifax at the beginning of August. From 1793, New Brunswick entered upon a period of severe depression, and the Loyalist fathers, who had imagined their province as the centre of a "renovated empire",[25] were disillusioned. With the outbreak of war with France, Halifax, not Saint John, became the strategic military centre and also the focal point of commercial intelligence and trade. Besides drawing off the trade of Saint John, Halifax merchants charged exorbitant rates to forward British goods to New Brunswick. The already difficult situation was exaggerated by the signing of the Treaty of Amity and Commerce between England and the United States in 1794. Designed by England to buy the goodwill of the United States, the treaty took away from the British provinces the lucrative trade with the West Indies. "The great ships of New Brunswick no longer put to sea."[26] When the Scott brothers arrived from Greenock, Scotland, in March 1799, to found what was to grow into a renowned shipbuilding industry, Saint John had no vessels of any size. Moreover, many settlers, despairing of the prospects for their province, were leaving New Brunswick for Canada; the exodus to the Niagara peninsula had already begun. The population of New Brunswick had not increased according to the expectations of its founding fathers.

The Marriotts, then, were forced to contend with an unfavourable economic climate in Saint John from which the elite, who might have been expected to lead the way in support of the theatre, suffered most. It is hardly surprising that the Marriotts were at no point able to sustain themselves solely from their theatrical endeavours, despite the fact that they clearly tried strenuously and persistently to attract patrons. For two months following their arrival in the city, Marriott ran a combination restaurant, butchershop, winestore, and barbershop. An early vendor of fast-foods, he provided "*Dinners* dressed and sent out at an hour's notice", and served on the premises "*Soups, Broths, Beef* and *Mutton Steaks*, at the lowest prices, at a minute's warning".[27] The occupation of barber, especially, was one often taken up by actors, for it was "not uncommon in those days to find actors officiating with the razor when a dull theatrical season or some other reason prompted a change of occupation".[28] The next enterprises Marriott undertook to keep him financially solvent were those of educator and hotelkeeper. In March he opened a school to teach English grammar, reading, writing, drawing, ciphering, and fencing. In April he opened the Thespian Hotel on Tyng (now Princess) Street.

The theatre, his main endeavour, was hindered by other problems not of his making. Weather delayed the opening of his amphitheatre, and illness among the actors forced postponement and even changes of programme. The company was unable to offer productions frequently enough to sustain itself over a period of time, though it is unlikely that the small population of the city could have supported more. All things considered, it made sense that the Marriotts should give up the struggle and return to Halifax where the conditions for theatre were more propitious.

Even during the depression of the 1790's Saint John could support, as we have seen, a short amateur season. The amateurs were not dependent on the theatre for their livelihood. They could be satisfied with the small audiences Mallard's must have held and they could, moreover, be assured of the encouragement of relatives and friends. If there was not wide enough support to sustain professional theatre, there was at least interest among the younger generation of the merchant and professional classes and a willingness to provide for themselves what could not be had otherwise. Thus, just over a year after the departure of the Marriotts, another amateur season of dramatic activity was in preparation.

The City Council minutes for October 3, 1800, contain a peti-

The Exchange Coffee House at the corner of King and Prince William Streets. The Mallard House appears on the left, on King Street.
(New Brunswick Museum)

Old City Hall, Market Square, given to the New Brunswick Museum by the New Brunswick Historical Society. (New Brunswick Museum)

tion from William Botsford, George Leonard Jr., Charles Peters, and William Simonds, applying on their own behalf and that of other young men of the city for permission "to fit up the city hall for the purpose of a theatre". The City Hall, a two storey building on Market Square, had been erected in 1797. On its second floor, above the market and the police lock-up and accessible by an out-side staircase and balcony, were the Council Chambers and Court Room where the young men found space suitable for less weighty purposes. The minutes record that the petition was granted on con-dition that the users guarantee to repair any damage, yield to an in-spection by three aldermen at the close of the season, and insure the building to the amount of £1000 against fire caused by its use as a theatre.

The gentlemen who initiated the project were older than the amateurs who had conducted the first two seasons at Mallard's Tav-ern. William Botsford was twenty-seven, and Charles Peters was his senior by one year. Because all were established in their profes-sions, they could better afford to take the financial risks that reno-vation of the City Hall involved. William Simonds was a store-keeper, a descendent of the prominent pre-Loyalist Simonds family. The other three, all of Loyalist stock, were lawyers at the beginning of impressive careers. George Leonard was the son of the Hon. George Leonard, formerly of Plymouth, Massachusetts, and now a Legislative Councillor for New Brunswick resident in Sussex. William Botsford's father was Amos, Loyalist agent and first Speaker of the New Brunswick House of Assembly, and Charles Peters was son to James, Loyalist agent. William Botsford, himself a graduate of Yale, would go on to become Recorder of Saint John, Solicitor-General, and judge. Charles Peters would become a judge in the Court of Vice Admiralty, Attorney General, and Common Clerk of Saint John.

Although the players were mainly amateurs, they seem to have called in professional assistance at least for the first produc-tion, and perhaps for the full season; the "M^r & Mrs Mariniett" in-cluded in the cast list for *Cheap Living* and *Cross Purposes* on Janu-ary 14 are almost certainly the Mariotts, recalled from Halifax. According to John S. Ellegood, himself one of the company, the other actors in the opening production were "Mr J. Allan, Mr Just(?), Mr Sangster, Mr Phair, Mr E^d Leonard, Mr Sands, Mr W. Ca....., Mr C. Peters, Michel Ryan, Mr W. Botsford, W. Chipman Junr Doctor Emerson, & myself".[29] Ellegood was Sir Toby Bumper in *School for Scandal* (performed twice in February),[30] to which Mary Odell contributed a prologue, raising and answering ques-

13

tions that would be repeated frequently in the succeeding years of
the nineteenth century:

> . . . . where's the person, pray
> Who goes for moral lessons to a play?
> In theatres do Beaux and Ladies search
> For truths which they are sure to find at Church?
> For antidotes against domestic strife,
> For guides of conduct, or for rules of life?
> Does age here learn to excuse the faults of Youth?
> Do Beauties learn discretion? — Lovers truth? —
> No — though with sage instruction plays are fraught;
> You come to be *amused*, not to be *taught*.[31]

The beneficial effect of the theatre, according to Miss Odell, can be
summed up thus:

> Hence may result a calm and constant ray
> Of inbred joy, not subject to decay;
> Approved by reason and sustain'd by truth,
> It sheds new lustre on the bloom of Youth,
> And, to the verge of Life's eventful Stage,
> Lights up the eye and gilds the brow of Age.

Between mid-January and mid-March 1801, the energetic
company presented a season of four completely different programmes, three of which were performed more than once, all to packed
houses. Rehearsal of four full-length comedies and four afterpieces
in two months meant a heavy schedule for actors with busy lives
outside their recreation. Perhaps the pace was too hectic to continue, for the theatre in City Hall is not heard of again.

Further evidence of interest in drama during the difficult
1790's is provided by two pieces written in New Brunswick. In 1795,
Edward Winslow penned his pamphlet, *Substance of the Debates in
the Young Robin Hood Society*, published, the title page alleges, 'at
the Request of a Number of the KING'S faithful Subjects in
New-Brunswick".[32] Following in the tradition of the American
propaganda play like Sewell's *A Cure for the Spleen*, Winslow's political satire sets out to persuade its readers and in so doing ignores
all the rules for dramatic construction. More properly a dramatic
sketch than a play, it contains little action, no stage directions, but
much sharp, pungent wit and several fine, cleverly drawn images.
Debates in the Young Robin Hood Society deals with issues of vital
interest to Saint John. It is Winslow's defence of government by an
appointed Loyalist elite, and simultaneously a defence of reason
and education. It focuses on the controversy surrounding the Carle-

ton government's intention to develop Fredericton and the inland agricultural areas of New Brunswick through legislative initiative and in defiance of those who favoured development of the coastal areas and decentralization of power. Specifically, it is a reply to James Glennie's pamphlet entitled *Substance of Mr. Glenie's Address to the Freeholders of the County of Sunbury*. In this urgent political debate, which had been aggravated by the trade depression, the gentlemanly values of the Loyalist fathers as sound precepts for the development of the province were on trial. Though their influence continued to be felt for decades, the debate was lost, and this would eventually have an effect on the tastes of the populace even in the elitist bastions of arts and letters.

The second piece was Lt. Adam Allan's verse drama *The New Gentle Shepherd*, an adaptation of Allan Ramsay's *The Gentle Shepherd*. Allan was born in Dumfries, Scotland, and emigrated to the colonies, where he held a Lieutenant's commission in the Queen's Rangers. A Loyalist, he was one of the first settlers at Saint Anne's Point (now Fredericton), his house being one of four there in 1785, and he continued to live in York County until his death in 1823 at the age of sixty-five. He may have made his adaptation while commanding a post at Grand Falls in 1798, during a period of unrest between the United States and the provinces.[33] Though Allan was never a resident of Saint John, his work found a readership there. The *Royal Gazette* announced publication of his play in September 1798, and three years later gave evidence of its continued popularity with an announcement of an "improved edition".

Lt. Allan, in an address to the public prefaced to his volume, says that his intent was to divest Ramsay's play of the shackles of its Scottish dialect. Although the original version had gone through several editions in Scotland and Ireland, it was little known in England and America "because the dialect in which it was written was not generally understood by the natives of those countries".[34] Allan set out to rectify this. Although for the most part faithful to the Scottish text, he added a preface and an epilogue, added a third scene to Act IV, made some alterations in the songs and other parts of the play, substituted simple, direct stage directions for Ramsay's long poetic ones, and generally improved the stageworthiness of his source. The result was a charming five-act comedy containing many characteristic features of the pastoral romantic mode. It was, however, never acted in New Brunswick.

From 1801, prosperity slowly began to work its way back to New Brunswick. After 1806 the economy showed a pronounced upsurge, and the province again sent a fleet of ships around the world.

Provincial trade of all sorts increased, assisted in part by the Free Ports Act of 1807. In 1808 New Brunswick's exports to the West Indies rose 150 percent over the preceding year, and, with the closure of the Baltic to British ships, her timber found a ready market in Britain.

The new prosperity, however, was not immediately reflected in the theatre. For seven years after the 1801 season in City Hall, the people of Saint John saw no drama apart from one performance of Garrick's *Catherine and Petruchio* given by a company from the Theatre Royal, Halifax, in May 1803. Not until 1809 did the theatre become active again.

The evening of February 3, 1809, saw the opening of the Drury Lane Theatre, the first building in Saint John to be used solely as a theatre. The story of its erection is one of a spirit of adventure, persistence, and co-operation between gentlemen of the garrison and of the city. The idea for the project came from officers at Fort Howe. There seems to have been little time spent in planning; rather, the undertaking evolved almost spontaneously out of the enthusiasm of the officers of the 101st Regiment under their commander, Major George O'Malley, an enthusiasm which they managed to convey to their civilian associates and, after opening night, to the general public.

During one of the coldest Januarys in memory, the new theatre took shape. "Many of the gentlemen of the City, while they very cheerfully subscribed to so laudable a work, conceived it to be beyond the bounds of possibility that a Theatre . . . could have been prepared for an exhibition in the course of the winter",[35] but the military men were indefatigable in their exertions. The project involved the rebuilding of an existing shell of a building on the corner of Union Street and Drury Lane (now a parking lot for Brooke Bond) and more than doubling its size. When the renovated structure was finished, it contained a 56 by 26 foot auditorium with boxes, pit, and gallery; a Green Room for rehearsals; sundry other rooms which could be used for workshops, storage, or meeting places; a cellar and a garret.[36] Nothing is known of the stage except that it was dressed with a "variety of Scenery", but it would have been small, with a proscenium arch and a narrow apron, and it was probably raked. Artificial light would have been provided by candles or oil lamps. The first night audience found the theatre an "astonishing spectacle", "complete", and "perfect in its arrangements".

A crowded house greeted the opening programme, J. G. Holman's 1796 musical comedy *Abroad and at Home* and that favorite of Saint John amateurs, *All the World's a Stage*. Although the plays

16

had been ready on January 30, work on the theatre was not quite finished in time, so the opening had to be postponed four days. The audience was "crowded and respectable"; the theatre's location in the fashionable district of York Point was not only convenient for the regimental gentlemen stationed in Portland but must have attracted Loyalist and pre-Loyalist families like the Chipmans, Leonards, and Hazens who had their homes there. Tickets, at 5s. for a box, 4 s. for the pit, and 3s. for the gallery, were considerably more expensive than any before in Saint John. There is no doubt, then, that the new theatre became a gathering place for the well-to-do and the intellectual elite.

The opening night passed satisfactorily for all concerned. The reviewer for the *Royal Gazette* found that "the several characters of the Drama were supported with singular correctness and spirit" and enthused: "What will not perseverance accomplish, when animated by the disinterested zeal and public spirit, which have thus so unexpectedly laid the foundation of an institution, that will, we trust, long continue a source of rational amusement and pleasure to our society".[37]

The company, in an overt indication of its sympathies, called itself His Majesty's Servants. Only two of the young actors are known by name. They are Captain McCormick of the 101st Regiment and Edward Jarvis, a twenty-one year old college student and son of Loyalist Munson Jarvis, a hardware merchant and overseas trader.

All of the plays the young men performed in the short season, which lasted only until May 2, were British comedies and melodramas, most of them belonging to the eighteenth century. The oldest piece was T. Sheridan's *The Brave Irishman* (1737), and the newest was George Colman's very successful *John Bull*, which ran for forty-seven nights at Covent Garden in 1803 and earned its author £1200. In addition, the repertoire included two Thomas Morton plays, *Zorinski* and *Speed the Plough*, another George Colman, *The Poor Gentleman*, and Bickerstaffe's *Doctor Last in His Chariot*. The company managed two programmes in February, March, and April, and one in May, performing a total of ten separate scripts. But there were problems when soldiers on duty tried to commit themselves to production dates, and twice performances had to be postponed when military obligations prevented an actor from appearing at the theatre.

Unfortunately for theatre, the 101st Regiment was sent to the West Indies in July 1809. In appreciation of his contributions to the life of Saint John, the Common Council presented Major O'Malley

17

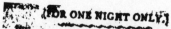

[FOR ONE NIGHT ONLY.]

Theatre, Drury-Lane, Saint John.

ON WEDNESDAY, MAY 16,

MR. POWELL will give his *Attick Entertainment,*

The Evening Brush,

, FOR

Rubbing off the Rust of care.

Subject for Laughter,

Butchers in Heroicks—Tragedy Taylors—
Wooden Actors—Blunderers and Bogglers—
An Actor reading his part without eyes, &c. &c.

To be interspersed with several appropriate
COMIC SONGS, viz:

Shakespeare's Seven Ages of Human Life,
Darby Logan's passage from Dublin to London,
The Coach Box,
The Golden Days of good Queen Bess.

To which will be added, a Whimsical and Critical
Dissertation on Noses:

The Ruby Nose,
Roman Nose of old Ben Blunderbuss,
The Prognosticating Snout of Goody Screech-
Owl, &c. &c.

The whole to conclude with a SONG,

Modernized by MR. POWELL,

Giving a whimsical description of the

BATTLE of the NILE,

to be Sung in the character of a *French Officer.*

N. B. The Doors to be opened at Seven o'Clock, and
the Performance to commence at half an hour after.

BY PERMISSION.

At Mr. JARVIS's Store.

Mr. MARRIOTT,

RESPECTFULLY informs the
Ladies and Gentlemen of SAINT
JOHN, that being assisted by a Lady and
Gentleman of this City, he is enabled
to get up a whole PLAY and a Con-
cert of Instrumental Music—which
will be performed on MONDAY
Evening, the 25th Instant—

A *Celebrated Tragedy,*
CALLED

DOUGLASS;

OR

The Noble Scotch Shepherd.

Young Norval, Mrs. Marriott,
Old Norval, A Gentleman,
Glenalvon, Mr. Marriott,
Lord Randolph, A Gentleman,
Servants, filled by others
Lady Randolph, By a Lady of this
City.

Anna, by a young Lady instructed for
the purpose.

A Bengal Light,

By which the audience will be able
to discern 2000 faces and persons in the
dark, and the place appear as light as
day.

A Scots Song, called
" To the Green Wood gang wi me," by a
Lady of St. John.

The whole to conclude with a grand
Artificial FIRE WORK.

SAINT JOHN THEATRE.

SECOND NIGHT of the GRAND MELO-DRAMA, called

TEKELI;

Or, The Siege of Montgatz.

On Wednesday Evening September 17, 1817,

Will be presented, (for the Second time,) the Grand Melo-Drama, in Three Acts, called

TEKELI;

Or, The Siege of Montgatz.

With New Scenery, Machinery, Decorations, &c. as performed upwards of 40 Nights at the Theatre Royal, London, is written by Theodore Hook, Esq. author of " The Fortress, &c."—Wall at the Original Music.

HUNGARIANS.

ACT 1.—SCENE I.

REPRESENTS A FOREST.

ACT 2.—SCENE I.

THE MILL OF KEBEN.

RIVER TORZA.

A WOODEN BRIDGE ACROSS THE TORZA.

HALL.

For Freedom and Our Country,

THE FORTRESS OF MONTGATZ.

A Combat between Alexina and Edmund

FREEDOM TO HIS COUNTRY.

The Evening's Entertainment to conclude with the much admired Farce, in Two acts, called

Irishman in London.

Tickets, *Five Shillings* each, to be had of Mr. Jarvis, at the Theatre, where places may be taken.

18

with the freedom of the city. The *Royal Gazette* of July 24 contains his appreciative response:

> The approbation which they have been pleased to express of my conduct, during my command of this Garrison, is truly gratifying to my feelings, and I beg you will assure them that I shall ever entertain a pleasing remembrance of the happy time I have spent amongst them, and a heartfelt solicitude for their future welfare.

Sadly, His Majesty's Servants did not survive the loss of the regiment. The civilian complement, unable or unwilling to cope on their own, sold the theatre building, together with "Wardrobe and Appurtenances", to an unknown buyer at a public auction on November 1, having made it a condition of sale that the purchaser should "during the continuance of the term keep the same for the purpose of a Theatre only".[38] If the newspapers are a reliable guide, he did not keep to his bargain, for they indicate that the theatre was silent until 1815 with one exception. That exception was a performance, on May 16, 1810, of C. S. Powell's one-man variety show, *The Evening Brush for Rubbing Off the Rust of Care*. It was Powell's way of finishing a three-and-a-half month period of residence in Saint John during which he operated a dancing school; his Halifax Theatre had fallen on dark days, forcing him to seek other means of remuneration.

The absence of theatrical performances from Saint John at this time cannot be blamed on a lack of material prosperity, for during the last years of the Napoleonic War the city was enjoying an unprecedented degree of prosperity, stimulated in part by the War of 1812. William M. Jarvis remembers how the 1812 conflict enhanced his grandfather Munson Jarvis' business:

> The result of the state of affairs in the United States was the establishment of a large contraband trade along the Maine border, perfectly legitimate however from the New Brunswick standpoint. Purchasers of manufactured goods came to St. John from the United States, the dead stock was cleared out and the goods were sold as rapidly as they could be imported. The same thing probably occurred with other St. John merchants, and the foundation was laid at St. John for a period of prosperity which the city long afterwards enjoyed.[39]

In a letter to Jonathan Odell, the first Provincial Secretary of New Brunswick, Ward Chipman described how the increase of commerce had altered the landscape of Saint John by 1814:

The number of houses, stores, wharves and other buildings and improvements that have been erected and made in the City since the declaration of war by the American States, is by far greater than within any equal period of time before that declaration, and new buildings in still greater proportion are now in progress and contemplation, and such is the demand for houses that rents have increased the present year more than forty per cent upon their former amounts.[40]

By 1809 Saint John had the money, the facility, and an expanding population to support theatre; nevertheless, the 1809 venture in Drury Lane did not become permanent because the officers, who were its backbone, were removed. The gentlemen from the city, if Jarvis is typical, were young, either students or at the edge of careers. Perhaps their own flexible circumstances made them unlikely founders of a permanent theatre, perhaps they were more interested in making money, or perhaps there was simply no strong leadership among them. Leadership, after all, from the outset had come from the military men whose enthusiasm and vision had carried along the sceptical civilian gentlemen.

More resourceful were the young men who operated the Drury Lane Theatre in 1815 and 1816. Neville Parker and James Lyster were seventeen. Parker was studying law and would be admitted to the Bar in 1819; Lyster was soon to become a tailor. With them were Isaac Ketchum, who opened a dry goods business in 1819, James Lyster's brother William, I. Johnston, and Messrs. McDuff, Randall, Sutherland, and Watkins about whom nothing is known.

For two years Parker and his friends catered to the same elite audience that His Majesty's Servants had drawn in 1809, and tickets were still expensive at 5s. for a box and 3s.9d. for the gallery. Both seasons opened with performances for charity. In 1815 the anonymous *Barnaby Brittle; or a Wife at Her Wit's End* and Charles Kemble's *Point of Honour* each earned £5 for poor relief, while in January of the following year, Cherry's *The Soldier's Daughter* and Dibdin's *The Jew and the Doctor* contributed £20 to the relief of "unfortunate sufferers at the battle of Waterloo".

Scripts for the main part of the 1815 season, from April through August, were selected from the ones received in response to a newspaper advertisement placed by the company. Apart from Home's *Douglas*, the repertoire included only comedy. Most popular was Charles Macklin's comedy of humours, *Love A-la-Mode*, which was played four times. Its character types were amusing: Sir Archy MacSarcasm (a Scotsman), Squire Groom (an Englishman),

Mordecai (a Jew), and Sir Callaghan O'Brallaghan (an Irishman and the successful suitor of Sir Theodore Goodchild's ward Charlotte). George Colman's *Heir at Law* was performed twice, once with *Love A-la-Mode* and once with *Miss in Her Teens*, the farce which in 1747 began Garrick's long reign at London's Drury Lane Theatre. Thomas Morton's melodramatic love story *A Cure for the Heartache* and the ever popular *John Bull* were two more mainpieces, and the farces of *The Toothache* and *Raising the Wind* were typical afterpieces. The same types of English comedy, and some of the same titles, were performed in Halifax in the early 1800's.

The 1816 season in Drury Lane was brief indeed, consisting of only two known programmes apart from the initial benefit one, but the second is particularly interesting, for it marks the production of the first locally written script. This was a two-act farce entitled "The Sailor's Return; or Jack's Cure for the Hystericks", by a "youth in St. John". In contrast, the other programme was a classic, Oliver Goldsmith's *She Stoops to Conquer*, which, as all the other amateur productions apparently did, "gave general satisfaction to the audience". The level of expectation, we presume, cannot have been high. The role of Tony Lumpkin was "much better performed than expected" and that of Miss Neville " as well as expected". The part of Mr. Hardcastle was thought to be "well conceived", and Miss Hardcastle, "considering the transformation he had to undergo from the masculine to personate the feminine gender", proved the actor's comic genius. The scenery was "good and well managed", the house "well lighted and comfortable", and the costumes as appropriate as "any that have heretofore made their appearance".[41]

It is a great pity that the Drury Lane Theatre was not still available when a company of professional actors came to Saint John the next summer.[42] By then the building had been lost to theatre for a year, sold at auction on July 16, 1816, this time with no proviso that it remain a theatre. Thus Mr. Price had to bring his company to Mr. Green's new building on the south side of King Street, just down from the Masonic Hall on the corner of King and Studholm (now Charlotte). The building, then leased by Ralph Munson Jarvis, can hardly have been adequate for theatrical productions. Since tickets were all at the uniform price of 5s., there can have been no division of the auditorium into boxes, pit, and gallery. About the stage, too, nothing is known, but however small or makeshift its dimensions, it was forced to contain a quantity of scenery. For Act II scene i of *Tekeli; or the Siege of Montgatz*, the whole of the centre stage was "open to the RIVER TORZA". The playbill describes it like this:

On the right a practicable WINDMILL;
on the left a WATER MILL,
with Rolling Water;
A WOODEN BRIDGE ACROSS THE TORZA,
Running from the right hand of the centre to the upper part of
the Stage on the left. The distant Country bounds
the View.[43]

For Act I Scene i the stage had to represent a forest with a large oak and other smaller trees and for the last scene of Act III the fortress of Montgatz with its battlements, towers, and walls.

Notwithstanding the difficulties, the company announced a season of regular productions on Mondays, Wednesdays, and Fridays at 7:30, beginning on July 23 with J. Tobin's twelve-year-old comedy *The Honeymoon; or How to Rule a Wife*. From then until early October they offered a mixture of Shakespearean tragedy, comedy, and melodrama. A number of plays, such as *Everyone Has His Fault, The Soldier's Daughter*, and *Love A-la-Mode*, had been performed earlier by the amateurs. Others, such as George Colman's *The Battle of Hexham*, were by authors already popular with Saint John audiences. Townley's 1759 satirical farce *High Life Below Stairs* aimed at the pretensions of servants, which had caused a riot of footmen during its second performance at London's Drury Lane, could still evoke a response from Saint Johners. *Tekeli*, written in 1806 by Theodore Hook at the early age of eighteen and, boasted the playbill, "performed upwards of 60 Nights in the Theatres Royal, London, to overflowing Houses", was indicative of the growing public taste for spectacle, but only Isaac Pocock's melodramatic treatment of a charming heroine falsely accused of stealing a silver spoon actually taken by a magpie (*The Magpie and the Maid*, 1815) was less than ten years old. The cautious selection of plays shows only the performance route of British plays through the American theatre to the provinces; the arrival of a professional company did not alter or develop the tastes of the Saint John audience.

Price's company came to Saint John from Halifax where it had been performing at the small Fairbanks Wharf Theatre since the fall of 1816. The manager was also the leading man, and Mrs. Charles Young was leading lady. They played opposite each other in tragedy, as Romeo and Juliet and Macbeth and Lady Macbeth, and assumed major roles in the comedies and melodramas — as Captain Irwin and Miss Wooburn in *Everyone Has His Fault*, Gondibert and Adelaide in *The Battle of Hexham*, Murtock Delany and Louisa in *Irishman in London*, and Lovel and Kitty in *High Life Below Stairs*.

The Haligonians thought that, as an actor, Price excelled in tragedy, though his style was marred by a tendency to exaggerated declamation and violent actions. His conception of the character of Macbeth, however, was pronounced perfect, particularly in the scene following the murder of Duncan where "horror and remorse could not have been better depicted or expressed than they were by Mr. Price both in his countenance and voice".[44]

Mrs. Young was a rather small woman, well formed and of a beautiful complexion, who counted her admirers by the thousands, but the reviewer for the Halifax *Free Press*, writing anonymously as Peeping Tom, thought these were not assets suitable for tragedy, especially since she aspirated loudly at every breath. Veritas, reviewing for Halifax's *Acadian Recorder*, was kinder. He thought she looked "uncommonly well" as Lady Macbeth and that "her fine voice alone would render her a pleasing performer on any stage".[45] Divided critical opinion was not new to Mrs. Young, for Boston and Philadelphia had appreciated her but New York never had, even though one newspaper in 1809 predicted that "with application on her part and encouragement on that of the managers, she will very soon rise to be of considerable importance".[46] Mrs. Aldis, who shared the honours with Price in Dimond's afterpiece *Hunter of the Alps* and who played Lady Irwin in *Everyone Has His Fault* and Queen Margaret in *The Battle of Hexham*, was evidently a larger woman. Veritas thought that her figure was "calculated for tragedy" and that "if her voice were better she would do great justice to some of the noblest characters that are admired on the English stage".[47]

Supporting female roles were taken by Mrs. Foster and Mrs. Charnock. Mrs. Charnock appeared infrequently, perhaps because Peeping Tom was right in saying she had no acting ability. Mrs. Foster, Mrs. Young's sister-in-law, was particularly useful in the company because of her clear and distinct singing voice. Her talents were heard to advantage especially in the comic songs which frequently filled the interval between the mainpiece and the afterpiece. Other chief members of the company were Mr. Charnock, the once-upon-a-time shipmaster who won the public's favour with the easy manner in which he played comic characters, and Mr. Placide who also excelled in comedy. Lesser members and supernumeraries included Messrs. Robinson, Armstrong, Carey, Kelly, and Conroy, and Masters Stanley and Every. Mr. Aldis looked after the house, including the sale of tickets.

It is hard to assess the merits of the company or their reception in Saint John, since no newspaper saw fit to review their performances, though the absence of reviews does not in itself indicate a poor response, as plays had only rarely been reviewed before. Although Mrs. Young had once played Desdemona to Thomas Cooper's Othello, and Mrs. Aldis had played important roles in New York such as Alicia in *Jane Shore* and the Queen in *Hamlet*, members of the company had experience almost exclusively in supporting and even minor roles. Any of the audience who had been privileged to attend Covent Garden or Drury Lane would certainly have realized that this company was inferior. Most of the audience, though, would have been in no position to make comparisons. Probably the truth lies somewhere between the extremes of uncritical acceptance and snobbish negativism found in the Halifax press. While it is unlikely that the company wilfully murdered plays to the extent Peeping Tom alleged they did, it is possible, even probable, that they underestimated the sophistication of the provincial audiences, as he also alleged — although their choice of repertoire was directly in accordance with proven taste. In Halifax the company did not usually draw full houses, but had sufficient response for Price to manage successive spring seasons there in 1817 and 1818 and to extend the 1818 season through the summer. He then left, turning the company over to Charles Betterton who had been brought to the Park Theatre from Covent Garden in 1816, for the winter and spring of 1818-1819. Squeezed between the spring season in Halifax and the busier fall-winter season in the United States, the two-and-a-half month visit to Saint John was only an interlude in the company's attempts to make inroads into the eastern provinces.

Besides a small and inadequate facility in both Saint John and Halifax, Price and his company had to contend with opposition to the theatre from the local press. The opposition was not directed against Price specifically, but against the stage in general, and erupted into a lively debate with eloquent spokesmen on both sides. In Saint John, whose Loyalist values had from the beginning embraced the theatre with other art forms, this was the first voiced disapproval of dramatic performance and a sign of the strength of new, Puritan elements in the city. The *City Gazette* was leader of the opposition, a role which would intensify under the editorship of the Reverend Alexander McLeod between 1826 and 1831, while the *New Brunswick Courier*, always a supporter of drama, rose to the defence. The arguments were the same heard earlier in Britain and America, on the one side, that actors were an infamous lot whose profession endangered public morality and, on the other, that "the Theatre has generally proved the font of Public spirit and morality".[48] Detractors wanted to prohibit stage plays, while supporters agreed that "an extended and populous town . . . ought to support an handsome and a well conducted Theatre".[49] The same arguments would be replayed over and over in succeeding years; the opposition would sometimes be a significant force to reckon with, but never could it suppress the theatre entirely.

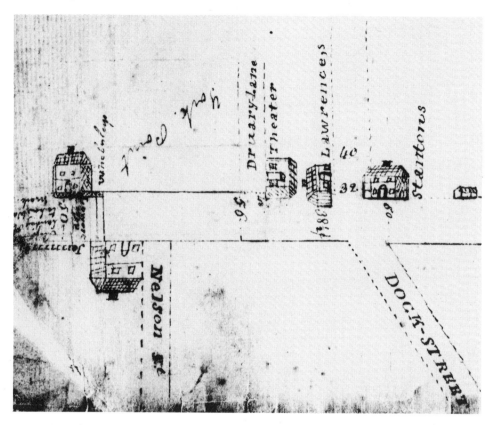

Map showing the location of the Drury Lane Theatre on Union Street, between Dock Street and Drury Lane. (New Brunswick Museum)

The Northern and Eastern Panoramic View of St. John, New Brunswick. Pendleton's Lithography, Boston. Coloured Lithography, c. 1835.
(Public Archives of Canada)

26

ii
Hopley's Theatre to the Prince of Wales

The years following the close of the War of 1812 saw a continuation of the economic growth that the war period had generated. Saint John carried on a brisk trade with Europe, the West Indies, and the United States. Its merchants, many of whom were Scottish, tended to become "commission merchants and shipbrokers, usually owners of a store and one or two vessels taking fish and lumber to the West Indies, bringing back rum and molasses and sugar, or taking lumber to Great Britain, carrying manufactured goods thence to the West Indies and returning to Saint John with West Indies products".[1] Increasingly, the staple article for export was squared timber, 114,116 tons of which were shipped in 1824.

By the mid 1820's Saint John was a bustling city, taking full advantage of its excellent harbour and the high tides which enabled even the largest ships to discharge their cargoes at the wharves in safety. Loyalists and their descendents still constituted the core of the 1200 people living in Saint John and Portland, but they were now outnumbered by immigrants, chiefly Scots and Irish who had arrived on the returning timber ships. The mixed population is reflected in the assortment of churches — two Anglican churches, a Church of Scotland kirk, a Catholic chapel, two Methodist chapels, and a Baptist meeting-house. Among other buildings the city had a grammar school and a madras school, two public libraries, three printing offices, a chamber of commerce, a provincial bank, a court house, a marine hospital, a poor house, a jail, and new barracks at Lower Cove.[2]

Then in 1825 Saint John, with the rest of New Brunswick, was affected adversely by a recession in Europe. A gentleman who was there described with passion what happened:

I wish, Sir, that you had seen the horror and vexation which

27

sat upon the countenances of all at St. John's, when the melancholy tidings of the disastrous events in Great Britain were ascertained to be correct. The tale of their vessels lying in the docks of London or Liverpool, without a bidder . . . showed them that they were indeed undone; not only that all their golden visions had vanished, but that the earnings also of many years of industry and frugality had been dissipated. St. John's presented a picture of almost total bankruptcy. I myself just escaped insolvency; but I had some thousands of pounds. Where are they?[3]

Even though this emotional appeal is probably an exaggeration, still the number of vessels built in Saint John declined from nineteen in 1825 and did not recover fully before 1832, increasing thereafter to a new high in 1840.[4]

Nevertheless, in 1828 a traveller to Saint John was impressed with its achievements and potential:

Fifty years ago the site of this thriving city was covered with trees, and only a few straggling huts existed within its harbour. This was its condition at the peace of 1783; and when we now view it, with its population of above 8000; its stately houses, its public buildings, its warehouses, its wharves, and with the majestic ships which crowd its port, we are more than lost in forming even a conjecture of what it will become in less than a century. Its position will ever command the trade of the vast and fertile country, watered by the lakes and streams of the river St. John.[5]

It seems surprising that there was so little theatre in the thriving port city between 1818 and 1828. In fact, in no ten year period since the arrival of the Loyalists had there been so little theatre. Mr. Cody's Long Room (formerly the Exchange Coffee House) was the setting for most of what there was. In July 1819 the East-India Jugglers exhibited there, and Messrs. McGleary and Jones from Dublin, Glasgow, New York, and Montreal gave readings on June 14, 1820.[6] In 1822 and 1823 there were several performances by amateurs, who dubbed Cody's the Amateur Theatre. Miss Powell, daughter of the late C. S. Powell, who like her father before her was running a dancing school in Saint John, played Lady Randolph in two productions of *Douglas* in the spring of 1822. In September plays were performed for the benefit of the Irish emigrants, there were two more productions in November, and tickets for *She Stoops to Conquer* on August 30, 1823, were obtainable from merchant and ship-owner Thomas Millidge.[7] In October 1825 Messrs.

Stewart and Hooper presented "Scenes from celebrated Plays" in aid of "Sufferers by the late Fires throughout the Province".[8] Apparently amateur drama, scarce as it was, was still promoted by the elite as a means of assisting the needy.

One reason for the paucity of dramatic performances was, undoubtedly, the absence of a proper facility. Another may well have been the "peculiar cast" of the inhabitants. Many of the merchants in the shipbuilding business were transient persons with no local attachments, whose intention was to return to their native country with all the money they could make, and who were thus uninterested in culture.[9] The population base of interested persons was still too small to provide stimulation for theatre on any continuing basis. Saint John had to wait until a professional company thought it could reap a harvest there.

A new era for theatre commenced on June 2, 1828. Not only did that day begin the first season of professional theatre since 1817, but it introduced the first of three successive theatre seasons. The actors who performed in 1828 were the first ones to come back again. This is a small but significant step forward toward the time, nearly twenty years later, when Saint John would have uninterrupted summer theatre seasons.

The announcement of the opening of the 1828 theatre season was given more than a month in advance. The *Courier* of May 10 proclaimed that the managers had rented "the new and commodious Building erected by Mr. HOPLEY, and [that they] intend fitting it up in a superior style, with entire New Scenery, Dresses, and Decorations, for Theatrical Entertainments". The advertisement also offered assurance to the public that "Proper Officers will be in attendance rigidly to enforce order".

Mr. Hopley's building, known in this period simply as the Theatre, stood on lots 233 and 234 on the south side of Union Street, each lot fronting on Union for 40 feet and extending back for 100 feet to the Old Burial Ground. It had been built as a Circus in time to house what appears to have been the first circus performance to visit Saint John in August and September 1824.[10] While the *Courier* was right in saying that Mr. Hopley owned the building in 1828, it was probably mistaken in implying that he built it. There is confusion with the traditional understanding of its origins as these have been expressed by Clarence Ward in the *Saint John Globe* of October 7, 1905:

> One of old St. John's landmarks was Hopley's Tavern and Theatre, situated on the southwest corner of Sydney and Union streets. John Hopley came to St. John from Ireland in

1815, and about the year 1822 he erected his tavern and theatre on this corner. It was always called the "Golden Ball Corner". . . . The major tavern adjoined the theatre and stood on the corner of Union and Sydney streets. It was to this building that the golden ball was attached.

If John indeed came in 1815, he has disappeared without a trace. On the other hand Joseph Hopley, native of Ireland and a mariner, applied for freeman status in 1822 and could then buy land.[11] On May 5, 1825, he purchased the two lots on which the Circus stood from Ebenezer Smith and William Rudolphson for £251.[12] Nine days later, the *Courier* informed patrons that tickets for Master Henderson's "ELEGANT and EXTRAORDINARY PERFORMANCES on the WIRE" could be had from Joseph Hopley at the Circus. On August 3, 1825, he bought the inn next door on the Golden Ball corner; its relative value in relation to the circus property can be seen in the high purchase price of £1400.[13] Thus, in 1828 Joseph Hopley was, at age 40, owner both of the building which was converted to hold the theatrical performances and also of the inn next door which, legend says, provided accommodation for the acting company. We know little more about him except that he and his wife Margaret had five children and that he died in October 1845 "in the 57th year of his age, after a long and tedious illness".[14]

Little firm description of the Theatre is available. It was a wooden structure with a pit and tiers of boxes whose seating capacity was approximately 800. We know that the stage was about forty feet deep, because, for a production of *El-Hyder* on July 27, 1829, it was extended twenty feet to show the processions to best advantage, making it nearly sixty feet deep.[15] When utilized as a theatre the building had a plank floor, most of whose space must have been occupied with the hard backless benches that stood in the pit, but the floor could be removed and replaced by sawdust and tanbark if a circus was in town.[16] A writer reminiscing much later recalled: "As the rear of the theatre was not very tightly constructed, the boys who could not always get money to purchase tickets to enter by the front, would frequently enter by the rear and climb up, unobserved, and take their seats gratis".[17] This defect made for disorderly conditions with which even the officers in attendance could not cope satisfactorily, and Mr. Hopley found it necessary to make improvements. Prior to the opening of the 1829 season, he announced alterations "for the better preventing of disorderly persons from intruding or from occupying the space directly under the Boxes. — There was much need of this improvement; for that Section of the Theatre could be but partially lighted; thereby affording an

30

opportunity of *Rowing* without the possibility of detecting the disturbers".[18]

The company that opened the Theatre in 1828 was led by actor-manager Cornelius A. Logan from the New York and Boston theatres. Mr. William Hardy of London, New York, and Boston was scene painter, and Mr. Hart from the Montreal and Boston theatres was stage manager. The backbone of the acting company was the Riddle family, Mr. and Mrs. Riddle, Miss Riddle, Miss E. Riddle, and Master Riddle. In addition there were Mr. and Mrs. Herbert and Mr. Adams.[19] Mr. Logan was leading man and Mrs. Riddle his leading lady.

In August, Logan brought two stars from the American stage to Saint John. The first was Arthur Keene, called by some "the best professional male singer in America",[20] who came to perform the roles of Harry Bertram in the melodramatic opera *Guy Mannering* and of Captain Belvill in Brooke's pastoral opera *Rosina*. Keene had been born in Ireland and made his American debut at the Park Theatre, New York, in 1817 as Harry Bertram, a role he played many times afterwards. Since each performance took place in a crowded hall, Saint John audiences cannot have been disappointed in him. Said the *Courier* of August 9, "We have never at any time seen it [the house] filled by such a numerous assemblage of the most respectable part of the community". Frederick Brown, the American tragedian, came next. Born in London, his first American appearance had been at the Federal Street theatre in Boston. No stranger to Canada, he had played in Halifax in 1818 and 1819 under Price's management, and he had been first manager of the Theatre Royal, Montreal, in 1825. Logan had been able to obtain him for one night only. Accordingly, he starred as Damon in Banim and Sheil's *Damon and Pythias; or a Trial of Friendship* for Mr. Hardy's benefit on August 25.

A large proportion of the Saint John public was prepared to give Logan's company a fair trial. On one evening near the beginning of the season, the proceeds were $300 (£75), and the *City Gazette* estimated that in a week of four performances receipts probably equalled £300.[21] At ticket prices of 5s. for a box and 2s.6d. for the pit, this would mean that up to 600 persons daily were frequenting the Theatre early in June. Mid-month, Mr. Logan reduced tickets for the boxes to 3s. 9d. and for the pit to 2s. (one-half price for children under twelve) and the number of performances from four to three. While this was undoubtedly done, as the *City Gazette* believed, to increase the number of spectators on each occasion, it can hardly have increased the weekly total, and so is presumably in-

31

dicative of the company's desire to play nightly to capacity houses and to a falling off of audience numbers.

The June 2 opening of *The Honeymoon; or How to Rule a Wife* exceeded the expectations of many in attendance. The performance was thought to have gone off well, "making due allowance for the short time afforded to the Actors for preparing themselves to appear on the Stage, in consequence of their having to superintend the arrangements of scenery and other theatrical apparatus".[22] By the end of the month patrons had noticed a "very visible improvement", and a "general feeling of satisfaction" prevailed.[23] The actors seem to have been competent but unexceptional. The public's favorite was easily Miss Riddle, whose Cora in *Pizzaro* was considered equal to that of any actress on the American boards and who "carried the palm" as Albina Mandeville in *The Will*. While the others "did ample justice" to their parts, excelling "principally in the performance of light pieces", she acquitted herself with excellence.[24]

For three months the company performed, on Monday, Wednesday, and Friday at 8:00 p.m., an assortment of comedy, tragedy, "melodramatic spectacle", "melodramatic opera", "pastoral opera", "musical farce", "oriental drama", and plain melodrama. Some of the tragedies and many of the farcical afterpieces belonged to the eighteenth century: Home's *Douglas* and Sheridan's *Pizzaro*, Macready's *The Village Lawyer* and *The Irishman in London*, Hoare's *No Song No Supper*, Inchbald's *Animal Magnetism; or How to Raise the Dead* and *Mogul Tale; or The Cobbler's Descent in a Balloon*, and Bickerstaffe's *The Romp*. The comedies and melodramas were more recent. Among new works was John Poole's comedy, *Paul Pry*, which had enjoyed a hugely successful run of 114 nights in its first (1825) season at London's Haymarket. Others included Knowles' tragedy *William Tell* (1825), Pocock's *Rob Roy MacGregor Campbell* (1818) and Moncrieff's *The Spectre Bridegroom* (1821). *The Hunter of the Alps*, *The Soldier's Daughter*, and *The Magpie and the Maid* were already familiar to Saint John audiences.

The newer works speak of the growing taste for spectacle, for music and dance. George Colman the Younger, whose dramas were particularly representative of late Georgian comedy, summed up the new demand for spectacle in a prologue he wrote in 1794:

> Since the preference we know
> Is for pagaentry and shew,
> 'Twere a pity the public to balk —
> And when people appear

32

Quite unable to hear
'Tis undoubtedly needless to talk.
Let your Shakspears and Jonsons go hang, go hang!
Let your Otways and Drydens go drown!
Give us but elephants and white bulls enough,
And we'll take in all the town.
Brave boys![25]

The new spectacular drama made scenic demands on the company as well as on the theatre structure, and Mr. Hardy at least was equal to the challenge. The scenery for the thrilling drama of *Therese, the Orphan of Geneva* (1821) was said to be "elegant"; the scene of the "burning of the Pavillion produced a grand effect", so nearly approaching reality that "some persons in the Boxes seemed alarmed for the safety of the building".[26] There were "new Scenery, Dresses and Decorations" for the "grand, Oriental, Melo-Dramatic spectacle" *Timour the Tartar*, but whether the performance was as splendid as the one in 1830 for which a whole stud of horses was brought on stage, we do not know.[27] Excitement had scarcely abated from these two extravaganzas when the company spent lavishly on *The Forty Thieves*. When that drama was first produced in Boston in March 1810, the theatre was closed for ten days in preparation. By opening night the managers had spent two thousand dollars, but so great was the success of the piece that the standing-room only audience quickly enabled them to recoupe their losses and much more.[28] Mr. Hardy did himself "much credit" in the effects he created for the Saint John production: "The first scene the CORAL GROTTO, representing the Palace of the Fairy of the Lake, has almost magical effect, but the appearance of the CAR, drawn by SWANS, was hailed with rapturous applause".[29]

Despite such enthusiastic appreciation, the Theatre had its opponents in the community from the beginning. To Mr. McLeod of the *City Gazette* the Theatre was an "insidious enemy", and he declined to publish its advertisements. Under the guise of deep concern for the welfare of his fellow citizens, he complained that "by attending the Theatre, very many people, who can but ill afford it, allow themselves to be cajoled out of their money, in support of an institution which to say the least of it, is altogether useless, and to maintain a profession, which as to any practical and positive good it has ever produced, may be fairly considered as a blank in creation".[30] Those who could afford it, Mr. McLeod believed, should spend both their money and their time more profitably. By July 23, the *British Colonist* thought it necessary to reject the "growing snarls of Pseudo Critics" and to insist that "the Establishment of a 'regular Theatre' has been a public benefit to our improving community". The management constantly provided reassurance in its advertisements that strictest order and decorum would be enforced. The reviewer of the *Colonist* recommended *Therese* because it inculcated "lessons of virtue" and advocated the "cause of religion and virtue", and the *Courier* encouraged those hesitant to attend by pointing out that "a number of respectable citizens are frequent attenders".[31] More encouragement could be derived from the the Mayor's patronage which was announced on every advertisement.

Still, the opposition was intransigent, and the announcement of the opening of the 1829 season brought a volley of protests from press and pulpit which reached even to the Mayor's office and to the Grand Jury. First was a letter to the editor of the *City Gazette* on March 25, citing an instance of robberies following a production of the *Beggar's Opera* in London, to show how criminals have learned their trade at the theatre. The letter began:

> Mr. Editor, — I am extremely sorry that Dr. Johnson's 'Dancing Dogs' have again taken up their abode among us. I had thought that the Public were sufficiently gulled last season by these here fellows, not to encourage them any more.

Next, a letter to the editor of the *Courier*, on April 11, included extracts from a sermon preached "on the occasion of the fall of the Brunswick Theatre in London" on the text: "The man that wandereth out of the way of understanding shall remain in the Congregation of the dead (Prov.21c.16v.)". Among the alleged evil effects of the drama were inflammation of the passions, imparting of an unrealistic picture of life, and especially —

> Company. — This, at the Theatre, is awful. The admission there of persons of professionally evil life, is a source of great gain and accounts for the mystery of so shameless a Toleration. . .
> Hours. — Late hours: and how are our youth exposed, by being disgorged into the streets from the doors of the play-house at midnight; when piety and decorum have withdrawn to the quiet domestic pavillion, and when most of what remains without is given up to the sons of Belial!

The Mayor had refused to sanction the reopening of the Theatre, but the company, ignoring him, opened anyway on May 11 and brazenly ran "By Permission of His Worship the Mayor" on their advertisements. In his charge to the Grand Jury, reported in the June 6 *Courier*, he said he had received petitions from a number of citizens charging that theatrical amusements had an immoral tendency and were thus injurious to society. A number of persons living in the vicinity had allegedly also complained of tumult and disorder at the doors. The Mayor was especially concerned, considering "the pecuniary difficulties of the times", to remove temptation from persons who could ill afford to waste their money on recreation, and also to protect the youth from possible harmful influences. Because he was not sure that his authority extended to jurisdiction over the Theatre, he commended the matter to the Grand Jury for a verdict. Seventeen out of twenty-one jurymen accepted his offer of free tickets in order to examine the nuisance at first hand, but they failed to present a report. Finally, the Jury decided it would not be expedient to suppress the Theatre, so its season was allowed to go forward without, however, the encouragement of the Mayor's permission on the publicity. Mr. McLeod found himself "utterly at a loss to assign motives for the strong interest which some of our good citizens have manifested in its favor".[32]

Despite opposition (or perhaps because of it) large audiences occupied the Theatre. The company stood fast. When rumour circulated that Mr. Hart's role as Mawworm in *The Hyprocrite* slandered the character of the clergy, Hart chose the same piece for his benefit, to give sceptical persons a chance to judge for themselves. The next night the company began the evening with the prologue to Massinger's *The Roman Actor*, "The Stage Defended". On the eve of their departure for Halifax in August, they said that success had exceeded their expectations and they intended to revisit Saint John soon.

For the 1829 season Messrs. Logan, Hardy and Hart and the Herberts had returned, as had Miss Riddle, now Mrs. W. H. Smith and accompanied by her husband. The other Riddles and Mr. Adams were missing. Mrs. Parker, Miss Robbins, and Messrs. Kelsey (leading man) and Frithey were newcomers to the company. An entirely different programme was presented, except for the repetition of *Rob Roy MacGregor Campbell* and *Douglas*. The season opener, instead of *The Honeymoon; or How to Rule a Wife*, was *Wives, as They Were, and Maids as They Are* (1797). This season, like the last, paid token attention to Shakespeare. Instead of *Othello*, there was *Romeo and Juliet*, with Mrs. Parker as Juliet, and *Macbeth*, "with the whole of the Music, Chorusses, Incantations of Witches, &c.", starring Mr. Kelsey and Miss Robbins. Comic songs in the interludes were provided by Mr. Herbert and Mrs. Parker and dances by Mrs. Smith and Mrs. Parker. For the most part the company performed romantic melodramas like *The Bleeding Nun; or the Forest of Rosenwald, Cataract of the Ganges; or the Rajah's Daughter, The*

Forest of Bondy; or the Dog of Montargis, and *El-Hyder; or the Chief of the Ghaut Mountains*. They were catering, in a more extravagant manner, to the taste for spectacle they had awakened in 1828. *El-Hyder* used horses in procession, and *The Cataract of the Ganges* required horses and "a cataract of REAL WATER". *The Forest of Bondy* needed a dog who would rush at the throat of his master's murderer. Scenery and decorations for all pieces were said to be new. A favorite of the season was Knowles' *Brian Boroihme; or the Maid of Erin*, performed with "the original Music as performed in the principal Theatres, in England and America, with the most unprecedented success". In its last production of the season, for Mr. Herbert's benefit on July 13, it was coupled with *Tom and Jerry; or Life in London*, the "Grand, Classic, Comic, Operatic, Didactic, Moralistic, Aristophanic, Localic, Terpsichoric, Panoramic, Extravaganza Burletta" about "Fun, Frolic, Fashion and Flash" in London.[33]

Logan's company did not return to Saint John in 1830. Instead, W. C. Forbes, from New York and Philadelphia,[34] opened the Theatre on April 12 for what he expected would only be a short season of six nights. Instead, he returned briefly at the end of May, took the company to Fredericton and the Miramichi as planned, and then returned early in July for three months. During that time he moved the time of performance from 7:15 in April to 8:30 in July, reduced ticket prices in May to 2s.6d. for the boxes and 1s.3d. for the pit, "owing to the depression of the times", and increased the frequency of performance from three nights a week to five. The only member of Logan's company who was with him initially was Mr. Hart, the stage-manager.

Forbes' company included New York born Westervelt Walstein who had performed in New York, Boston, and Philadelphia, Mr. and Mrs. Forrest from the Philadelphia theatres, and Mr. A. Dickson, whose personations of Irish characters evoked a ready response from Saint John's Irish element. In July he brought as a star Thomas Cooper, the British-born actor who in 1798 had made a reputation for himself as a Shakespearean and tragedian at the Park Street Theatre, New York. In 1830 Cooper was nearing the end of a career during which he was regarded as America's leading classic actor. His "masterly" performances of Othello, Pizzaro, and of Zanga in Dr. Young's *Revenge; or the Moorish Captive* were applauded in Saint John by "fashionable" audiences. One reviewer called his impersonation of Othello "a fine specimen of acting". Lovers of the drama were pleased with the quality of the performances which they vowed had never been surpassed in the province and were pleased also with a repertoire that offered "the most intellectual treats that the catalogue of the legitimate Drama can supply".[35] In late August Forbes added to the company as leading players Mr. and Mrs. W. H. Smith, and also Mrs. Riddle and her daughter Eliza. In September, when the Smiths had of necessity to return hastily to Boston, he replaced them with Mr. and Mrs. William Pelby and their daughter Ophelia.

The highlight of the Smiths' brief stay was a production of Douglas Jerrold's new (1829) nautical drama, *Black-Eyed Susan*, whose hero, William, was to become the stereotype of the stage sailor. The plot of the play is an uncomplicated one enlivened with songs and with sailors' hornpipes. Turning on a simple coincidence which at the last moment saves William from hanging and returns him to his sweet young bride Emily, it sets forth the orthodox message of nineteenth century melodrama: that virtue is rewarded and villainy punished. The play's first London run amounted to 300 nights. So great was its popularity that T. P. Cooke, who played William, "not only found half of London flocking . . . to see him; but was actually called upon, after acting in the play, as a first piece, at the Surrey Theatre, to drive off in his sailor's dress, and act in it again on the same night, as the last piece at Covent Garden Theatre".[36] In Saint John W. H. Smith played William, and Mrs. Smith was Susan.

The engagement of the Pelbys maintained the standard Forbes had been trying to set. The senior Pelbys were favorites in Boston (William was manager of the Tremont Theatre in 1827), and popular especially in tragic roles. For Forbes they played the leading roles in *The Merchant of Venice* and *Macbeth*, Mr. Pelby in particular winning praise for his "tragic powers". Mrs. Pelby was the erring but repentant wife, Mrs. Haller, in Kotzebue's *The Stranger*, and in the sensational tragedy *Bertram; or the Castle of St. Aldobrand* her husband played the Gothic hero-villain Bertram who finds his beloved Imogine married to his enemy St. Aldobrand. Full of fierce passions and despair, revenge, murder, and madness, the latter play may well have impressed audiences in Saint John as it did in London, where spectators were "swept into rapture" by Keane's dazzling performance.[37]

The dramatic menu offered in the three year period from 1828 to 1830 clearly reflects the new tastes in the theatre in London and America. Plays had been rapidly moving away from the refined immorality of the eighteenth century comedy of manners and from the desciplined precision of the language of that century; instead they were being influenced by the romantic, the Gothic, the exotic, and the moral. Plots became rather thin as incidents and spectacle both increased. As writer Elizabeth Inchbald complained, "The stage delights the eye far oftener than the ear".[38] Polite society was forsaking the theatre in the whole of the English speaking world, and it was becoming instead a gathering place for the middle and lower classes. The composition of the audience in Saint John changed too, following suit.

There are a great many signs that the clientele that supported Hopley's Theatre was different in nature from the one that had supported drama in Saint John's earliest years. The Theatre itself was located in a far from fashionable suburb, backed by the cemetery and near the rocky, uneven street along which "the jail, the poorhouse and the dead house had been placed . . . as if they were being located in an out of the way place where they would not obtrude themselves on the notice of the general public".[39] Union Street, on which it stood, was the highway that connected the city with Portland and Simonds and thus with the rest of the province. Important as it was for traffic, it was not at this time 'respectable'.

Mr. Hopley himself was representative of the change that had taken place. Of Irish, rather than Loyalist background, he was one of a large immigrant population that had altered the character of the city. The Irish who had settled in Saint John in ever increasing numbers since 1815 had been forced to leave their homelands because of agricultural depressions or unavailability of work. The "ignorant poor and priest-ridden", as the Chief Justice of Upper Canada termed them, they swelled the population of labourers in Saint John.[40] They also seem quickly to have become patrons of the Theatre, as the number of Irish pieces in the programmes attests.

The population of Saint John could now be divided into three segments in respect to theatre. Polite society, consisting of descendents of the Loyalists and the prosperous merchants, would not have gone readily to Hopley's. If they did, the disorderliness would have discouraged them. Despite frequent references in the press to the respectability of the audience and despite the efforts of Mr. Forbes in 1830 to offer more plays that might attract them, the elite must have been a minority in attendance at the Theatre. A small but vocal Protestant clique stayed away from the Theatre on principle. Saint John, of course, shared this characteristic also with other cities. On October 28, 1829, Mary Merritt complained from Boston to her son in Saint John about her unsuccessful attempts to see a play: "I cannot get anyone to go with me, the people here are all too pious".[41] A larger, less educated, and generally less prosperous group, liberally sprinkled with Irishmen, formed the bulk of the audience. These were the people most affected by hard times, for whom especially ticket prices were lowered, and about whom Mr. McLeod worried — people like the man who could not pay his creditors and yet was seen with his wife and daughter going to the Theatre, servants, and, of course, the young.[42]

If polite society was not the dominant presence in the Theatre, the intellectual elite nonetheless turned naturally to the dramatic form as a means of expression. In 1833, there appeared in the *Courier* serialized portions of a three-act political satire, "The Triumph of Intrigue", under the simple pseudonym 'O.P.', which may well be abbreviated Latin for Public Opinion. For two years the *Courier* had been waging a war with letters and editorials against the policies of Thomas Baillie, the Commissioner of Crown Lands, and the anonymous play was one weapon. Essentially, the plot unfolds the schemes of Wily oh' Deil and Tommy to outwit the Scottish squire and thus to transfer power over the Estate to themselves, taking it away from the twelve domestics. The squire, who has been appointed by the "Laird" to "superveese his praperty, collect the siller, and execute justice", is the Lieutenant Governor Sir Archibald Campbell, who had recently led the British troops to victory in Burma. Tommy is, of course, Thomas Baillie and the appropriately named Wily oh' Deil his father-in-law. The twelve domestics all belong to the legislative council of the estate, New Brunswick.

The sharpness of the attack on the British-appointed Campbell is felt very early, when Johny Fairchild (John A. Beckwith), leader of the domestics, in his first speech compares the new province to a forest and the crown appointments to rapacious wolves. In Act III, O. P., acting as commentator, reinforces Johny's opinion while explaining the play's title: "Our Estate has long been the *fishing ground* for the Leviathans of Office; the industry of the poor man has been their prey; the cry of oppression has been overpowered by the recriminating din of disloyalty; the truth has been *rebutted* by prejudice; and intrigue has triumphed over the just rights of the Tenantry and the dignity of the Estate".

Though the *Courier* of March 9 said it was "the wish of several spirited Gentlemen in this City to take characters in the Drama, and get it up as a Play, for the Benefit of the Poor", the script was clearly written to be read, not performed. The characters are suitably stereotypes whose primary function is to communicate the playwright's thought, but each has his own unique vitality and is believable within the scope of the play. While the dialogue sparkles with images, the speeches, for the most part, are long and rhetorical rather than conversational.

Despite Forbes' long 1830 theatre season which lasted, with interruptions, from April to November, Hopley's Theatre was silent in 1831 and largely remained so until 1838.[43] Perhaps part of the reason might have been the controversy resulting from an accidental death which took place on stage on Friday, August 6, 1830. On that date, the theatre company reenacted the Battle of Waterloo with the assistance of some soldiers from the barracks in Lower Cove. Unfortunately, the soldiers became carried away in the excitement of the mock combat, until a ramrod was plunged more than three inches into the forehead of one John Hale. A heated debate then ensued in the press, with Mr. McLeod of the *City Gazette* condemning the inhumanity of the actors and the sinfulness of the drama in general, and with Mr. Walstein replying on behalf of the actors in the *Courier*.[44]

Since the times were then difficult for Mr. Hopley, on October 1, 1831, he advertised for sale the Golden Ball and the Theatre. On October 31, having found no buyer, he mortgaged the Theatre for £400 to Gabriel Rossiter of Fredericton. On March 29 of the following year, he obtained a £932 mortgage from Thomas Millidge on the Golden Ball Inn. Although both were one year mortgages, he repaid neither until December 1837, immediately after which he consolidated his loans by mortgaging the combined properties to Millidge for £1212.[45]

Shortly thereafter, in the spring of 1838, the Theatre once again became the scene for regular dramatic performances. The manager of the company was W. S. Deverna, the stage manager John Nickinson, and the prompter Mr. Addis. The previous autumn Deverna had been responsible for stage fixtures and machinery at the opening of the new Olympic Theatre in New York, where he worked with Nickinson who became one of the prominent members of the Olympic company and an artist of whom, said Odell, "one cannot speak too respectfully".[46]

Hopley's Theatre opened in 1838 without the cloud of controversy that enveloped it a decade previous, and with a greater air of respectability than the drama had enjoyed since 1817. The earliest playbill which has so far come to light, for *Othello* on July 23, is headed with a coat of arms underneath which is written, "By Permission of His Worship the Mayor".[47] Further prestige accrued when, on August 9, the Lieutenant-Governor Sir John Harvey attended a production of *The Soldier's Daughter*, even though the arrival of his entourage interrupted the performance:

> The play commenced at the usual hour, and was in the second act when His Excellency and Lady Harvey arrived. The house, both boxes and pit, rose, and greeted the veteran and his lady, with three hearty cheers. The national anthem was then played by the excellent Band of the 11th Regiment, and the play proceeded.[48]

THEATRE.

The Manager has the pleasure of announcing that he has succeeded in making an Engagement *for a Few NIGHTS ONLY*, with the Celebrated English TRAGEDIAN

Mr. Vandenhoff,

From the *Theatres Royal, Drury Lane, Covent Garden,* and *Haymarket,* who will make his first appearance in St. John, This Evening in the Character of

MACBETH.

As also a Re-Engagement with

Mrs. Anderson,

For a few Nights Only.

LADY MACBETH,	Mrs. ANDERSON.
MACDUFF, -	Mr. FREDERICK

WEDNESDAY EVENING, JUNE 24, 1840.

Will be performed Shakspeare's TRAGEDY of

MACBETH,
King of Scotland.

With all the Original Music, &c.

MACBETH,	-	Mr. VANDENHOFF,
MACDUFF,	-	Mr. FREDERICKS,
BANQUO,	(his first appearance here,)	Mr. HENRIE,
Donalbain,	-	Miss Buloid.
Malcolm,	-	Mr. Young,
Bleeding Captain,	-	Mr. Milner,
Physician,	-	Miss Buloid.
King Duncan,	-	Mr. Preston,
Rosse,	-	Mr. Stuart,
Hecate,	-	Mr. Hardy,
1st Witch,	-	Mr. Lansing.
2d. Witch,	-	Mrs. Lansing.
3d. Witch,	-	Mr. Collins.
1st Apparition,	-	Miss Lewis.
2d. Apparition,	-	Miss Foster.
LADY MACBETH,		Mrs. ANDERSON.
Gentlewoman,		Miss Lewis.

SONG, 'Rory O'More' Mrs. LANSING

To conclude with the Farce of

Lover's Quarrels.

Don Carlos.	-	Mr. Young,
Sancho,	-	Mr. Lansing,
Lopez.	-	Mr. Milner,
Donna Leonora.	-	Miss Buloid.
Jacintha,	-	Mrs. Lansing.

Mr. Vandenhoff

Will make his second appearance To-Morrow Evening,
THURSDAY.

Admission to the Boxes and Parquette 4s,—to the
GALLERY, 2s.

Places for the Boxes and Parquette can be secured daily
on application to Mr. FIELD at the Box Office.

Smoking prohibited in all parts of the Theatre.

VIVAT REGINA!

June 24.   W. P. SANCTON, Printer.

Vandenhoff in MacBeth, *a playbill.* (Harvard Theatre Collection)

James Hackett as Falstaff.
(New York Public Library)

Junius Brutus Booth as Sir Giles Overreach engraving from a watercolor by W. Heath
(Theatre and Music Collection Museum of the city of New York)

41

Deverna charged 4s. admission to the boxes and 2s. for the pit, prices considerably higher than in 1830. His company included Mrs. and Mrs. Anderson, Miss Sands and Mrs. Tessier, Messrs. Taylor, Bellamy, Miller, Milner, Brown, Smith, Raffile, and Rasimi, and his stars Miss Angelica and the Harrisons. Miss Angelica was one of a group of Parisian dancers who had made their debut at the Lafayette Theatre, New York in 1828; Deverna's playbill advertised her as a "danseuse" and "comedienne" of London, New York, and Philadelphia. The Harrisons, he said, were from the "principal London theatres" and "recently the leading Performers in the 'Park Theatre', New York". They had, in fact, made their American debut in 1833 as Othello and Desdemona, parts which were judged to be far above their abilities, and they were soon regular members of a company;[49] in Saint John, though, they could play roles denied them elsewhere. Of Deverna's company, only Mrs. Anderson and the Harrisons were spoken of in the press. Mrs. Anderson elicited much applause for her performance of Lady Anne in *Richard III*, Mrs. Harrison's Queen Elizabeth was "a piece of good acting", while Mr. Harrison as Richard was "thrilling and had the audience perfectly at his command" through skilful employment of his muscular figure and his flexible, harmonious voice — the dreaming scene in the last act especially was "a splendid piece of acting, and although his rushing to the front of the stage and falling on his knees was not contemplated by the author, yet the effect was great, and added to the interest of the scene".[50]

In July, while Mr. Deverna was attracting an audience to Hopley's with solid scripts such as *Othello*, *Richard III*, *George Barnwell; or the London Merchant*, and *Douglas*, Fuller's Olympic Circus and Magic Theatre (or Olympic Amphitheatre) was successfully wooing the masses, first on a lot near the Catholic chapel and then on Charlotte Street near the St. John Hotel. Each programme of equestrian exercises and feats of strength and skill included pantomime and comic songs, concluding with a dramatic piece such as *The Cobbler's Daughter* or *The German Farmer*. In October, after Deverna had gone, Fuller's company occupied Hopley's Theatre/Circus. For 3s.6d. and 1s.9d. they offered spectacular pieces like *The Forty Thieves* and *Blue Beard; or the Enchanted Castle*, during both of which a number of horses appeared on stage. Scenes for each production were advertised. Act I of *Blue Beard* featured "A Grand Triumphal Procession of Horse and Foot and Blue Beard and Fatima in a splendid chariot, drawn by three Horses abreast", and Act II was to show the "death of Abolamique, who sinks amid a shower of fire from above and a volume of flame from beneath".[51]

Not surprisingly, Fuller found the Theatre rather small for his purposes.

The next three years brought more stability to Joseph Hopley's Theatre. During those years, it was managed by Henry W. Preston, a favorite actor and for some years manager of a theatre in Albany, New York, who recruited the most notable international stars yet seen in Saint John. Performances were given four times a week, on Monday, Wednesday, Friday, and Saturday, and ticket prices were constant at 4s. and 2s.

The 1839 season opened on May 29 with J. S. Knowles' *The Wife; or a Tale of Mantua*. The performance, which had the permission of His Worship the Mayor, commenced with "God Save the Queen". Preston said he had "recently refitted and ornamented" the Theatre (although in what way we do not know) and smoking was strictly prohibited in it. The choice of scripts offered during the season indicates that he was catering to polite public taste. He produced Bulwer's *The Lady of Lyons*, Garrick's *Catharine and Petruchio* (starring Mr. Rodney and Mrs. Preston), Shakespeare's *King Lear* for Mr. Fitzgerald's benefit, *Merchant of Venice*, Acts I and II of *Richard III* and Act III of *Hamlet* (in which, in a reversal of the practice of the young gentlemen amateurs at Mallard's, the women played the men's roles — Mrs. Preston as Richard III and Mrs. Charles as Hamlet).[52] For variety, the repertoire included also *Edgard the Idiot*, which the *Commercial News* found "a Drama of peculiar construction" whose production, nevertheless, had "created a great excitement both in London, and lately at the Theatre in Halifax",[53] *The Tower of Nesle; or the Chamber of Death* for Mrs. Chapman's benefit, and an operatic play, *Pedlar's Acre; or the Wife of Seven Husbands*, starring Mrs. Gibbs. Preston recruited his company in New York, returning there in mid-August to enlist Mrs. Gibbs and Mr. Freer. The season then continued to November 9, apart from an interruption in late September and early October during which the Olympic Circus occupied the Theatre, and Mr. Preston went to Halifax.

Mrs. Gibbs, formerly Miss Graddon, was, as the *Commercial News* claimed, "a celebrated English actress and songstress", for she had earned a reputation in opera in London before her American debut in New Orleans in 1835. Saint John audiences were impressed with her "rich and melodious voice", especially her "exquisite" warbling. Charles Freer, who had only recently arrived in America from the English provincial theatres, was an ambitious young man determined to make himself known to managers and theatres, and soon his ability to "jump, with astonishing ease, from tragedy to crudest melodrama, and back again" was recognized.[54]

Shylock and Edgard the Idiot were two of his earliest American roles. He had performed at the Park Theatre in May 1839, just prior to Mrs. Gibbs' benefit there. The reviewer for the *Commercial News*, who had seen him in the United States, found him "a clever actor — yet not an astonishing one". His personal appearance was much in his favour, but his voice was too gutteral, with "a pulpit vein in it", to give maximum effect to his reading.[55]

The Saint John papers termed Mr. Fitzgerald "a fine looking fellow", who undertook a wide variety of characters but whose stage presence was marred by too polished a gait, which reminded one reviewer of Gulliver watching his steps in Lilliput for fear lest "he should carry away some of the chimney tops". J. R. Hall, who played comic parts like Jemmy Twitcher in *The Golden Farmer* and the Dutch Major in *The White Horse of the Peppers*, was a vivacious actor with an expressive face. Mr. Bellamy, an Irishman, could keep the audience "in a Roar", and J. S. Charles was a clever actor who improved during the season. Mrs. Preston's skills were sufficient to prompt the expectation that her name would "soon be numbered among those actresses who have already attained a high histrionic eminence". Mrs. J. S. Charles was a favorite with the critics: "Eulogium . . . would be wasted upon her, and could add nothing in favour of the reputation she has long since acquired".[56]

Preston's careful management in his first Saint John season won him sufficient of what he flatteringly described as "a distinguished patronage" to warrant even more ambitious action in 1840. Accordingly, he embarked on two projects at considerable expense, one the remodelling of the Theatre and the other the acquisition of some famous stars. He rebuilt the interior of the Theatre. He raised the stage some feet above its former level, provided new, comfortable, and elegant boxes and gallery, and turned the pit into a parquet "similar to the New Orleans Camp Theatre — where the ladies, and those who generally frequent the dress circle, can be seen to the best possible advantage".[57] Formerly, the pit was occupied by the 'lower' classes and by youth and the boxes by the elite; now, with the alteration of the pit to a parquet, more seating was made available to the elite, and the former pitters were banished to the gallery. The higher cost of tickets to the boxes and parquet, both set at 4s., versus 2s. to the gallery, was intended to facilitate a change in the composition of the audience. Accoustics were improved when the sides of the house were "ceiled and deafened". The whole exterior was painted and "otherwise ornamented", and the scenery was newly designed by Messrs. Hardy and Milner and their assistants. The *Morning News* congratulated Mr. Preston on his taste and agreed with the *Courier* that no pains or expense had been spared in turning the Theatre into "one of the chief characteristics of our city".[58] When Preston announced the coming, during the season, of John Vandenhoff and his daughter, Fanny Fitzwilliam, and Junius Brutus Booth, the press could hardly believe the good fortune: "If so, our Theatrical firmament will be dazzled by stars which have illumined the Metropolitan boards with unusual splendour. Vandenhoof, [sic] is among the very few distinguished Tragedians of the present day. Booth's Richard is inimitable".[59] Preston kept his promises, although Booth did not appear until 1841.

In addition, the manager employed a strong company from the New York, Boston, and New Orleans theatres. The *Morning News* was pleased: "As regards the company . . . we must say, that Mr. Preston seems to have understood the metal of his corps, and good taste of a St. John audience, before he made his engagements".[60] Most of the company were making their first appearance in Saint John, but Mr. Hardy, scene painter and stage manager, had been there eleven years previously. Mrs. Anderson, leading lady until the Vandenhoffs' arrival, had visited Saint John in 1830 as Miss Pelby. Mrs. Preston and the charming Miss Buloid, wife of actor W. Abbott, also assumed major roles. Dubliner William S. Fredericks from Covent Garden and the Park Theatre, was leading man. He had made his American debut at the Park as Virginius in 1836, sunk "down into a respectable position in the stock company",[61] and by 1838 had risen to play title roles there and in Philadelphia. The travelled reviewer for the *Morning News* had often seen him on the American boards.

The 1840 season opened on Monday, June 15, with Bulwer's *The Lady of Lyons*, advertised as a "fashionable play in five Acts", starring Mrs. Anderson as Pauline and Mr. Fredericks as Claude Melnotte, a role he had played "upwards of Fifty nights" with British actress Ellen Tree. There followed such staple fare as Kotzebue's melodrama *The Stranger*, Rowe's verse tragedy *Jane Shore*, Garrick's *Catharine and Petruchio*, and also a new play, Knowles' *Love; or the Countess and the Serf* (1839), all with Mrs. Anderson and Mr. Fredericks in the title roles.

Preston's coup of the year was undoubtedly his presentation of the distinguished English tragedian John Vandenhoff and his daughter. Between June 24 and July 6 he appeared as Macbeth, Othello, Hamlet, Cato in Addison's tragedy of that name, Master Walter in *The Hunchback*, Shylock in *The Merchant of Venice*, and Mercutio in *Romeo and Juliet*. Miss Vandenhoff starred opposite him as Portia, Ophelia, Juliet, and as Julia in *The Hunchback*. Their performances were attended by "numerous and respectable" audiences, so that by July 1 the Theatre had become "quite a fash-

45

ionable place of resort". The reviewer of *Romeo and Juliet* was ecstatic: "We were transported as if by magic, across the wide Atlantic and up the expanded Mediteranean: and saw before us, not the
imitators but the *originals*. . . . We saw no *acting*; we saw *life* as it
was some hundreds of years ago, as it is now, and ever will be —
and nothing else. This is what we call 'holding the mirror up to
nature'".[62] Vandenhoff had given the role of Romeo to Fredericks
and taken Mercutio for himself because, the reviewer assumed,
conscious of his own powers, he was jealous of no rival. Miss Vandenhoff was called for after the final curtain "and if her little heart
did not swell, almost to bursting, with the plaudits loud and long,
she must be an ANGEL! — what an angel!!!" Mr. Preston had
spared neither expense nor ingenuity in setting the scene but put
forth an "extraordinary outlay" in getting up "the choicest 'floating
capital' of the cis-atlantic Theatrical world".[63]

A change of pace from the largely Shakespearean repertoire of
the Vandenhoffs was provided by four nights of Mrs. Fanny Fitzwilliam, English comic actress and vocalist, as Widow Brady in Garrick's *The Irish Widow* and as Peggy Thrift in his *The Country Girl*.
Mrs. Fitzwilliam came to Saint John following eight months in
America, during which she travelled upwards of 8,000 miles, performed 200 nights, and added $20,000 to her fortune. Saint John
audiences were enthralled by her performances: "The brilliancy of
her voice, the vivacity of her acting, and the rapidity with which she
dressed, looked and played the various characters she assumed,
perfectly bewitched the audience. . . . Let every body see her, for
every body should do so. The language has not words to describe
her".[64]

After Mrs. Fitzwilliam's departure for engagements in New
York and England, the Vandenhoffs returned once more to contribute their services in Otway's *Venice Preserved* for Mr. Fredericks' benefit on July 13. This may well have been the social highlight
of the season, for Lieutenant-Governor Harvey was in attendance:

> His Excellency the Lieut. Governor, and suite, entered the
> Theatre about the middle of the first act, when the Orchestra
> struck up the National Anthem — during which Jaffier and
> Belvidera, who were then on stage, had not a word to say — as
> a matter of course. The Anthem over, three cheers were given
> in honor of His Excellency, which he acknowledged, in a few
> words — which we could not distinctly hear.[65]

This was also to have been the Vandenhoffs' last appearance. After
a few nights, however, on which Preston gave the Theatre over to
Madame La Conte's dancers, they gave three more performances.

On July 22 the house was "crowded to excess" for Knowles' comedy *The Hunchback*. On the other hand, his verse tragedy *Virginius* had "a very slender audience" on the 24th. A cynical article on the theatre and public taste which appeared in the *Morning News* in response to it leaves one puzzled about the truth of the Vandenhoffs' reception in Saint John:

> It is somewhat strange that wherever these distinguished artists have appeared, they have met with the most cordial reception, always playing to full and fashionable houses — while in St. John, they have nearly met with (must we say it) — *defeat.* . . . and how is it that in our city he is not better under stood when the intelligence of the community is not inferior to any other under the sun? Something is out of joint, and we will now endeavour to point that something out, according to our notion of *things*.
> 'Tis true, on several occasions Mr. and Miss Vandenhoff have played to good houses — *fashionable* houses; but on those occasions, we believe, it was only FASHION, that drew the people together, and not *taste* for the play or the players. It is only necessary for the manager, to announce, that his Theatre is to be visited by some person of distinction, to insure for himself a good and FASHIONABLE house; he may rely upon a bumper as often as he has an opportunity of doing so. Apropos — How would it do for Mr. Preston to import a few Earls, Knights, or Squires, (not half-squires, for they are already as *thick* as hops about a Brew-house,) in the capacity of box STARS, (no doubt they would bring their own *stars* besides,) in order to have *attraction* in the house? They would *draw* well — aye, ten times better than those histrionic geniuses *whose abilities are their only recommendation*! The age is sadly out of repair.[66]

Earlier in the month, the same newspaper had commented on the "overflowing and fashionable audiences" which nightly visited the Theatre, and the *Courier* of July 25 remarked that the Vandenhoffs had, on every occasion, drawn overflowing houses. Preston, though, did not prolong their engagement, on the grounds that the public had become familiar with their merits, so we may assume that the novelty of the famous stars was wearing off and with it box office receipts. The Vandenhoffs made their last appearance in a comedy, Shakespeare's *As You Like It*, on July 27. For the remaining two weeks of the season, Mr. Fredericks and Mrs. Preston led the company.

On June 17, 1841, Preston opened his Theatre on Union Street once more, with a company that, the press announced, "for strength and talent" had never been surpassed in Saint John and with the internationally acclaimed tragedian Junius Brutus Booth as his star. Over the preceding week various members of the company, including the Booths, had registered at the St. John Hotel. A mixture of youth and age, they included actors who were yet to make their reputations and others whose heyday was past; only Mr. and Mrs. Chapman had been with Preston in Saint John before. Twenty-five year old Cockney Charles M. Walcot had only recently arrived from England. Although he had performed in Philadelphia, he had yet to make the New York debut from which he would rise to become one of the best comedians of the mid-nineteenth century and a rival to James H. Hackett. Sixty year old John Barnes had once been the idol of Park Theatre audiences, but in recent years he had been playing the minor theatres and touring on the southern circuit with his wife Mary and daughter Charlotte, both of whom were with him in Saint John. Sadly, it was to be Barnes' last tour, for a month later, in Halifax, he suffocated when a carbuncle broke in his throat. Charles Howard, of Covent Garden, had made his American debut in the opening programme of the National Theatre in 1836. J. S. Shaw was a delineator of Irish characters, and English born Mrs. Pritchard had acted in New York and Philadelphia. Comedienne Mary Ann Rock, of "the Theatres Royal, London, Dublin, and Edinburgh" had delighted Bowery audiences from 1827 to 1832 with her vivacity and skill. After nearly a decade of performing in her native Britain, she had returned for a couple of seasons to a New York that had largely forgotten her. Like all the others, she was in Saint John during a lull in the American theatre season.[67]

Preston had planned a star-filled season. In addition to Booth, he brought George H. Hill, better known as Yankee Hill, and James H. Hackett. Bostonian Hill had acquired an unrivalled reputation on both sides of the Atlantic for his representations of Yankee characters. Preceded by extensive press publicity, he came to Saint John on July 24 to perform for "one night only" with "beautiful and accomplished ballad singer" Miss Reynolds. Presumably success was the reason he was still there on the 30th. Hackett, whose name, the *Morning News* said, "is such a tower of strength both in the States and in London", appeared only on July 26 in "three of his most celebrated characters", Falstaff, Colonel Nimrod Wildfire, and M. Mallet.

Preston must have meant the highlight of the season, nevertheless, to be the appearance, from June 17 to June 30, of Junius Brutus Booth, in roles for which he had earned international acclaim — Sir Giles Overreach in Massenger's *A New Way to Pay Old*

48

Debts, Sir Edward Mortimer in Colman's *The Iron Chest*, and Hamlet. He opened as Hamlet, with Miss Rock as Ophelia, Mrs. Preston as the Queen, and Mr. Howard as the Ghost. The review in the *Morning News* was lengthy but detached, complimentary but not emotional, as if its author were used to seeing actors of Booth's reputation every week:

> Mr. Booth acted the character with great ability. He is evidently a tragedian of the first walk, and appears to have studied deeply 'to suit the action to the word, the word to the action'. In voice, gesture, and stature, he may almost be called the counterpart of the younger Kean. Nature has stamped tragedy on his brow, nor can he apparently smile without an effort. His enunciation, notwithstanding a deep and gutteral voice, is peculiarly clear and distinct. We were struck forcibly by his soliloquy 'to be or not to be' — and never remember to have heard it pronounced with more pathos and depth of feeling by any actor of the day, not excepting Kemble, Macready, Forrest, Kean or Vandenhoff. It was indeed a rich intellectual feast to watch the secret and silent working of his mind as he approached 'the oppressor's wrong, the proud man's contumely'.[68]

Though he was accustomed to crowded houses wherever he played in Europe, England, or the United States, Booth played to nearly empty benches on his first two nights in Saint John, prompting the reviewer for the *Weekly Chronicle* to worry about the reputation of Saint John's citizens: "We hope that he will not be allowed to depart under the impression that we do not possess either taste or liberality. We also trust he will be taught that we prefer the language of Shakespeare, delivered with the eloquence of a Cicero, to the buffoonery of a circus or the roar of wild beasts in a menagerie".[69] The *Chronicle*'s pointed barb referred to the fact that masses of people were regularly attending the circus on Carleton Street where, just a week before, a large group of disorderly spectators had caused extensive damage to the tents and injured a number of citizens.

Behaviour in the Theatre on Booth's opening night was not decorous either, provoking the *Chronicle*, in its search for means to attract more patrons for the actor, to announce:

> We think the order, as well as the respectability of the house, would be improved, by keeping the constables, who are paid for their attendance, in their proper station, i.e. at the doors. We last night saw two of those knights of the mace . . . sitting

on the front seat of the parquette, with their hats on, and their heels on the back of the orchestra, luxuriating in a most un-'oriental fashion'. This should be corrected.[70]

In addition, the paper thought that, "in the present depressed state of trade", ticket prices should be put down to 2s.6d. and 1s.3d.

Neither noisy behaviour in the Theatre, nor expensive tickets, nor the verdict of the press that Booth's supporting players were only "tolerable good seconds . . . certainly not below mediocrity" was, of course, the real reason for the poor reception which greeted him; famous actor that he was, Booth simply could not compete with the circus. By his third night, however, the larger audience in attendance at the Theatre encouraged the *Morning News* to remark hopefully that "he appears to be coming gradually into notice".[71]

After Booth's last performance on June 20, 1841, Hopley's Theatre stood empty until Mrs. Fanny Fitzwilliam and the playwright and comedian J. B. Buckstone came for three days in late September 1842, enroute to Halifax and England at the close of an American tour. A review following their last performance indicated that at least some of Saint John's population were missing the drama:

> On Friday evening the inimitable Buckstone and Fitzwilliam, closed their performances in St. John. The house on the occasion was strongly patronised, which circumstance strongly evinced that a taste for the Drama, has not become entirely obsolete in St. John. We always were of opinion that a Theatre here in the winter season, would receive very liberal encouragement — that is, in good times; and we trust that Saint John, next winter, will be in a condition to sustain the Drama in its legitimate purity. During the three nights of the past week's enjoyment, we felt very much like living once more; we felt like being in one of the large cities of the world, where a man can enjoy himself, no matter how dismal the times, or poor his circumstances. We trust to have an opportunity of *living* again this winter, for it is hard for one in the hey-day of his life, to be compelled to monopolize miserable thoughts.[72]

Nevertheless, the dearth of professional theatre lasted until 1845, when Preston again returned as manager. Until then, the only professional attractions were itinerant entertainers like Signor Blitz, mesmerist, and the armless S. K. G. Nellis who could do amazing tricks with his feet.

The wistful reviewer of Mrs. Fitzwilliam and Mr. Buckstone alluded to hard times in Saint John, as the *Weekly Chronicle* had done a year earlier, and the city had indeed entered upon a period of severe depression. This may well be the reason Preston's 1841 season was so short, and it is almost certainly why he did not return until 1845, when times had begun to improve.

The city had entered the 1840's optimistically. The population of the eastern peninsula had swelled to 19,281, with the combined populations of city and county reaching 32,957. Buildings of brick, wood, and stone were rising with a rapidity that prompted the *Commercial News* to ask, "Are they rearing another New York, — will these enterprising people cover all these bold hills with their habitations?"[73] In January 1841, the New York *Sun* marvelled at the city which was "increasing in wealth and population with a rapidity surpassing any city in the Union".[74] But by January 1842, the *Morning News* was reporting that upwards of 4,000 individuals depended on public charity for support and that 600 more were unable to meet their debts: "If times do not soon alter for the better", it predicted, "we will be like the shipwrecked mariner, obliged to turn to work and eat one another for food". Many stores were closed; few people walked the once busy hub of King and Prince William Streets during the day, and at night the city stood silent in total darkness, for the City Council could not afford to light the street lamps. The *New Brunswicker* blamed the city governors, and their extravagance was undoubtedly one factor in the problem, as were the several serious fires that had destroyed homes and businesses since 1837; but the whole of New Brunswick languished in depression, largely because the British preference for timber had been considerably reduced.[75]

In the circumstances, it is significant that "a goodly number of the young men" of the city sought to fill the gap the absence of a professional theatre company had left. Encouraged by the *Morning News*, they formed the Saint John Histrionic Society on October 10, 1842, and not wasting any time, they opened at the Theatre on the 27th before an audience of 400. With the assistance of some ladies from the community they presented the twin comic bill of *Charles II; or the Merry Monarch* and *Dying for Love*. Although the actors were thought to have "hung down their heads a little on the first night", the lady who played the Countess "walked the stage like Majesty itself", and all were expected to acquire more confidence with experience.[76]

Until the end of the year the Society faithfully offered a new programme once a week — including Colman's *Iron Chest*, Jerrold's domestic drama *Rent Day*, Wilks' romantic melodrama *Wenlock of Wenlock*, and the ever popular tragedy of *Douglas*, plus appropriate afterpieces, songs and dances, all backed by scenes painted by Mr. Slader. They made every effort to attend to the comfort of their audience. Between the first and second week, partitions were erected and stoves placed in the lobbies of the Theatre, and other unnamed alterations and improvements were made. Officers were employed to enforce order. Proceeds, as promised, were given to charity, and the Band of the 30th Regiment provided the music. Tickets, at the beginning of the season, were 2s.6d. for boxes and parquet and only 1s.3d. for the gallery, but even so patronage was slender enough that the company found it wise to make special concessions to the ladies. Accordingly, prices to admit ladies to the boxes and parquet were reduced to 1s.3d., and new season prices reflected the same concessions: "For one Gentleman 20s.; one Gentleman and Lady 25s; one Gentleman and two Ladies, 30 s."

From January through September 1843, the Histrionic Society performed more or less weekly — more or less because in February they performed twice weekly, and in the first half of March and in July and August they closed the Theatre. Scripts included the opera of *Rob Roy*, *The Merchant of Venice*, *MacBeth*, *Othello*, *Robber of the Rhine*, and *Wenlock of Wenlock* again. Audiences cannot usually have been large, for the attendance of 300 persons at *The Dumb Girl of Genoa* on February 13 was sufficient to warrant the comment that "the public have at length exhibited some signs of theatrical animation". Normally, however, the company met with approval from the reviewers "for the quick and efficient manner in which they have brought forward new pieces", for "their exertions to please", as well as for their "extraordinary talent". Only occasionally were they criticized publicly, once for relying on the prompter too much and another time for uttering sailors' oaths (in the interlude "Scenes in the Forecastle") that some of the ladies considered "not very appropos for the stage". After September, the Society is not heard of again.

By May of the next year, though, another society of young men had formed, calling itself the Saint John Amateurs and announcing its intention of giving a theatrical performance once a month "during the season". *Othello* was the first production on May 15, but thenceforth the Amateurs did not advertise. While it is thus impossible to know if they did in fact perform monthly, they were still identifiable in the spring of 1845, for Preston used some of them to fill up his new company at the Theatre.

The company with which Henry Preston opened on March 5, 1845, was not a strong one. Led by himself and by Miss Hildreth, a stock actress "from the Boston Theatres", it included Miss Reiner, and Messrs. Charles Howard, James, Williams, and Edgar. Pre-

THEATRE.

Benefit of Miss M'Bride !

Miss M'BRIDE *respectfully announces to the Ladies of Saint John, that her Benefit is appointed to take place on*

FRIDAY EVENING, SEPTEMBER 5, 1845,

When will be presented the following novel and attractive Bill of Entertainment, which she trusts will meet with their approbation.

Last appearance of MR. FREER and MISS M'BRIDE !

SHAKSPEARE's *beautiful* COMEDY *of*
AS YOU LIKE IT,
in which several of the Gentlemen of the Dramatic Amateur Association will appear, who have most kindly volunteered their aid.

FRIDAY Evening, September 5th, will be performed, Shakspeare's
Comedy of
AS YOU LIKE IT ;

Jacques,	. . . .	Mr. FREER,
Orlando,	. . . . .	By a Gentleman Amateur,
Duke,		
Amiens,	. . . .	By Gentlemen Amateurs.
Oliver,		
ROSALIND,	. . . .	Miss M'BRIDE.

After the Comedy, MISS M'BRIDE *will dance a Scotch* PAS SEUL, *arranged from the much admired Overture of Guy Mannering.*

To conclude with *Shannon's* Comedy, in 2 Acts, of THE
YOUTHFUL QUEEN ;

Steinberg,	. . . . . .	Mr. FREER,
The Youthful Queen,	. . . .	Miss M'BRIDE.

☞ *That the performance may be over at an early hour, the Curtain will rise at 8 o'clock.*
SAINT JOHN, SEPTEMBER 4, 1845.

R. Shives, Printer.

ston, understanding the Saint John audience, opened with Kotzebue's *The Stranger*, which he advertised as a "Moral and Intellectual Play"; a farce for the Irish, *Irishman's Blunders*; and a song
written by "a Gentleman of Fredericton". Prices were 3s. for the
parquet and boxes and 1s.6d. for the gallery, but these were dropped in the second week to 2s.6d. and 1s.3d. For the rest of the
month he catered to the mixed tastes of his audience, with a legitimate mainpiece like *Hamlet* or *Pizarro* and a lighter afterpiece such
as *Irish Haymaker*. Then, on March 31, he presented a "New Play,
entitled the PROVINCIAL ASSOCIATION: or, TAXING EACH
OTHER", billed as an "Original and truly admirable Tragi-Comedy", and precipitated a riot such as the Theatre had never seen.

Preston had acquired the play in Fredericton from its author,
Thomas Hill, editor of the *Loyalist* — a "miserable wretch", Mr.
Fenety, editor of the *Morning News*, called him. Hill had penned
the play during two busy weeks in the legislature for use in the new
hall Preston intended to fit out as "The People's Olympic Theatre".
It was in preparation by February 8, for the *Loyalist* of that date
says its appearance is "expected shortly to be announced", but it
did not appear before Preston transferred his company to Saint
John.

If Preston was not fully aware of the emotional fever inherent
in the political subject, Hill must have been, but no one can have
been prepared for the full force of what was to come. At a time
when the battle between 'protection' and 'free trade' waged hot and
when an association calling itself the Provincial Association had
been formed to combat government policy, the title alone was
enough to spark trouble. Without knowing or caring whether the
play was, as the *Herald* afterwards said, no more than "a sportive
delineation of the incident on which it was founded" or, as Hill
claimed, merely a "quiet satire . . . upon the extreme measures of
the Association", the protectionists of the Association descended
on the Theatre determined to suppress it. In this they succeeded
temporarily, "for so violent was the tumult in the theatre and in the
street that it was impossible for the performers to get a hearing".
Still not satisfied, "they proceeded to injure the building, by breaking the doors, pulling down the stove pipes, and materially injuring
the adjoining premises".[77] Unintimidated, Preston tried again on
Wednesday, April 2, when again the Theatre was crowded, and
again there were attacks on the stove pipes. Once more hissing,
hooting, whistling, and stamping prevented the play from being
heard, and the crowd outside, armed with clubs and sticks, broke
down the doors and attacked benches and spectators alike.[78]

When Preston announced another performance for Monday,

April 7, there was some question whether the Mayor would allow it. Mr. Fenety, a vociferous opponent of Hill's play, which he declared designed to bring contempt on the "respectability" and "moral rectitude" of "certain well-known members of this community" and their wives, wrote about the uncertainty in mock heroic tones:

> Monday was a day big with events; and the signs of the times at an early hour gave strong indications of the fate of Rome, and of Caesar. This was the day appointed for the repetition at the Theatre of the piece called the "Provincial Association" — 1 o'clock (broad day light) was the hour set apart for raising the curtain. Placards were posted about the streets, intimating to the public, that tickets of admission could be had at the modest price of 5s a piece — that the gallery was to be closed, (to keep out the noise, we presume).[79]

The lengthy satire went on to recount the events of the day, which culminated in the arrest of Mr. Preston on unspecified charges just at curtain time, his release on bail, and the eventual completion of the performance. This time the high ticket prices kept out the Provincial Association's paid rioters, and there was no row. Still another production was allowed to go forward on the afternoon of Friday, April 11, without incident.

The controversy in the press concluded with the *Herald*'s condemnation of the *Morning News*' second hand reporting as "egregiously untrue" and "flagrantly abusive of individuals" and with Thomas Hill's defence in the *Loyalist*.[80] Hill said the plot and characters were "almost wholly *ideal*", not caricatures, and he promised to vindicate himself by publication of the manuscript. This he did, for from May 22 until the end of the year the back page of the *Loyalist* carried this notice:

The Provincial Association

The Tragi-Comedy, under the above title, is now published, in a Pamphlet form, and can be had at the Book Stores in St. John and Fredericton — Price 1s.3d.

It is our loss that no copy of that pamphlet seems to have survived.

Another political play of the same year has survived though. Less interesting because it was never performed, it is a "farce" in four short acts entitled "Political Intrigue; or the Best Way to Tar One Another", published unsigned in the *Morning News* on October 20. The play is set in the seat of government, Patridge Island, which even has its own Downing Street. Three buildings are conspicuous — the Guard House, the Hospital, and the Light House, and the functions of government are carried out in them. The *dramatis personae* are Sir Solomon Colebox (Governor of the Island), Hon. Lucey Seaco Swamco (Secretary of the Island), R. J. Squaretoes (Chief Commander of the Light House), Hon. Blownard Blucher (Prime Minister), and X. Y. Z. Ready, Esq. The slight plot concerns the attempts of Swamco and Squaretoes to "lay on the tar" to Sir Solomon in Blucher's absence in order to induce him to appoint two of their friends to public office. The plot is foiled when Blucher returns and the names, which have already been published in the *Fisherman's [Royal] Gazette*, are withdrawn. In a light-hearted but cutting way, the play deals with the problem of political patronage and, in its island setting, with the isolation of government from the people.

Perhaps the fuss surrounding *The Provincial Association* had the effect such controversies often do, of drawing more people to the scene, for Preston's season continued unabated through April and May with such well-known plays as *School for Scandal* and *The Heir at Law*. Preston was doing well enough that on April 18 the *Herald* could announce that workmen had "commenced operations on the building in Duke-street, commonly known as the Tabernacle, for the purpose of fitting it up as a Theatre, which in point of structure, beauty, capacity, and arrangement, will in every respect be convenient to the wishes, convenience, and accommodation of the gentry of Saint John". The new theatre, to be named the Prince of Wales, stood on the corner of Duke and Sydney Streets. By the time of its opening on June 23, the large wooden building had been refashioned from a place of worship into an "elegant place of amusement . . . complete in all its interior departments, viz. — select and comfortable Boxes, both public and private, roomy Saloons, airy entrances, spacious galleries, pit, &c. &c."[81] At 5s. tickets to the dress circle were expensive, but the less-well-off could sit in the second tier of boxes for only 2s.3d. or in the pit for 1s.3d.

By the end of June, Preston had added to his company Miss McBride as leading lady, and at the end of July he engaged Charles Freer as his leading man. The repertoire he offered was mostly familiar: *The Hunchback*, *The Lady of Lyons*, *The Soldier's Daughter*, *William Tell*, *Black-Eyed Susan*, *Hamlet*, and *Macbeth*. Only rarely did he experiment, as with *The Seven Clerks; or the Denouncer* by the author of the popular *Wenlock of Wenlock*. Generally the thrice-weekly performances were well patronized, unless the circus was in town. Preston's biggest problem was with the quality of his actors. Often he used local people, and sometimes, like the occasion on which "one of the principals of our own Histrionic Association" played Claude Melnotte, they were enthusiastically received, but the professionals he had been able to recruit were much inferior to those he had brought to Saint John before. The *Morning News*, always good at sarcasm, let its feeling on this subject be known in its review of *As You Like It*, for Miss McBride's farewell benefit on September 5:

> The *prima donna* of the evening — Miss McBride — sustained the character of Rosalynd admirably, and we did not know which to admire most, the exhibition which she made in the tights, or her clever *naiveté* when ambling in disguise with her lover — our Charley! By the hokey, if some of those lean chaps of pharoah's kine, forming Preston's *stock*, could only manage . . . to raise a pair of legs a piece, to compare with those which Rosalynd displayed, they would have something to recommend them. By the way, there is one poor unfortunate fellow, who always strikes our fancy; his legs would make capital broom handles; and however much *calf* there may be about his acting, in that region where the calf should be, there is none whatever. Rosalynd should bequeath him her's. . . . PRESTON always excels in what he undertakes — therefore we would like to see him excel in bringing forward a few more excellent actors on the boards.[82]

Unfortunately, the life of the Prince of Wales was to be short. Fire started in the stoves used for heating after a performance on December 4. By the time it was discovered nothing could be done, and the theatre was destroyed by five o'clock the next morning. Few, if any, of the effects of the performers were saved. Preston lost scenery, properties, every item in his valuable wardrobe, his collection of books, in short "everything theatrical . . . which a professional career of nearly twenty years had enabled him to accomplish".[83] Some suspected arson, but the reason for the fire was generally supposed to have been "the careless and inefficient manner in which the pipes were put up".

Saint John was now left without a theatre. The theatre at the Golden Ball, which can never have been very satisfactory, lay dormant since the illness and death of Joseph Hopley. Either it was unfit even for renovation or Mr. Preston had neither the heart nor the means to try again. It stood unused until fire severely damaged it in November 1854 and lingered on as an eyesore until flames finally transformed it into a smoking ruin in October 1874.

View of King Square (Coloured lithography)

58

iii
Lanergan's Lyceum in the Golden Age

Shipbuilding, railway construction, the struggle for responsible government, and the debate pro and con Confederation characterized the period which has been described as Saint John's Golden Age. During the 1850's the city was one of the most prominent in British North America;[1] during the 1860's, when 261 new vessels were launched, she dwarfed all other Maritime ports in shipbuilding. The wave of prosperity, which was to continue until a worldwide depression had its effect in 1874, made itself felt in all areas of life. While Saint John's bankers and builders were mingling with others in the world business centres of London, New York, and Boston, new hotels were being built at home to accommodate the thousands of tourists who were coming to visit. In 1853 a fine suspension bridge made the west side of the city less isolated, while the People's Street Railway in 1866 linked Market Slip to Indiantown. The main streets were gradually being paved, and King Square, which in the forties had been a mud slough, had been improved by the city, its pathways laid out in the shape of a Union Jack, and trees planted. The shopping district boasted dry goods and fashion shops which some claimed to equal those of Broadway and Washington Street in New York, and which the Quebec *Gazette* said outfitted ladies in as becoming a manner as in any North American community.

There were problems, too, with which the city government, headed by a mayor now elected by the people instead of appointed by the provincial government, was attempting to deal. Particularly pressing were problems of sanitation, police, and fire protection. The cholera epidemic of 1854 drew attention to the accumulation of filth from decomposed animal matter in the slaughterhouses and from the absence of privies in overcrowded areas, and led to an

59

1855 report recommending the prohibition of open drains running over the sidewalk, the distribution of water to the poor in dry weather, and the removal of slaughterhouses from the city.[2] The city's youth were the major concern of the police chief, especially the "squads of boys from eight to sixteen years of age, who belong to no school, who have no regular lawful employment, and whose only business is to loaf up and down the wharves and streets of our City, seeking for an opportunity to commit some petty theft, or otherwise annoy honest and peaceable citizens".[3] Hundreds of teens of both sexes, he complained, nightly congregated at the head and foot of King Street. His difficulties were compounded by the 287 taverns which received licences in 1864, the unlicensed beer shops "where prostitutes and persons of notoriously bad character congregate", and by the gambling houses to which the police were frequently called to evict disorderly persons but where they had no authority to enter.

Nevertheless, a visitor to the city could somehow ignore these black spots and notice only the positive aspects. One such visitor, the editor of the Boston *Advertiser*, was captivated by the lively intelligence and refined tastes of those of the 27,317 inhabitants he encountered in the summer of 1861:

> St. John is a city . . . of whose refinement, intelligence and culture we can scarcely speak our high opinion without violating the behests of courteous hospitalities there received. . . . A well stocked museum of natural history proves the scientific taste of the people, as that in music is attested by the repeated and eager visits of the principal mistresses of song (no less than three first-class artists gave concerts there during the period of our excursion), while half a dozen presses show that the inhabitants are fond of reading newspapers, and that they enjoy political and sectarian discussions with uncommon zest.[4]

In 1857, according to the *Morning News* of January 17, more opportunities existed than ever before for music education; never had Saint John been so well supplied with competent teachers. In the same year theatre too entered a new phase, for J. W. Lanergan opened his Dramatic Lyceum on the south side of King Square and offered the first of his many annual summer seasons, thus beginning a pattern of regular theatre that would continue without interruption into the twentieth century. The Dramatic Lyceum itself would continue in active use until displaced by the more elegant Academy of Music in the 1870's and finally destroyed by the Great Fire of 1877.

The years between the Prince of Wales and the Dramatic Lyceum had been lean ones for theatrical entertainment in Saint John. The late 1840's had produced only scattered entertainments of a popular nature, such as Rockwell and Stone's circus, ventriloquist and magician Signor Blitz, Spanish magician Signor Francis, Parker's Ethiopian Operatic Troupe, Barnum's General Tom Thumb (weight 15 pounds, height 28 inches), and Nova Scotia giant Angus McCaskill. To such exhibitions the people were "much attracted", reported Abraham Gesner in his 1847 publication, *New Brunswick; with Notes for Emigrants.*[5]

The second half of the forties was an extremely difficult period for a city that had scarcely recovered from the severe depression of the earlier part of the decade. In 1846 immigration from Ireland speeded up, as more and more tenants were evicted from their lands following the famine of 1845 and the repeal of the Corn Laws in 1846, bringing about an acute problem in Saint John in 1847 because of the high proportion of persons who arrived with typhus and made the establishment of a quarantine station on Partridge Island a necessity.[6] The thousands of Irish who came, tempted to hope for a better life by misleading accounts such as the Rev. W. C. Atkinson's *Historical and Statistical Account of New Brunswick*, which described the province glowingly as a colony "watered by noble rivers, whose fertile alluvial banks team with riches",[7] had difficulty winning acceptance into the new community. Their arrival flooded the labour market and introduced into Saint John the same problems of violence, lawlessness, drunkenness, poverty, and religious strife they had left behind. The "pleasures enjoyed by the rational part of the community" contrasted markedly, said Gesner, with the "outrages committed by the lower classes of Irish.[8]

By the early 1850's, however, the worst of the difficulties were over, the tension that had erupted in the York Point Riot of 1849 had eased, immigration had settled down, and the fortunes of an overcrowded community were turned around. In 1852 amateurs of the 72nd Regiment from Fredericton performed twice in St. Stephen's Hall, and Frank Maybee announced an intention that never materialized to establish a Dramatic Athenaeum in the former Friary on Horsfield Street. During 1852 and 1853 the famous Heron family of vocalists included dramatic sketches in the concerts they gave in the Mechanics' Institute, and in 1855 included the full length *Lady of Lyons* in their repertory. In 1854 Yankee Hill brought his New Orleans Opera Troupe to the Institute for a brief stay.

When Lanergan, Sanford, and Fiske's Star Company opened on July 25, 1856, in the former dining room of the St. John Hotel, the city was ripe to be harvested by an enterprising theatrical manager such as James West Lanergan proved to be. Lanergan's own association with the drama began early. As a child he is said to have read widely in Shakespeare and other Elizabethan dramatists. At sixteen, he was at the head of an amateur dramatic company. When success in that role prompted him to adopt the stage for his career, he joined the strolling company of 'old Bill Dinneford', whose circuit included New England towns from Lawrence to Portsmouth. In 1849, at nineteen, he became a member of the stock company of the newly opened Portland Museum under Joseph Proctor, the lessee. Though he was hired for utility, he made such rapid progress in the company that within four weeks he was being trusted with responsible roles. The season at the Museum terminated abruptly, and after several months of precarious existence, Lanergan went to Boston for an appearance at the Lyceum. There he met George Wyatt, joined his company, and remained with him until 1852 (apart from a three month interlude at the Museum), much of the time as leading man. In the fall of 1852 he organized his own travelling company, which illness forced him to give up after only one successful season. For the next three years he was a member of the stock company at the Broadway Theatre, New York, after which he entered into partnership with Edward Sanford and Moses Fiske to form the Star Company, or as it was also called, the New York Dramatic Company, which toured the New England States in 1856.[9]

The Star Company, whose membership was drawn from the Broadway Theatre and from the new Boston Theatre, had Messrs. Lanergan and Sanford as its leading men; Fiske was the comedian; W. Pratt, author of *Ten Nights in a Bar-room*, was first old man, and Caroline E. Bernard was leading lady.[10] From the opening production of Tom Taylor's serious comedy *Still Waters Run Deep*, starring Mr. Lanergan as John Mildmay, performances went on nightly in the St. John Hotel until August 20, when the company had to leave to honour engagements in Springfield, Massachusetts. Seats were inexpensive at 1s.3d. (1s. 10½d. reserved). The hall was small and inadequate, but it was always full, and there was no other. Although the Mechanics' Institute had been erected in 1840 on Carleton Street, its directors would not allow its lecture hall to be used regularly for dramatic purposes. Lanergan adhered to his promise to produce the legitimate drama,[11] and, furthermore, he saw to it that the evenings ended early — although his programme was usually a double bill, he would omit the afterpiece if the main attraction was too lengthy. His repertoire included *Love's Sacrifice*, *Damon and Pythias*, *Othello*, *The Hunchback*, *The Lady of Lyons*, *George Barnwell*, *All That Glitters is Not Gold*, with nothing new or controversial.

62

The discreet management of Lanergan, Sanford, and Fiske did much to improve the reputation of theatre in Saint John. "It cannot be denied", the *Morning News* asserted on August 11, "that the taste for Theatricals has undergone a decided improvement here since the stay of the Star Company". So great was their success that from August 7 the *News* was arguing for the erection of a permanent building of suitable dimensions. The company too must have been pleased with its reception, for on his return to Boston, agent W. H. Thomas spoke "in warm terms of the hospitality of the people of New Brunswick, where, notwithstanding the company were all Americans, they made warm friends, and were treated with a cordiality that has left an impression upon their hearts never to be effaced".[12]

Since Lanergan already realized that "the place afforded a good and profitable field for permanent dramatic business",[13] he was easily induced to return to Saint John for the winter of 1856-1857 to select a site in the centre of the city suitable for a "commodious and comfortable hall for dramatic, musical, and other purposes" and to make arrangements for its erection. On March 18, 1857, he leased a property on the south side of King Square belonging to broker John Ansley. The property included lots fronting on King Square for 33 feet and running back 132 feet, together with a 14 foot wide alleyway that followed the adjoining lot for 100 feet. Lanergan obtained the property for a term of ten years, with an option to renew for further five year terms, at a yearly rent of £80 to be paid in four quarterly payments.[14] He was then ready to proceed with his plan to construct a properly ventilated hall with all the modern improvements and capable of seating from 800 to 1000 people. Design he made the responsibility of architect William Campbell, who had rebuilt the Sadler's Wells Theatre in London. Opening night was scheduled for June 1.

In the meantime, from December 24, 1856, Lanergan put on nightly performances in the St. John Hotel, accommodating himself to the inconvenience of being unable to introduce adequate scenery in the cramped quarters. His company now consisted of Mrs. Lanergan (the former Miss Bernard), Mr. and Mrs. Wallace from the New York Museum, Miss Winthrop and Mr. Adams of the Boston Museum, George Tyrell from Cincinnati, and Messrs. Holmes, Parker, and Stone from the National Theatre in Boston. Sanford and Fiske had not returned. As might be expected, the company had good houses and generous applause. The parts were all pronounced "well sustained", "decidedly good", or "creditably performed", and Lanergan's choice of scripts was approved from a moral as well as an artistic standpoint; W. H. Smith's *Drunkard*, for instance, was admired as a drama in which "the miseries consequent on a life of intemperance and debauchery are so faithfully and graphically portrayed that the effect cannot be otherwise than beneficial".[15]

By the end of April, when the St. John Dramatic Lyceum was rising on the same King Square site which in the next century would hold the Imperial Theatre, two other new theatres had been proposed, and one of them was about to open. In early February 1857, William Warren of Boston arrived in Saint John, supposedly to start work immediately on a theatre large enough to accommodate 2000 persons and situated centrally. Its dimensions were to be 80 by 100 feet and 40 feet high. It was to contain a parquet and three galleries and to surpass in its internal arrangements some of the Boston theatres. The initiators were William and Robert Warren, business agent and manager respectively of the Metropolitan Troupe of musicians and comedians who had performed in Saint John for a week in December 1856. The two men announced in February that tenders would be called for a building to be completed in August, but nothing more was heard.

More successful was the Royal Provincial Theatre which opened on May 11 in a remodelled room of Mr. Paddock's brick building on Prince William Street, into which access had been provided through a new covered entrance from Duke Street. The room was "neatly and comfortably fitted up and furnished with handsome scenery and all other appurtenances requisite to produce stage effects";[16] seats in the reserved section were cushioned. The manager was G. K. Dickenson of London and New York, billed as the "author, adapter and translator of many excellent plays",[17] and the company was chosen, as was customary, from the theatres of Boston and New York. The company performed regularly for a month in plays like *Hamlet*, *The Lady of Lyons*, and *Camille*; Mr. Dickenson received good reviews, though the rest of the company was considered mediocre. If the theatre was used after June 10, however, its performances were not advertised. Unfortunately, about four o'clock one Sunday morning late in October, fire broke out in the upper storey. Although it was out by six, the interior was destroyed, along with the scenery belonging to the Provincial Theatre.

The Dramatic Lyceum, on the other hand, was just beginning. As anticipation mounted with the progress of the construction through late April, May, and early June, the press carried detailed descriptions of the building.[18] Its exterior, which was to be finished in an Italian style, was 33 by 124 feet. Inside, the auditorium was 78 feet long, and the stage was 30 feet deep with a proscenium opening of 20 by 17 feet. Those "usual sources of annoyance in a theatre", the pit and gallery, were being done away with and the auditorium

64

Lanergan's Dramatic Lyceum (New Brunswick Museum)

J. W. Lanergan
(Harvard Theatre Collection)

65

divided into a parquet to seat 550 people comfortably, a dress circle to seat 300 persons, two private boxes, and four family boxes capable of holding six and nine persons each, with a separate entrance to each department. The dress circle was supported by eight heavy doric columns of birch. At its rear was a cloak or retiring room for the ladies, "a very essential feature in all well regulated Theatres". For accessibility, the ticket office was situated close to the entrance to the parquet and dress circle. Seating in every part of the building was arranged for both comfort and convenience, and the slope from the stage to the rear seats was to be gradual so that nothing could intervene "to prevent the hearing or obstruct the view of the actors".

The Lyceum was designed to overcome the problem of poor ventilation that plagued all other public buildings in Saint John. Three ventilators, each twelve feet in diameter at the base, were to be located in the roof, one over the stage, and two over the auditorium. These would ensure, together with "proper apertures in the walls", for "the free circulation of pure air", as well as serving for both interior and exterior adornment. Heat was to be provided by two small stoves near the front of the building, one at the right and the other at the left of the entrance. Lighting would be with gas.

By no means a pretentious building either within or without, the Lyceum was significant as the first theatre in Saint John to be designed and built as such, and it would amply serve the purposes for which it was intended. Not nearly so large as the Boston Theatre opened in 1854, whose auditorium was 90 feet in diameter and whose stage had a proscenium opening of 48 by 21 feet, nor so elegant, it would be packed with audiences "made up of the *elite* and respectable portions of society . . . Railway Commissioners, Apothecaries, embrio Mayors and members of Government . . . Insurance Brokers from Rocky Hill, Aldermen and Councillors, South Wharf Huxters, Shoemakers and Bankers",[19] and even ladies with their poodles. Lanergan would spare no effort "in order to maintain the drama in the high and respectable position it ought to occupy".[20] To that end, he intended to sell no intoxicating liquors on the premises and to employ "proper officers to enforce an orderly deportment among the younger part of the audience".[21] Drama at the Lyceum, nevertheless, would always be opposed by some members of the local populace, such as the Reverend G. M. Armstrong, rector of St. John's (Stone) Church and the author of this letter:

My dear Mr. Jarvis,
I was not at home yesterday when your note arrived asking me

for a copy of the rule I brought forward at our last Teachers meeting. It is as follows — "No person can be admitted to become, or remain a Teacher who does not agree to abstain from attendance at balls, dances, and theatres, and whose principles are not in accordance with those of this Church of England". I do hope that you will agree to the requirement of this rule and continue one of our Teachers, but should it be otherwise I do not object to your taking your class next Sunday as you proposed in that case.[22]

On June 15 the Dramatic Lyceum opened, two weeks behind schedule, with Bulwer's comedy *Money* and the farce of *Mr. and Mrs. Peter White*, for which Lanergan had employed a company of twenty. *Money*, featuring Mr. Lanergan as Alfred Evelyn, Mrs. Lanergan as Clara Douglas, and comedian F. F. Buxton as Graves, was considered by the moralistic reviewer for the *Morning News* as an appropriate choice for Saint John, for it aptly illustrated that

'Tis a very good world we live in,
To lend, or to spend, or to give in, —
But to beg, or to borrow, or get a man's own,
'Tis the very worst world that ever was known.[23]

Moreover, the play was judged as well performed as members of the audience had seen it in New York and London. Artistically, the entire event was termed a decided success. There were, however, some unforeseen problems with the building itself. The back seats of the dress circle were not elevated sufficiently, while the seats against the wall were useless for sitting, and people actually stood on them with dirty boots in order to see over heads (although some people stood up when there was no need of it). Only from the first or second tier of seats in the boxes could a view be had of the stage without standing. Fortunately, the parquet seats were fine. Likewise, the arrangements of the orchestra, stage, scenery, and for lighting were very good, the best, in fact, that the reviewer for the *Courier* had seen on such a small scale of building; the scenery, designed by Mr. Strong, was particularly worthy of mention.[24]

In his first season at the Dramatic Lyceum, from June 15 to September 1, 1857, Lanergan produced more than thirty-six different double bills. Audiences saw Shakespeare, Sheridan, Knowles, Bulwer, dramatizations from Walter Scott, and melodramas such as *Bluebeard; or Fatal Results of Curiosity*. By the beginning of the second week, the theatre was being called a "fashionable place of public resort" attended by "numerous and brilliant audiences" and becoming increasingly popular. On the whole the entertainments were considered to be "judiciously selected and ably performed", with Mrs. Lanergan in particular being singled out for her acting ability, but the reviews were not entirely uncritical. The *Courier* disliked the dramatized versions of both Mrs. Stowe's tale of *Dred* and Scott's *Lady of the Lake*. It considered the first ill-suited to the stage and said of the second: "Like most adaptations to the stage of compositions not designed originally for that purpose, both the dialogue and incident failed in creating the same interest when acted as when read".[25]

If the audiences were intelligent, as well as fashionable, they were also much more polite in their behaviour than the patrons of Hopley's and the Prince of Wales had been, and newspaper reviews frequently commented on this, expressing their optimism for the future and gratitude to Mr. Lanergan. On June 24 the *Morning News* reported: "We are pleased to say that none of that noise and rowdyism, so peculiar to the pit of a theatre, are observable at the Lyceum. So long as this state of things continues the Lyceum will do well". Two weeks later, on July 10, the same paper added: "There is none of that hissing and stamping formerly so prevalent, and Mr. Lanergan is deserving of praise for effecting this essential change". The problems annoying the Lyceum's patrons were minor in comparison to the disturbances at Hopley's, consisting as they did of distractions caused by gentlemen who went out during the intervals and failed to return to their seats until after the next act had begun, and of the bothersome chatter of other persons who insisted on conversing while the orchestra performed its pieces in the intermissions.

In August of 1857 Lanergan brought his first well-known star, tragedian Wyzeman Marshall, to play the roles of Ingomar, Cardinal Richelieu, Iago, and Hamlet. Marshall was an energetic man of commanding stature whose strong features were set off by black side-whiskers and a goatee. His dusky countenance and full, sonorous voice were eminently suited to the characters of heavy tragedy and romantic melodrama in which he excelled. Born in Hudson, New Hampshire, in September 1816, and raised in Boston, he had made his first stage appearance at Boston's Lion Theatre in 1836 and, only two years later, became a leading actor when he played Pizarro to the Elvira of Mrs. William Pelby. A good but not a great actor (like most of the stars Lanergan would bring), whose ambition was nevertheless to be at the top of his profession, he was thoroughly conversant with every branch of his profession.[26]

When Marshall did not receive as good houses in Saint John as might have been expected, the *Morning News* felt compelled to offer an explanation in defence of the absentees:

It must not be supposed that because the house is not filled to repletion during his engagement, that his talents are not understood in St. John. The reason is otherwise. Our people have not yet got into the dramatic vein. We have never had a good or respectable theatre until now. The attempts that have been made here from time to time have been of a low rowdy character; and people at length became disgusted with anything that savoured of theatrical representations. This prejudice has got to be overcome, and it is fast yielding. Mr. Lanergan has infused new life into the pit and boxes; the people are beginning to understand him; and in less than another year he will find his building entirely too small for his company.[27]

The patrons who did attend the Lyceum, though, were most enthusiastic about Marshall's acting; they ranked him with Macready, Vandenhoff, Booth, and Kean, pronounced his impersonation of Hamlet a "thrilling performance" and his work in general "highly pleasing and natural", a decided improvement upon the tendency to loud talking and violent gesticulation of which the August 15 *Courier* said some members of the company were guilty. Upon his return to Saint John for a week from August 1, 1859, he was billed as a favourite, and his audiences were good enough for Lanergan to extend his engagement for a second week. On that occasion he played in *Pizarro, Damon and Pythias, Two Gregories, The Lady of Lyons, Three Guardsmen, Catherine and Petruchio, Julius Caesar, Richelieu, Richard III, Rob Roy*, and *Virginius*. In 1860 he came back again to star as Hamlet, Iago, and Rob Roy.

Since J. W. Lanergan returned to Saint John with a company each summer season into the mid-1870's, it is impossible to deal with all his accomplishments in detail, but only to select some of the highlights. The reputation he won for himself in his first season bore fruit. Personally he was charming, full of anecdotes and a capital raconteur, warm-hearted and loyal in his friendships, firm in his opinions but willing to try new things. He impressed others with his "gentlemanly deportment and quiet unassuming manner", and he inspired confidence that under his management everything would be conducted "with propriety and decorum". The "intelligent and educated portion" of the citizenry, who had long desired "to see the legitimate drama, divested of evil accessories", established in the city, found their wishes being realised. Though the struggle for an audience was a constant one in the early years, and though the press for a long time believed it necessary to stress the respectability and morality of his productions, Lanergan's success was steady and sure; even in 1858, an American source said, he was in Saint John "coining money".

At the close of the Dramatic Lyceum's first summer season, in 1857, Lanergan transferred his company to St. John's, Newfoundland, after which it disbanded in Halifax. In Halifax, Lanergan found E. A. Sothern with a company that had been in residence at the Lyceum on Queen Street, just off Spring Garden Road, since June 1857. Sothern would later be known internationally as Lord Dundreary, after the role in *Our American Cousin* he created on stage, but then he was calling himself Douglas Stewart and was entirely unknown to fame. He made overtures to Lanergan to join forces with him for the winter, and so it was in Halifax, on February 16, 1858, that Lanergan appeared first as Iago, a part in which the New York *Express* later said he stood second to no American actor.[28]

In August 1858, after Lanergan had finished a short season in his own Dramatic Lyceum, Sothern brought to Saint John a company whose chief members were himself and Mrs. Sothern, Sarah Stevens, and Messrs. Raymond, Bland, and Briggs. His leading lady for the first week was Agnes Robertson, wife of Dion Boucicault, one of the most prolific and popular playwrights of the nineteenth century. The press was enraptured by Miss Robertson. The *Courier* of August 7 dubbed her "the 'Fairy Star'", "the greatest living actress in her peculiar line of business". "There is a bewitching fascination about her", it enthused, "that takes the heart by storm and enlists the sympathies of the audience throughout".

Sothern introduced Saint John to its first Boucicault play, *The Corsican Brothers*, whose plot hinges on the fact that the Corsican twins are linked by a sympathy that informs one if the other is in danger; when Louis is killed in a duel, Fabian sees his ghost and goes to avenge his brother. Before one of the largest houses yet assembled in the Lyceum, Sothern starred as the twin brothers "with great ability". Of particular attraction to audiences of the play everywhere were its two special scenic effects: one, the painting of a back-scene on a scrim — that is to say, on a linen or calico material that appeared solid when lighted from the front, but which became transparent with rear lighting to allow a scene behind it to be exposed — and the other the 'Corsican trap' which, by means of a slider and a line for pulling, allowed a ghost to rise through a trap door while drifting slowly from one side of the stage to the other. Although there is insufficient information to say with certainty that Lanergan had the requisite six feet below the stage for the proper functioning of the trap (the ghost might have been handled in some other way), the painted scenes could easily have been flown from

C. W. Couldock as Iago
(Harvard Theatre Collection)

F. S. Chanfrau as "Mose"
(Harvard Theatre Collection)

Little Cordelia Howard
(Harvard Theatre Collection)

Wyzeman Marshall
(Harvard Theatre Collection)

the fly gallery which ran along the top of the wing space on either side of the stage. The play would have had a magical enough effect on its audience even if a scrim alone were employed.

In addition to *The Corsican Brothers*, Sothern produced other works, such as *The Marble Heart; or the Sculptor's Dream* and *Camille*, in which he featured himself in leading roles. Armand Duval, in *Camille*, he had played for 150 successive nights at Wallack's Theatre, New York, opposite Matilda Heron. The *Morning News*, which found his performances electrifying always, thought he showed to his best advantage in this role, even though the *Courier* had earlier pronounced his rendition of Raphael in *The Marble Heart* "the *acme* of finished acting". He was extolled for his wonderful versatility, for an expressive face capable of showing "intense passion with terrible earnestness" and yet for his lightness and even droll impersonations.[29] All this may be just "indiscriminate puffing", of which the Halifax *Sun* said the Halifax papers were guilty, and certainly Saint John reviewers were not averse to puffery; but still, they had shown their critical side the previous season, therefore one assumes they were genuinely enthralled with the Sothern company, and probably overwhelmed that an actress of Agnes Robertson's stature should visit their boards.

Before Sothern's August season in the Dramatic Lyceum, Lanergan had run his own 1858 season from May 3 to June 18. He introduced no stars during that time but concentrated instead on consolidating the reputation for reliability he had acquired the previous year. Answering a criticism that patrons could not tell what play was being performed until they arrived at the theatre door, he placed regular advertisements, at 5s. a square, in the local papers. In these he announced the title of the plays, occasionally the leading players, curtain time at 8:00 p.m., and ticket prices of 1s.3d. for the parquet, 2s.6d. for the dress circle, and from $4.00 to $6.00 for a box. None of the previous season's company returned (Mr. Buxton had "paid the debt of nature"), and leading roles were taken by the Lanergans and by Mrs. H. D. Beissenherz, whose husband was leader of the orchestra. Mrs. Beissenherz, a large woman, undertook such challenging roles as Romeo and Richard III with, we are told, excellent results. The season's repertoire included Boucicault's new military drama *Jessie Brown; or the Relief of Lucknow* as well as the old *Douglas*. The Lyceum, commended in the press as a place where a "quiet and pleasant evening" could be spent and where "every comfort, besides the intellectual treat" was provided, continued to increase in popularity.

That winter the Lanergans spent in the West Indies. Lanergan chartered and fitted up a vessel expressly for the purpose, equipped it with moveable scenery, properties, and wardrobe, and furnished it with the comfort of members of his company in mind. They visited Demerara, Barbadoes, Trinidad, St. Thomas, Kingston in Jamaica, Antigua, and Nassau and reaped such substantial returns that the venture was continued for four more winters in succession. Then the outbreak of the American civil war in 1861 and the risks attendant upon it put an end to the lucrative project.[30]

Lanergan's 1859 season in Saint John, from July 12 to August 23, more than made up for the lack of visiting stars in 1858. For only the first and last weeks of the short season the company performed on its own, with L. P. Roys as leading man, Mrs. Lanergan as leading lady, and Moses Fiske as comedian, supported by Messrs. Beattie and Sheridan, Mrs. Fiske, and others. *Romeo and Juliet* was well received in the opening week, while Knowles' *The Wife* was dismissed as "very dull to look at" even when ably performed. *A New Way to Pay Old Debts*, *Paul Pry*, *Love's Sacrifice*, *Nick of the Woods*, and *Othello* were main pieces in the last week. July introduced C. W. Couldock, then aged 34, to New Brunswick, and in August Wyzeman Marshall was the star attraction.

Couldock opened in the role of Luke Fielding in *The Willow Copse*, a part he had made his own. For twenty-five years he toured North America with *The Willow Copse* as his chief attraction. Although Boucicault, its author, had not thought of Luke Fielding as a great part, the New York *Clipper* believed the actor "made the old English yeoman, in all his worth and integrity, so lifelike and conspicuous that all of the other characters paled like stars before the rising sun".[31] Couldock was known also in standard tragic roles and later, when the popularity of legitimate drama began to wane, for his portrayal of Peter Probity in *The Chimney Corner* and Dunstan Kirke in *Hazel Kirke*.

Born in London in 1815, Couldock had performed in England with Macready, Kean, Mme. Vestris, Charles Mathews, and Charlotte Cushman. In 1849 he came to North America at the invitation of Miss Cushman, made his debut with her at the old Broadway Theatre in *The Stranger*, and then appeared with her in Philadelphia, Boston, and New Orleans. His next engagement, in 1850, as a leading man at the Walnut Street Theatre, Philadelphia, was the one during which he acquired the role of Luke Fielding and which launched him as a touring star in his own right.

Clara Morris, herself an actress, vividly recalled his appearance and personality three years after his death in 1898. "He was squarely, solidly built, of medium height — never fat. His square, deeply lined, even furrowed face, was clean shaven". He wore a "suit of black cloth — always a size or two too large for him — and his never changing big hat of black felt". A man of unquestionable integrity, honourable, truthful, and warm-hearted, he had a quick temper to which he yielded at the least provocation, making mountains out of molehills, and "when he had just cause for anger he burst into paroxysms of rage, even of ferocity, that had they not been half unconscious acting, must have landed him in a mad house".[32]

In spite of his eccentricities, the *Morning Freeman* thought him, in 1859, "unquestionably the most finished dramatic artist that we have ever had amongst us", even though it also judged his voice "somewhat deficient in clearness and power".[33] The paper's assessments were based, not only on his performance of Luke Fielding, but also on his interpretations of Hamlet, King Lear, Shylock, Iago, Richelieu, and Louis XI. The *Courier*'s evaluation of him on July 30 is representative of opinion:

> Mr. Couldock came among us as the plain, unpretending actor, as he is the plain, unaffected gentleman; and he has met from a discerning public, a thorough trial, and an approving verdict. He is an artist — he has genius. He has portrayed accurately and without servile imitation the greatest creations of the poet — the most difficult characters of the stage. In every part we have seen him in he has borne himself up well alongside the best actors known to our generation. As Luke Fielding, in the Willow Copse, where the variety of emotion is great, and the general scope of the part powerful, he seemed born for the character, and the character seemed to be created especially for him. To be natural, simple, and yet as energetic as the character demands, is, to our mind, the highest excellence of the dramatic art, and this Mr. C. accomplished to a remarkable degree. He is a splendid *facial* actor, and his expressions are so perfect as to carry the beholder completely away with the spirit of the piece.

Overflowing houses and enthusiastic curtain calls greeted him every evening.

On his return to the Dramatic Lyceum in 1862, Couldock introduced some new characters, in particular Peter Probity, and repeated most of the old ones. This time the audience was not much enthused by his Iago (Lanergan had played his own Iago shortly before, and the audience liked it better), and Mrs. Lanergan as Desdemona monopolized the applause. In general that year, and during subsequent visits in 1866 and 1869, however, the press was generous with its praise. The enthusiasm of the *Daily News* on July 23, 1866, was typical: "His 'Richelieu', 'Luke Fielding', and 'King

Lear' are really masterpieces. To equal them may be possible, but to go beyond them is almost out of the question. There is a perfect naturalness in his manner, and his reading of the part harmonizes so well with the character, that one is tempted at times into the belief that a real and not imaginary 'Richelieu' or 'Luke Fielding' occupies the stage".

In Couldock, the Saint John critics found an excellent example of what they regarded as a natural actor — one who uttered his lines in tones intended to approximate normal speech and who involved his whole body, and particularly an expressive face, in as honest a representation as possible. To be natural, or to seem to be the character himself was, in the eyes of the press, the highest achievement of the actor. It had been so since the Lyceum's first season in 1857 when Wyzeman Marshall had received that tribute for his acting, and it would continue to be so throughout the Lyceum's reign in Saint John.

For the beginning of the 1860 summer season on June 4, the interior of the Dramatic Lyceum was refitted and redecorated, the problem with the seats in the dress circle overcome, and the auditorium extensively altered and provided with some new "select" seats. The theatre was now, in the words of the *Morning Freeman* "one of the neatest and most comfortable Theatres of its size on the Continent". Ticket prices were set at .50 for dress circle and orchestra stalls and .25 for the parquet, with reserved seats .25 extra — and at these prices they would remain. In an effort to preserve decorum in keeping with the Lyceum's image, ladies could not be admitted unless accompanied by a gentleman. The company, advertised as 'a large and efficient one" chosen from "the leading Theatres in the United States", again included L. P. Roys and the Fiskes and introduced as leading lady Lizzie Emmons, who quickly became a favourite. Miss Emmons, whose real name was Kelly, came originally from a prosperous Halifax family but had moved to Boston when her father lost his health and business. Her mother had Lizzie and her sisters trained for the stage as dancers, after which Lizzie enjoyed a brief career as a stock company actress until her sudden and premature death in Boston.

The first visiting stars of the season were little Cordelia Howard and her parents Mr. and Mrs. George C. Howard in the popular melodrama *Uncle Tom's Cabin*, which ran at the Lyceum for four nights from June 11 to 14, the longest run to date in Saint John of a single production and sufficient testimony to its popularity. George Howard had been lessee of the Troy Museum, New York, when Harriet Beecher Stowe's novel appeared, his wife Caroline was an actress in the company, and their daughter Cordelia a precocious

Mrs. Julia Bennett Barrow.

(Harvard Theatre Collection)

child-actress. Thinking the character of Eva would be a suitable vehicle for the child, Howard turned the story over to a cousin, George L. Aiken, also an actor in the company, for dramatization, with instructions that dramatic emphasis be built around the character of little Eva. Aiken initially constructed a three-act play which opened at the Troy Museum in September 1852 and ran for 100 nights. He then wrote a second three-act play which carried the story on from the death of Eva to the death of Uncle Tom.

Saint John audiences saw the combined six-act play consisting of thirty scenes, no act having fewer than four. By means of wings and drops and the addition of special pieces when needed, the setting was changed in production from the interiors of wealthy homes of the white owners to the plain cabins of the negroes, from city to country. We do not know how realistic Lanergan was able to make scenes like that of Eliza crossing the ice. A number of the scenes are tableaux, the most effective of which was probably the last, which revealed little Eva behind a scrim drop, surrounded by stage angels and bright clouds and riding a milk-white dove, blessing the kneeling figures of St. Clare and Uncle Tom, newly arrived to join her in heaven.

When Cordelia came to Saint John in 1860 she was twelve and at the end of her stage career. She had first performed the role of Eva at the age of four, at which time reviewers had described her as "one of the most delectable and affecting specimens of the *art dramatique* we ever beheld".[34] Presumably her father produced the script in Saint John as elsewhere and took the part of St. Clare, Eva's father, while Mrs. Howard played Topsy and doubled as Aunt Chloe "with wings and pads". There is no mention in the local papers of the other members of the original company — George Aiken as George Harris and George Selby, George Fox (Cordelia's uncle) as Phineas Fletcher and Gumption Cute, and Mrs. E. Fox (Cordelia's grandmother) as Miss Ophelia — and some members of Lanergan's regular company are mentioned in supporting roles, so presumably the relatives did not travel with the Howards on this occasion. Reactions to the productions were mixed: one critic thought Cordelia played Eva to perfection while another thought her insufficiently childlike, but all agreed that Mrs. Howard's Topsy was remarkable and that the scenery and music were exceptionally fine. The combined talents of this family, the *Morning Freeman* said, had made the moral drama almost tolerable. Considering the reputation that preceded the Howards, it is not surprising that the Lyceum was crowded.

While in Saint John Cordelia performed most of the other parts for which she was famous: Katey in *Little Katey, the Hot Corn*

Girl of New York, Ida May in *Ida May; or the Kidnapped Child*; Oliver Twist; the Strawberry Girl in *Fashion and Famine*, and the little Polish boy in *A Page of History*. Shortly afterwards she retired from the stage, married at the age of twenty, and lived to ninety-four, referring to herself in later life as "the Shirley Temple of my day". By the time of her retirement, her father had amassed a fortune from *Uncle Tom's Cabin* and other plays in which she starred.

The Howards finished on Saturday, June 23, and Mrs. Julia Bennett Barrow joined Lanergan's company on Monday the 25th. Mrs. Barrow, an English actress who had won an enviable reputation at the Haymarket in London before her American debut as Lady Teazle at the Broadway Theatre in 1851, came to Saint John preceded by enthusiastic commendations in the press. She was the leading actress of the Boston Theatre from its first season in 1854, and afterward directed her own company at the Howard Athenaeum. The New York *Albion* of March 1 said she was a blonde, extremely pretty woman, "prepossessing in her air and manner", whose movements were easy and graceful, and, added Saint John's *Morning Freeman*, she was "dashing and coquettish", the owner of a "decidedly neat foot and rather fascinating ankle that occasionally shew to very great advantage".[35] In fact, so powerful an actress was she, and so strong her presence on stage, that the more modest and retiring Lizzie Emmons, who was entirely without coquetry, was thoroughly overshadowed, enough that the *Morning Freeman* found it necessary to defend her abilities against attack from the *Courier*.

Mrs. Barrow's specialty was in Shakespearean roles, and in Saint John she played Juliet, as well as Rosalind in *As You Like It*. She was greeted with full houses, her appearance considered a complete triumph. For her benefit, she played Kate Hardcastle in Sheridan's *She Stoops to Conquer* to a large and fashionable audience of ladies and gentlemen; this was despite a heavy thunderstorm between seven and eight o'clock which could have been expected to keep many of the ladies especially inside. On each occasion she was well supported by Lanergan's company, in particular by Moses Fiske as Touchstone and Tony Lumpkin. The *Morning Freeman* was glad to see the return of the legitimate drama after the interlude of the Howards.

Mrs. Barrow introduced to Saint John a new play by Dion Boucicault that had opened at the Winter Garden in New York only in December 1859. It was *The Octoroon; or Life in Louisiana*, a play about slavery written to capitalize on the popularity of that subject since the success of *Uncle Tom's Cabin*. The timing of its performance in Saint John was presumably intended to take advantage of the Howard family's success two weeks earlier. *The Octoroon*'s plot tells how the papers that would free the heroine, Zoe the slave girl, "are stolen by a scoundrel who is photographed in the act, and then, by the light of a burning ship which eventually blows up, stabbed to death by a Redskin in full war-paint".[36] It was easily within the Lyceum's capability to show the burning ship by means of a scrim, in the way burning buildings were commonly shown: the ship would be painted on the scrim and flames painted on a back-drop; then the gradual introduction of rear-lighting would make the ship seem to be enveloped in the flames. Saint Johners, nevertheless, found the play "not of absorbing interest", although they could find no fault with Mrs. Barrow's performance of Zoe.

Wyzeman Marshall was the final visiting artist, and the season then closed on July 26 after benefits for the regular members of the company, all accompanied by songs, dances, and afterpieces, including the localized farce *Did You Ever Send Your Wife to Indiantown?*[37] Lanergan next took his company to Halifax, where he played until the end of August with Mrs. Barrow as his star. In July 1861, she returned for another week to Saint John enroute to Halifax, where she performed with her own company until the end of September.

Lanergan opened the Lyceum with a strong company in 1861. "The untoward state of affairs in the United States" had enabled him, in the words of the July 13 *Courier*, "to select a company of performers of eminent talent" and to bring forward "the largest, most effective and highly endowed theatrical *troupe* that has ever appeared in this Province". In addition, the Civil War sent northward noted artists like Madame Fabbri and Madame Anna Bishop, both of whom performed grand opera in July, Madame Fabbri to a "perfectly crammed" house. The major attraction of that year, immediately following Mrs. Barrow in July, was the character actor F. S. Chanfrau, who performed nightly, except Sunday, from July 29 to August 14.

Chanfrau's great gift for impersonation won him the role which brought him fame — the part of Mose, a New York firefighter. Born in 1824, he grew up in poverty and had an inauspicious beginning as an extra in the theatre. Then, in 1848, Benjamin Baker wrote *A Glance at New York* for a benefit at the Olympic Theatre, New York:

Chanfrau had often amused the members of the Olympic Company in the green-room and during the 'waits' at rehears-

al, by his imitations of the peculiar gait and various mannerisms of the New York Fire Boys.

With his hat tipped over his brow, his curly locks subdued, by much moist manipulation, into the well-known soap
locks; with a cigar standing out from his mouth at an angle of
45 degrees, or less, he would shove his hands in his pockets,
and in voice, dialect and slang, would relate such amusing descriptions of his personal experience, as would throw his auditors into roars of laughter.

Upon this hint Baker transformed *Corinthian Tom* into
Mose and requested Chanfrau to play the part.

And play it he did!

The picture was perfect. The shiny hat, red shirt, black
trousers, boots, cigar, and pea-jacket over his arm — *Mose*
was recognized the instant he walked on the stage as the living
embodiment of the well-known Fire Boy.[38]

Chanfrau acted the character of Mose at least twice in Saint
John during 1861, in *A Glance at New York* and in the "sensational
drama" *Linda, the Cigar Girl*. Because the newspapers printed
scarcely any reviews after Mrs. Barrow left, it is impossible to know
with what favour he was received. When he played Wool, a plantation darkie in *The Hidden Hand; or Scenes in New York and Dixie's
Land* on August 5, the *Courier* said he did all that could be done
with a subordinate part in the way of character acting; the paper
thought the script itself possessed no literary merit. Chanfrau also
performed Irish characters, like Ragged Pat in *Ireland as it is; or
Landlord, Middleman & Tenant*, Phelim O'Flannigan in
O'Flannigan and the Fairies, and Paddy Miles in *Paddy Miles' Boy*.
Other roles included Solon Shingle in *People's Lawyer* and Harry
Helm in the nautical drama *The Ocean Child; or the Mother and the
Maniac*. In August 1863 he played most of the same parts, but performed also as Lord Dundreary in *Our American Cousin* (E. A.
Sothern's role) and gave imitations of several well-known actors in-
cluding Charles Kean, Edwin Forrest, and Junius Brutus Booth.
That year the papers had more to say about him. His Lord Dundreary "displayed a versatility of talent to which very few actors can
lay claim. The entire change of voice, gait and manner was not
more remarkable than the rapidity with which changes of costume
were effected".[39] The audience was delighted, yet his portrayal of
the Yankee teamster, Solon Shingle, won him even more praise.
The *Courier* wrote: "In the delineation of the genuine Yankee, Mr.
Chanfrau has no superior on the stage; his inimitably grotesque hu-

Joseph Proctor in Nick of the Woods (Harvard Theatre Collection)

mor keeps the house in a continual roar of laughter, relieved at times by his wonderful command of pathos".[40]

Despite what appears to have been another successful summer season in 1861, Lanergan decided the attendance at the Lyceum was not sufficiently large to remunerate him for further financial outlay, and so he closed his theatre on August 31. In the last week he featured popular comedienne Lucille Western, following a week devoted to benefit performances for members of his company. For Mrs. Lanergan's benefit on August 23, he produced *Colleen Bawn; or the Brides of Garryowen* "with new Mechanical Effects, New Music, &c., and cast to the entire strength of the Company". In consequence of its length and importance, he included no afterpiece on the evening's programme, but only an Irish overture and assorted Irish songs in the intervals. The new play, written by Dion Boucicault in 1860, had played nightly in London for the past eight months and now starred Mrs. Lanergan as Eily O'Connor (Agnes Robertson's role) and Rachel Johnson[41] as Anne Chute, with comedian W. S. Lennox as Miles-na-Coppaleen. Lanergan summed up his view of the play's importance on his playbill: "Ireland, so rich in scenery, so full of romance and the warm tints of nature, has never until now been opened to the Dramatist. Irish Dramas have hitherto been exagerated [*sic*] farces representing low life, or scenes of abject servitude and suffering. Such is not a true picture of Irish society".[42] From this beginning, the play became one of the more popular pieces in the Lyceum's repertoire.

In 1862 Joseph Proctor and C. W. Couldock were the visiting stars with Lanergan's company. Proctor was known especially for his role of the wildman, the Jibbenainosay, in a piece adapted from Dr. Bird's story, *Nick of the Woods*. People called him 'Nick of the Woods', for he acted the part more than 2,000 times, performing it in every important city in England and America. When he played the role in Saint John on August 1 and 2, the *Courier* declared that the script "possesses no great merit, but abounds in striking situations, hair-breadth escapes, and gives a graphic picture of the hardships and dangers of frontier life".[43] Its performance, nevertheless, was received by a full house. Proctor also starred as Outahlanchet, an Indian chief, in what the playbill described as "the beautiful Drama" of *Outahlanchet; or the Lion of the Forest*. This script too, the *Morning News* said, was "generally uninteresting to theatregoers — except those who delight in scalping knives, tomahawks, muskets, thunder, lightning, and blood".[44]

During the long reign of the Dramatic Lyceum, other visiting stars on its boards included English tragedian Charles Dillon and the renowned Boston-born tragedian E. L. Davenport with his wife. In 1866 Dillon made his first appearance before a Saint John audience as Virginius. A "man of commanding personal appearance, graceful in action, correct in speech, and without a demerit in his facial acting",[45] he performed the standard Shakespearean tragic roles Macbeth, Hamlet, and Othello, as well as his own specialty, Belphegor the Mountebank. In 1869 and 1870 the Davenports came to play opposite one another as Benedick and Beatrice, Charles Surface and Lady Teazle, Macbeth and Lady Macbeth, Othello and Emelia, and William and Susan.

The Lanergans themselves were accomplished artists. John Mildmay, in Tom Taylor's *Still Waters Run Deep*, was one of Mr. Lanergan's favourite roles. As Don Caesar de Bazan he was said to have no equal in America, once the elder Wallack left the stage. When he attempted Luke Fielding in *The Willow Copse*, the role Couldock had made familiar to Saint John, he "surprised those who have always looked upon Mr. Couldock's personation of the part as unapproachable by any other actor".[46] When he ventured forth as Iago in Shakespeare's *Othello*, he was following in the footsteps of Wyzeman Marshall, but his thoughtful, original approach won him an excellent review. The *Courier* of July 18, 1863, reported:

> His conception of this part is quite different from the stereotyped villain, who has so long held possession of the stage, and to our mind, much more true to Shakespeare's ideal. He makes him a genial social, companionable man, who veils his revengeful nature and hatred of Othello with consummate skill, and attaches to his interest all with whom he comes in contact. In embodying this conception of Iago, Mr. Lanergan exhibits the highest delineative power, which, aided by his fine physique and splendid voice, approaches the perfection of acting — which consists in the art of concealing art, and making the audience forget for the moment that the scene before them is not reality.

When he played the part in New York in 1866, with Charles Dillon as Othello, the New York *Express* of November 10 agreed with the *Courier*'s assessment, adding, "Lanergan has no superior on the American stage, (and from the samples sent us from London, we doubt if he has one in the English theatres)". His Hamlet too was "a gratifying improvement on the old stereotyped method of playing the part"; instead of "standing up and instructing the players in a harsh and dictatorial manner as is usually done, he seemed to comprehend that Hamlet was a philosopher".[47]

Caroline Lanergan played Desdemona to her husband's Iago, Ophelia to his Hamlet, and Juliana to his Duke Aranza (*The*

Honeymoon). She was known as Zoe in *The Octoroon*, Camille in *Camille; or the Fate of a Coquette*, Eily O'Connor in *Colleen Bawn*, and as Leah in *Leah the Forsaken*. But perhaps the part with which she was most closely identified was that of Fanchon in *Fanchon the Cricket*. The Lyceum company initially presented the script in August 1864, billing it as a new five-act sensation drama. Mrs. Lanergan was Fanchon then, and again in 1865. By the time she returned to the Lyceum with the role in 1866, she had acquired an international reputation for it, and the playbills contained excerpts from the reviews she had received on a tour of England. The Liverpool *Daily Courier* summed up the reports: "A graceful presence, expressive features, and effective voice, combine to make her a formidable rival to most successful English actresses whose line is that popularly understood as melodrama".[48] The Saint John papers were equally generous with their praise. The *Daily News* of June 22, 1866, declared her rendition of the cricket "a masterpiece of genius". Her "smiles, her tears and her passions were so natural that she held and swayed the feeling of the audience at her will".

To support themselves and the visiting stars they imported, the Lanergans regularly employed a strong stock company numbering between twenty and twenty-five members, many of whom were drawn from the Boston Theatre.[49] One favourite among these was 'Nick' T. Davenport who, in the minor role of Fag in *The Rivals*, had in 1854 spoken the first dramatic lines ever uttered publicly from the stage of the new Boston Theatre. Davenport moved from Laertes to Mercutio in *Romeo and Juliet* to young Marlow in *She Stoops to Conquer*, acting all "in good style, as indeed he does everything entrusted to him".[50] With Lanergan from 1859 until his premature death in 1867, Davenport was gifted as a comic and often helped to enliven the farces. Some actors, like J. B. Fuller, became welcome and familiar faces because they returned to Saint John so often. Fuller, who replaced Lemoyne as old man in 1862, stayed through the whole of the Lyceum period (except for an absence in 1866), performing roles like Polonius, Capulet, Hardcastle, Aminidab Sleek, and Armand's father in *Camille* "very carefully and correctly". Yet probably the favourite of the company, during the long time he was in residence, was W. S. Lennox, rated by some as one of the best low comedians of his day.[51] On August 11, 1862, at the end of his second season in Saint John, the *Morning News* summarized public opinion: "No one member of Mr. Lanergan's corps has been more painstaking, displayed more talent, or made himself more popular than Mr. Lennox. His admirable delineations of the humorous side of human nature have been the life of the Lyceum, and have contributed in no small degree to make it a place of popular resort, where the cares of a day may be forgotten in witnessing the triumph of a genial disposition". As Jacques in *As You Like It*, he was perfectly at home, "at times convulsing the audience with laughter by his drollery; as a low comedian it would be difficult to find his superior". As Launcelot in *The Merchant of Venice*, he brought down the house repeatedly, and his Tony Lumpkin was equally a hit. Already a veteran actor with ten years of experience on the stages of Philadelphia, Boston, and New York when he came to the Lyceum in 1861 at the age of 28, Lennox gave way to Wiggens in 1864, to Fiske and to Scallon in 1865 and 1866, but returned in 1868 to play all the rest of the Lanergan seasons.

Saint John's theatre-goers were slow to warm to Rachel Johnson, the stock company's leading lady from 1861 to 1863. As Miss Neville in *She stoops to Conquer*, she gave only "indifferent" support to Mrs. Barrow on July 24, 1861. As Dora Sunnyside in *The Octoroon* on August 13, 1862 (with Mrs. Lanergan as Zoe), she was "perfect in all except the facial acting". But as Lucretia Borgia on August 19 she was an unqualified success: "The varied and sudden ebullitions of feeling, from love to hate, from passionate revenge to agonizing remorse, were portrayed with that perfect naturalness, that grace and ease which go to make up the sum of good acting".[52] On her first appearance in 1863, as Mrs. Haller in *The Stranger* on June 29, she was "received with marked demonstrations of pleasure",[53] and for the rest of the season she received only praise. She was Lady Audley in the first Saint John production of *Lady Audley's Secret*, Miss Hardcastle in *She Stoops to Conquer*, Amelia in *The Robbers*; her Juliet was "almost perfection and drew tears of sympathy", and her Mariana in *The Wife* was "perfection itself". She was ably supported by Misses Cutler, Farwell, Adams, Lizzie Gale, and especially by Louisa Morse in the parts of older women — Mrs. Hardcastle, Juliet's nurse, and Mrs. Malaprop. Part of Lanergan's company in 1863 and 1864, Miss Morse was listed in 1866 but failed to appear, and her presence was constant from 1869.

W. H. Whalley made his first appearance as leading man of the 1862 season on July 11 as Rolla in Sheridan's tragedy *Pizarro; or the Death of Rolla*, with L. P. Roys as Pizzaro. Whalley looked the part. He was tall, with a commanding appearance and an "air of manliness which compels respect". Unfortunately only a small audience witnessed his excellent performance, for the script of *Pizarro*, the *Colonial Empire* thought, contained too many blemishes for a "sensitive audience". In July 1863 he played Rolla again, acted Robert Audley opposite Rachel Johnson, and was commended for the spirited and correct manner in which he portrayed Ingomar, the barbarian. In 1864 J. W. Hanley became leading actor, playing

Dramatic Lyceum Souvenir (New Brunswick Museum)

Othello, Romeo, Ingomar, the naive hero Bob Brierly in *The Ticket-of-Leave Man*, and the dashing Captain Absolute in *The Rivals* — his acting style praised for its "naturalness" and his delivery for its absence of rant. The next year Mr. and Mrs. Claude Hamilton were leading members of the troupe. Mrs. Hamilton cannot have been outstanding, for the papers say little about her, and her husband received more attention. Though the roughness of his voice made him unsatisfactory as the young lover Romeo, the eloquence of his presentation of Alfred Evelyn in Bulwer's *Money* "drew tears to strong men's eyes".[54]

There were substantial changes in the personnel of the company in 1866 and again in 1867. Apart from the Davenports, the J. H. Brownes, Fuller, and prompter W. H. Danvers, the company was new in 1866. For the first month of the season George Clair was leading man, performing as Othello, Richard III, the Stranger, Claude Melnotte, and Jack Long (a role he had played 474 times). Then on Saturday, July 11, Frank Roche, who was to be one of the most popular of the Lyceum's leading actors, made his Saint John debut as Bob Brierly. The *Daily News* was pleased: "Mr. Roche is in every sense of the term an actor, and one, too, of no ordinary calibre".[55] From this beginning, he went on to act Othello, Macbeth, Shaun the Post, Orlando, and black-eyed Susan's William, winning always commendation for the "naturalness" of his acting. His impersonation of the Stranger was "a master piece of acting — a brilliant conception — a life like representation".[56] His Joe Morgan, in the moral drama *Ten Nights in a Bar-room*, was "so truthful a representation of that character that at times we fancied, we saw not the *actor*, but the *real* Simon Pure inebriate, who, step by step, approached to the very brink of ruin".[57] Of his Claude Melnotte the *True Humorist*, denying flattery, said: "Mr. Roche's voice is full and round; his elocution faultless; his conception of the text complete; and at times, in the more eloquent passages, one would imagine his acting to be real".[58]

Petite Rachel Noah was juvenile lady in 1866. In 1867 she was part of a strong female complement at the Lyceum which included Mrs. Lanergan, Susie Cluer, Susan Flood, and also Mrs. D. R. Allen, who starred in important roles such as Lucretia Borgia and Catherine Duval (in Phillips' *Dead Heart*). Rachel Noah played a variety of parts: Desdemona, Colleen Bawn, Lady Anne in Richard III, black-eyed Susan, and supporting roles such as Nerissa to Mrs. Lanergan's Portia. The *True Humorist* enthused over her portrayal of Margot in the comic drama *Margot! The Poultry Dealer*: "We love that girl's acting — every movement is so graceful and true — every emotion so natural, every sentence so distinct".[59] Yet the

Humorist, in a clear case of puffery, reserved for Mrs. Allen, with Mr. Roche, the title of best dramatic artist to visit the Loyalist city. Miss Noah's reputation was a cumulative one, as she and her husband Shirley France returned to the Lyceum year after year.

Whether or not he was provided with visiting stars, Lanergan's custom was to produce each year a number of well-worn plays and also to introduce some of the more popular new ones. If the latter succeeded, as they generally did, they became part of the standard repertoire. Thus, some plays were performed time and time again.[60]

Three of the new plays introduced in one typical year, 1864, were *Fanchon the Cricket*, *Leah the Forsaken*, and *Ticket-of-Leave Man*. When *Leah* opened in Saint John in July, it had just reached its 211th performance in London, and Mr. Lanergan had played Nathan for ten weeks during its New York and Philadelphia run. He presented the play for five nights at the Dramatic Lyceum, featuring himself as Nathan and his wife as Leah. Two years later the playbill for a June 29 performance advertised: "The Favourite Play Again! By Request!" The July 2 *Daily News* explained that Mrs. Lanergan's interpretation of the title role was at least part of the reason for the play's popularity: "The manner in which she read the varied feelings, passions and emotions of the female soul in all the different circumstances to which she was exposed . . . was the work of a mistress in her art". Tom Taylor's drama *Ticket-of-Leave Man* ran for six nights in July 1864. It, too, had created quite a sensation in London and had attracted crowded houses on 130 nights in New York. On its initial night in Saint John, it was greeted by a packed house, but the critic for the *News* was so taken up with the discomfort of a hot evening and the slowness of the scene changes that he did not comment on the play. A few days later, however, he judged it "one of the most effective we have ever seen enacted", and fully deserving of its popularity. By the time of its second annual repetition, in July 1866, it was being billed as "the most popular drama in the language", and the playbill for June 17, 1867, speaks of a revival of "the greatest drama in modern times". By way of enticement to prospective patrons of the Lyceum, it quoted from *The London Times* an allegedly true story to illustrate the beneficial effects of attendance at the play:

> A clerk, who absconded from Liverpool with £2500, the property of his employers and after visiting many places, arriving in Birmingham about 5 o'clock, after taking some refreshments, went to the theatre, to while away an hour. As it happened, the piece which was being performed on the occasion of this visit was *The Ticket-of-Leave Man*. And the guilty man seems

to have drawn a moral from the representation; for when the scene in which the interview between Hawkshaw, the detective, and the 'Ticket-of-Leave Man' took place, Parker, the clerk, became so affected that he went out of the theatre, got three envelopes, and sent £1500 back to his employers.[61]

Thus, the playbill advertised: "Every Father, Every Mother, Every Sister, Every Brother, Every Mechanic, Every Banker, Every Merchant, Every Clerk, Every Professional Man, In fact, everybody should see this GREAT MORAL PLAY".

The highlight of another season, 1868, was the introduction of Augustin Daly's *Under the Gaslight*, which had set a new standard for sensations at the Worrell Sisters' Theatre, New York, in 1867. It had its first London production in July 1868, the same month Lanergan brought it to Saint John. Billed in Saint John as a "very exciting and wonderfully effective Drama, full of Novel Effects and Startling Situations",[62] and produced with all the original music, it was, of course, admired for its scenic representations and spectacular effects, in particular the pier scene and the railroad scene — "Down Express Train Passes at 10.30, p.m." Much less successful were the productions of Watts Phillips' latest senstation, *Maud's Peril*, in which the critics failed to see any intrinsic merit, and of *The League of Sierra Madre*, a drama written by Beatrice Jones of Saint John. The latter was the romantic tale of a Mexican who abandoned his wife, retreated to the mountains to lead a band of outlaws, abducted a wealthy heiress, and was finally regenerated through the death of his young wife. The *New Dominion and True Humorist* tried to overlook "any little delinquencies and contradictions" which could be attributed to a first attempt at dramatic writing, but it had more trouble ignoring what it considered inappropriate subject matter for an authoress: "This is not the arena where we would expect woman, in the dignity, and the gentleness, and the modesty of her sex, to gather garlands with which to decorate her literary genius. 'Tis the rough, stern, rugged nature of man for which such scenes are fitted, and who . . . can depict the outlaw's life and crimes without blushing at the indelicacies which woman's pen would refuse to trace".[63]

On the whole, the tastes of the Saint John audiences (or at least of those members who wrote reviews for the local papers) were sophisticated, refined, and up to date. They favoured the legitimate drama and new scripts in which they could see literary and artistic merit and tended to frown upon pieces which they deemed to rely too heavily on spectacle alone. In 1862, for instance, the *Courier* and the *Morning News* disliked the frontier plays *Nick of the Woods* and *Outahlanchet* in which Joseph Proctor starred, for the blood and thunder and hair-raising situations that were features of both were neither elevating nor realistic. On the other hand, the *Courier* the same year praised C. W. Couldock's piece *The Chimney Corner* as "a short two act domestic drama that depends for success not upon the adventitious aid of muslin waves or real water pumped from unknown depths, but the deep knowledge of human nature displayed by the author in every line of his production".[64] Good houses at some of the less subtly spectacular pieces suggest, however, that the audiences were not always as discerning as the critics. From time to time, nevertheless, the reviewers believed they could see the tastes of the populace improving, and, as in this review in the *Courier* of August 1, 1863, they commented on it:

> We are glad to perceive a great improvement in the public taste in Dramatic matters. Formerly the most attractive pieces were those abounding in thunder, blue fire, cold steel, and rant, and such pieces were sure to draw a large house. Of late the more legitimate drama has come to be appreciated, and it is quite interesting to see the good judgment displayed by the audiences, their keen appreciation of points, and their judicious applause when it is really deserved. Formerly the *piece* attracted the audience, and it was extremely difficult to get a good house on the repetition of even the best plays; now it is the *acting* that draws, and very frequently the third performance of a play is attended by as large an audience as the first, and this season the manager has frequently been requested to repeat for the third time an entertainment in which the acting has been more than usually good.

In its remarks on the opening weeks of the 1864 season, the *Courier* noted the audience's increasing appreciation of "natural acting" (that is, of intended realism in the actor's interpretation of his role), observing that the intelligence of the well-timed applause gave evidence "that they perceive and enjoy the fine points of the actor".[65] From the position of the late twentieth century, it is difficult to think of the inflated tones of *Colleen Bawn*, *The Octoroon*, *Ticket-of-Leave Man*, or other plays of their ilk in terms of naturalism, but from the perspective of the mid-nineteenth century the subject matter of these plays marked a trend towards realism, and the desire for realism in acting them is part of the same trend. In the early days of the Lyceum some members of the stock company had stressed volume above intonation: the 1862 reviews repeatedly criticized L. P. Roys for his tendency to rant, and on July 21, the *Colonial Empire* questioned sarcastically, "Is it to be understood that any member of this excellent company is unhappily deaf?" Increasingly, however, reviews commended the actors for the carefulness of their enunciation, for truthfulness in their representation of emotion, and for the gracefulness of their bearing.

In 1864, during a performance of *Jessie Brown* in which an actor named Bock took the role of Achmet, there was a moment of greater realism than either the script or the company envisaged:

> At that time the stage manager for Mr. Lanergan was Mr. J. H. Browne, and he had an impediment in his speech; but like the most of stuttering people, he could sing without the defect being noticed. In *Jessie Brown* the character of "Achmet" is drawn up from the stage, by a rope being tied around his neck, and at a given signal the body disappears from the sight of the audience. It is a very striking and powerful scene. In this case, the rope was not fastened correctly around the iron collar used to prevent the actor from suffocation, and the members of Mr. Lanergan's company, himself included, were surprised to see Mr. Browne, his eyes starting out of his head, and his hair fairly standing on end, rush over to them, exclaiming:
> "M — m — m — m — m — m — y   g — o — o — d
> go — o — d —
> His stuttering prevented him getting any further, until Mr. Lanergan said, kindly:
> "Sing it, Mr. Browne,"
> "Mr. Browne complied, and in a melodious voice he sung:
> "My goodness, boys, Bock is hung,
> No doubt about that!
> The man is hung — the rope has slipped!"
> By this time it was understood by the assembled Thespians, and a rush was made for the fly gallery, the rope cut, and Mr. Bock's life saved after hard work, and the attendance of two physicians.[66]

Even in a well-run theatre, and in spite of thorough preparation and planning, such calamities could occur. On another occasion in the Lyceum, a less potentially serious misfortune happened at the end of the first act of *The Chimney Corner*. Mr. Couldock, as Peter Probity, was lamenting the supposed dishonesty of his son. He arose from the supper table and said: "Patty, get me my hat and coat! I will follow him to the end of the world, though He above knows — "

> Just as he had got thus far, he was thunder struck to see a man roll out of the flies overhead, and fall crash upon the table,

smashing all the crockery, and upsetting everything. The audience roared with the laughter, the curtain was lowered when the solution to the matter was that one of Mr. Dorman's assistants on the stage had been out to a party the night before, and not wishing to be seen and feeling very tired and sleepy, had secreted himself on the paint bridge, about 25 feet above the stage, and was having a nap, had probably tried to turn over while sleeping, and the bridge being very narrow, had landed on the supper table below.[67]

From 1857 until the autumn of 1867, Lanergan's was the only professional dramatic company apart from E. A. Sothern's to spend an extended time in Saint John. The situation changed when Wilson and Clarke came to the Mechanics' Institute for a season that lasted from October 26 to December 18, 1867. The company, managed by G. E. Wilson and 'Funny' Clarke with F. W. Beattie as stage manager, produced plays that Lanergan's Lyceum had made familiar — *Fanchon the Cricket*, *Uncle Tom's Cabin*, *Toodles*, *Nick of the Woods*, *The Octoroon*. They charged only .25 admission, introduced Saturday matinees, and, by the quality of their productions, overcame the city's initial prejudice against travelling companies.

A much less positive reception was afforded T. C. Howard's Olympic Company when they hired the Mechanics' Institute in April and May 1868. The company was so small that Howard (who was familiar to Saint Johners because he had acted with Lanergan in 1866 and 1867) was required to double or triple characters in order to fill out his casts, or else to cut the scripts. Frank Roche and Mrs. D. R. Allen were considered excellent, but inadequate support rendered their positions impossible. Moreover, false claims in the advertising drew scorn from the *New Dominion*: "He can have the scenes painted expressly for every play, and yet have only about half a dozen altogether. He can get up 'the most wonderful effect ever produced in this City' . . . with less material than any other man we ever saw. He can advertise a 'full brass band' of *five* performers, and when he finds the people see the 'hoax' he can borrow from our own Amateurs".[68] Never, during his visit, was the Institute half full.

For nearly three months at the beginning of 1869, Wilson and Clarke again made Saint John a major stop on their Maritime tour. Despite the inadequacies of the Institute's stage, large audiences once more proclaimed themselves satisfied with the company's efforts; Mr. Clarke could make them laugh, and Mr. Wilson reminded them of Nick Davenport in voice and appearance. On their departure this time, a Boston paper said they had purchased a lot in

92

Saint John intending to erect a theatre in the summer of 1870, but when the company returned on March 28, 1870, calling itself Wilson & Clarke's Provincial Boston Theatre; no mention was made of a permanent building. The actors remained that year until May 6, leaving only a month before Lanergan opened the Lyceum on June 6.

Until 1872 Lanergan's company was unrivalled in Saint John during the summer months and, moreover, members of his company reached out to reap what harvest they could in Halifax which, with no permanent company, was not enjoying the same theatrical prosperity as Saint John. In August 1865 Fiske and Fuller took members of Lanergan's company to Halifax following the close of the Saint John Lyceum, and for the next two years Fiske recruited his own company and managed a summer season in Halifax while the Dramatic Lyceum was open. For three consecutive summer seasons from 1868, T. C. Howard's Olympic Company provided Haligonians with dramatic entertainment (presumably finding a better reception than they did in Saint John), and for four days in late July 1871, Lanergan took his own company to the cramped stage of Halifax's Temperance Hall.[69]

Each year with regularity Lanergan gave productions in his own Dramatic Lyceum Monday through Saturday in seasons whose length varied but usually lasted June through August. After that the King Square theatre closed to enable its actors to meet winter commitments in the United States and elsewhere. Lanergan himself, after the end of his West Indies venture, generally spent his winters in the United States. In the fall of 1862 he spent three weeks at the Boston Theatre, playing minor parts in support of Edwin Booth, and that winter (and again in 1866) was at Niblo's Garden in New York. In the fall of the next year he organized a company for a tour of the western States and made a circuit of Detroit, Milwaukee, and Peoria, Illinois that was so successful he repeated it for several more years. The response to him in Detroit was so warm that "a number of the most influential citizens . . . subscribed to a fund for erecting the Detroit Opera House, the original lesseeship of which was invested in Lanergan".[70]

By 1867 the *New Dominion and True Humorist* was calling for Lanergan to pull down his Saint John Dramatic Lyceum and build a bigger one, for the modest King Square establishment was considered inadequate for the "crowds of gay, orderly and intelligent persons" who nightly flocked there. Lanergan's response was to redecorate the Lyceum, add some new scenery, hire as orchestra leader Mr. Lothian, orchestra leader of the Boston Theatre, and generally prepare to make the 1868 season "the crowning one for the drama in St. John". He showed no indication of willingness to heed the opinion of the *New Dominion*'s editor that he could, "with more extensive accommodation and the constant employment of a scenic artist . . . do a more thriving business than in the drama-deluged cities of the United States".[71] Even in the summer of 1870, when some influential Saint John citizens had already taken steps to promote the construction of a more modern theatre, Lanergan showed no interest. That year he again freshened up his Lyceum: he re-tinted the walls, renewed the stair carpet, recovered the seats in the dress circle, added two rows of chairs in the orchestra stalls, saw that all seats were renumbered, repaired and cushioned, and, once more, repainted the scenery.

iv
The Academy of Music Era

The expansion and change that marked the beginning of the 1870's grew naturally out of the demand created by the overflowing audiences in Lanergan's Dramatic Lyceum. One small building could not accommodate all those whose interest in culture had been awakened by the yearly visits of Lanergan's troupe. The Lyceum, furthermore, had never been used for dramatic performance in the winter: in the autumn of 1867 it was used for church services, but even these had to be discontinued in November due to lack of heat, since Lanergan had built his theatre for summer use only. Consequently, once companies like the Wilson and Clarke Company began to visit the city in the winter, they were forced to perform in halls better equipped to keep out the frigid temperatures, particularly in the Mechanics' Institute which had not been constructed with dramatic performance in mind and whose directors had at one time opposed it on moral grounds. Though the Institute management had become more liberal and the hall renovated, it was still far from ideally suited to theatre. For these reasons, a more adequate structure than either the King Square Lyceum or the Mechanics' Institute was required. In the words of the *New Dominion and True Humorist*, Saint Johners had "acquired a taste for this kind of amusement" and would not be satisfied "until efforts are put forth to make the drama a permanent institution all the year round".[1] Hence, in April 1870 a group of Saint John's leading citizens brought before the Legislature a request for incorporation of a company to erect an Academy of Music. In September of the same year, Otis Small began construction of a block of buildings which would include a large lecture hall. Thus, by the spring of 1872 Saint John possessed four halls capable of holding between 800 and 1200 persons.

Victoria Hotel (New Brunswick Museum)

While the two new halls were under construction, Lanergan conducted his summer seasons as usual, and the Wilson and Clarke Company and another group of travelling players, the Flora Myers Company, relieved the winter monotony, but even in these engagements, some indications of change and growth were evident. In 1871 Lanergan, for the first time, felt the *New Dominion*'s cutting edge of criticism. While the paper did not hesitate to give praise where it believed it was due, as in the case of Dominick Murray's acting of Shaun the Post, it minced no words in voicing its disapproval, whether of the pitters' "depraved taste" for Oliver Doud Byron's murder-packed drama *Across the Continent*, the company's weak support of its stars, or the lack of historical accuracy in Kate Reignold's script of *Joan of Arc*. Increasingly it spoke out against inadequate stage management. The intervals between acts were intolerably long, and machinery was sometimes broken down, causing awkward pauses and spoiling some *tableaux* in *Joan of Arc*. Though it is possible that Lanergan was missing his former stage manager, J. H. Browne, there is no real reason to suspect that conditions at the Lyceum had deteriorated significantly. It is more likely that audiences, and reviewers especially, had simply become less tolerant. Lanergan had long since won his battle for respectability of the theatre, and the press no longer felt it necessary to defend him; because he had become an institution in the community, loved and supported consistently, it instead felt free to challenge him.

In the person of Flora Myers' agent, H. Price Webber, came evidence of the influence that Lanergan's theatre was having on some of Saint John's citizens. Webber had been born in Brixham, Devonshire, in 1845. As a teenager he fled to Halifax from a printer to whom he was apprenticed and there found a job on the *Nova Scotian* in the employ of the Hon. Joseph Howe.[2] Six months later he was in Saint John working on the *Globe* and, before long, becoming immersed in the cultural ferment of the 1860's, when Lanergan's summer theatre was spawning numerous amateur groups. Webber toured New Brunswick with the Saint John-based Home Circle Minstrels, the "Only Regularly Organized Troupe in New Brunswick".[3] In 1866 he played cornet in the band of M. B. Leavitt's Minstrels during their Saint John engagement. Then, in 1868 and 1869, while working as a compositor for the *New Dominion and True Humorist*, he was stage manager and performer in the newly formed Scribner Brothers Minstrel Troupe (or, as they were also known, Scribner Brothers Burlesque Opera Troupe and Brass Band). With them he travelled to Sussex, Pettitcodiac, Moncton, Shediac, Dorchester, Sackville, Amherst, and even Halifax ("to give Haligonians a chance to see what St. John can turn out in the 'burnt cork line'"[4]), entertaining in the songs, routines, and local hits of minstrelsy, and in burlesques like *Under the Rush Light*. Occasionally, he acted in legitimate drama with the St. John Dramatic Club. In 1870 he was manager of another new amateur variety troupe, the Provincial Variety Troupe, formed to embrace "some of the best talent that has been before the public in the past six years",[5] and he was also an actor and the stage manager of the Provincial Dramatic Society. In 1871, as agent for Flora Myers' Company, he was at the beginning of a long and respected career in the professional theatre which would involve management of the Boston Comedy Company for more than a quarter of a century.

With *Ticket-of-Leave Man*, *Fanchon the Cricket*, *Black-Eyed Susan*, and *Under the Gaslight*, the Flora Myers Company met with the same excellent success the Wilson and Clarke Company did with its similar repertoire. Webber was a versatile member of the company. He could sing, play the cornet, and impersonate a Southern gentleman to perfection. The Halifax papers praised him for his ability and business talents: the Flora Myers Company without Webber as its agent, said one reporter, "would be like playing *Hamlet* with Hamlet left out".[6] In the spring of 1872 he compounded his good fortune by marrying Edwina Grey, whose real name was Marcella Moore, an actress with the Flora Myers Company and former leading lady of Wilson and Clarke.

As travelling companies, the Wilson and Clarke Company and the Flora Myers Company were part of the new development in theatrical practice that would eventually undermine the resident stock company and revolutionize the actor-manager relationship. Still, in 1870, when resident stock companies were numerically at their peak in America, none of this could have been predicted, and the mood of optimism with which Saint John looked forward to a new era of theatre seemed warranted.

On July 15, 1870, this notice appeared in the *Daily News*: "The promoters and friends of the scheme to build an Academy of Music in this city are to hold a meeting this evening in the office of F. P. Robinson, Esq., on Canterbury Street, for the purpose of proceeding with the enterprise at an early day". The Legislature had passed the company's Act of Incorporation on April 7 but debarred it from building and from choosing a Board of Directors until $20,000 in capital stock had been subscribed.[7] Optimistically, the new Saint John Academy of Music Company proceeded with plans for a theatre on Germain Street, on a property known as the 'Marjoribanks lot' nearly opposite the foot of Horsfield Street and diagonally across from the elegant Victoria Hotel then under construction. Mr. Washburn of Boston, Architect for the Victoria Hotel, was engaged to draw the design.[8] Unfortunately, the money did not come in as fast as the planners had hoped, and on February 16, 1871, a special meeting of stockholders at the Waverley House found it necessary to appoint a committee to solicit further subscriptions in order that the amount pledged might be raised from $16,280 to the required $20,000. By the end of the month the financial goal had been reached. A second meeting at the Waverley House on March 9 completed the organization; a code of by-laws and regulations was adopted, and the following gentlemen were elected directors: Dr. George E. S. Keator, President, J. R. Armstrong, Secretary, Dr. Thomas W. Carritte, J. W. Beard, Frederick P. Robinson, and John Guthrie.[9] The work of erecting the building could now proceed at once, though the anticipated opening date of June 1, 1871, had become an impossibility.

On March 21, 1871, the 50 by 200 foot Germain Street property was purchased from F. P. Robinson and his wife Julie Claire for $5,420.[10] Early in May the ground was cleared and levelled at a cost of $1,620.15 in readiness for the foundation.[11] The contract for building the walls, putting on the roof and laying the floors was awarded to A. Christie & Co. for $12,300, the general finishing to the same contractor for $14,850, and extras for $2,000. Subcontracts were taken by Amos Fales for carrying, Mr. Chittick for the bannisters, and Michael Hennigar for mason work. By September the walls were almost complete when a severe storm blew two of them down; repairs were carried out, however, and the building was roofed-in before the onslaught of winter. In November the property was fenced along Germain Street to allow completion of the front. By the following April, the *Daily News* could record this progress: "The Academy of Music is being rapidly completed, the interior being arranged as fast as possible. The scenery is nearly all ready, and carpenters and painters are busy in furnishing other portions of the building. The sixth of May has been fixed for the opening".[12]

On May 1, the Academy was lit up for the first time for the pleasure of the friends of the directors. The main feature of the gas fittings was a "magnificent chandelier in the centre of the roof in the form of a sunburst, with one hundred and two jets, covered by a reflector of corrugated glass, coated on the back with silver".[13] Purchased from Tucker Manufacturing Company, New York, for $420, the sunburst threw a "soft yet brilliant light over the whole auditorium, doing away with the necessity of other gas lights except under the galleries, where a dozen double brackets [were] affixed to the walls. The stage foot-lights, twenty-two in number, [were] handsome argand burners, the tops of the chimnies being level with the stage floor".[14] The work of fitting the Academy for gas (presumably supplied by the St. John Gas Light Company) had been efficiently done by A. Rowan, the contractor.

From the street, the new brick Academy of Music presented a handsome and striking appearance. The front was finished with mastic in an ornate Italianate style, its fine carving standing out in relief from the dark brown background. According to the *Daily News* of May 6, the building was 50 feet wide and extended back 180 feet.[15] On the lower floor, either side of the grand entrance, were two shops, one of which had already been leased to a millinery business at $400 a year. Six sets of windows let in ample light to each of the two upper storeys, and the roof was flat and gravelled. Above the heavy cornice at the theatre's summit stood a bust of Her Majesty Queen Victoria and over the main entrance a bust of Shakespeare.

The grand entrance from Germain Street was 14 feet in width, its massive black walnut doors opening inward onto a hallway of pitch pine. Moving up the hallway, one passed the ticket office, then the stairs on each side going up to the floors above, and entered the parquet by one of its three aisles. The floor of the parquet (70 by 48) was of pitch pine, gently sloping toward the stage. Here one could sit in any of 546 hinged opera chairs, made of iron and upholstered with leather, and designed to be "neat, substantial and very comfortable". On the second storey the dress circle extended completely around the walls. It was supported by four iron pillars beneath and hung to the wall by iron braces secured through the brick. Four hundred and two persons could sit there on wooden settees, which were not cushioned and would soon be the subject of complaint both as an "eye sore" and also as "a sore trial to sit upon during a whole evening's entertainment". At the entrance to the dress circle, immediately over the main entrance, was located a ladies' powder room. From here, too, broad steps of pitch pine led up to the galleries. For those who preferred a better view of the audience than of the players, there were six private boxes near the stage, three on each side, all "handsomely fitted up" to provide accommodation for small parties; access could be had from the parquet and galleries. The third story contained a gallery where 100 'gods' could sit; a separate entrance on the north, with its own ticket office, provided access to this part of the building. The janitor's quarters, intended to occupy the front half of the third floor, had not yet been completed. Above all this was the loft with its endless arrangement of ropes, pulleys, and complicated stage machinery including apparatus for making thunder, rain, snow, and other effects. Around the whole interior of the theatre ran a beautiful cornice bearing an elaborate design. The interior walls were all tinted pink, but at the time of the opening the ceiling was still white, as were the ornate gallery fronts.

The 48 by 52 foot stage, equipped with four traps, had been "provided with everything necessary for dramatic and musical purposes" at a cost of $6,000. The scenery consisted of seventy-two wings, twenty pairs of flats, and many sets, including a practical bridge imported from Boston, which could be set up to extend the entire width of the stage. The drop scene, a representation of the Lake of Como, had been painted by Orrin Richards of the Boston Theatre. First-class arrangements had been made for calcium lights and other effects. Below the stage were carpenter and dressing rooms and four large furnaces considered sufficient to heat the building; from this floor an entrance to the yard permitted the performers access from Princess Street. Altogether, the *Daily News* said, the total cost of the structure was "in the vicinity of $50,000".[16]

It would be heartening to report that the opening of the Academy was a gala affair befitting its splendour, but such was not the case. The Board of Directors had devoted its energies to designing and building the theatre but had not devoted equal care to planning the use of it, and not until the end of April did they arrange a week long Musical Convention to mark the opening. The Convention (which was postponed from March when a snow blockade on the railway prevented performers arriving from Bangor and Boston) was to be directed by Mr. L. A. Torrens of Bangor, assisted by the Mendelssohn Quintette Club of Bangor. Its object was to gather together the musical talent of the province "for daily rehearsal of classical music, and thereby foster the taste and cultivate the vocal powers".[17] Daily sessions were to be held at 9:00 a.m. and 7:30 p.m. on Monday and Tuesday and at 9:00 a.m. and 2:00 p.m. on the other days. On Wednesday, Thursday, and Friday grand concerts were to be given at 8:00 p.m. and on Thursday and Friday afternoons matinees at 4:00 p.m.

Musically, the opening week was moderately successful, but financially it was a failure. At the first grand concert on Wednesday, May 8, a "well-filled hall" waited a half hour for the curtain to go up, for the train from Bangor was late, but before the members of the Quintette Club finally arrived, still in their travelling clothes and without their evening meal, sixty local singers on a terraced platform had filled the theatre with a sound that fairly tested its acoustic principles and found them ample. People came to the grand concerts but supported the matinees and rehearsals to a far lesser degree. The *Daily News* was probably stretching the truth when it said that the Academy was "filled" on Thursday "with an audience comprising the families of our best citizens",[18] (even though Lieutenant-Governor Wilmot did sit in his $25 box and was seen keeping time with his right hand). The *New Dominion* implied that Torrens did not break even on his venture. Since ticket prices were $1.00 or .50 depending on location, higher than at the Lyceum, people were reluctant to pay. Calling the $600 rental fee demanded of Torrens a "gross and contemptible extortion", the *New Dominion* complained: "It would have only been a graceful act to have allowed Mr. Torrens to give the opening and following concerts . . . at a fair and moderate rental. And yet our people grumble because they have to pay one dollar for an admission ticket. It is a poor rule which works but one way".[19]

An additional blight on the opening was the fact that the city had not cleaned up the street in front of the Academy. For the whole week of the Musical Convention it looked a perfect "Slough of Despond" — on either side a row of mud heaps, the accumulated rubbish of the winter, had been hastily raked together and not only presented a most disagreeable appearance to any one entering the theatre, but also emitted a most unsavory odour.

Until May 22 the Board of Directors did not know to what use the Academy of Music would be put during the summer. Nevertheless, with negotiations underway, they hired William Nannary (a local man and for some years Lanergan's business agent) as the Academy's box-office agent and also as editor of *Footlight Flashes*, a four-page paper of programmes, theatre news, and advertisements to be published whenever the theatre was open. Five hundred to 1500 copies of these were to be circulated each day, in addition to the copies sold daily on the trains coming in to the city. Finally, on the 22nd, the directors signed an agreement with Mr. Lanergan who, it appears, had yielded to persuasion to use the Academy instead of his own Lyceum.

Lanergan kept the Academy open for a short season from June 3 to July 27, and the press, after one heated objection to unnecessary noises behind the scenes, was nearly ecstatic in its praises of the performances, especially those by visiting artist Dominick Murray, Kate Reignolds, C. W. Couldock, Marietta Ravel, and Carlotta LeClerq. The *New Dominion*, not normally given to ecstasy, found itself caught up in a wave of enthusiasm for Miss Leclerq in *The Lady of Lyons*: "We feel bound to say that so great and so brilliant a performance as that given at the Academy of Music on Monday evening last never took place in our city before. . . . Miss LeClerq, as Pauline, won the hearts of the splendid audience which

102

turned out to greet her initial appearance in St John from the very first, and swayed them to and fro with the power of a diademed ruler".[20] Even prior to the first curtain of the season the *New Dominion* was in this unusually expansive humour, which called forth from it the strongest eulogy of Lanergan it had ever printed:

> His record has ever been a brilliant one. The 'ups' and 'downs' of the profession have come and gone, and Mr. Lanergan, in his long and arduous up-hill work, has never faltered. His aim was high and enobling; it is to his credit that he had never pandered to the rude tastes of blackguardism. He has lifted the dark veil which has hitherto shrouded the drama; and his entertainments have been the means of cementing together a love for the works of the dramatic authors, and an appreciation of the art of the great actors who have walked the boards, in their buckskin armor. The principal lights of the stage have, at great cost, been brought before our people in some of their grandest parts; and the regular stock company employed has ever been of first-class calibre. After many years of patient toil, Mr. Lanergan has, we are happy to say, had his efforts crowned with success; and all will unite with us in presenting congratulations to him in his new enterprise.[21]

At the end of Lanergan's brief season in the Academy, William Nannary took twenty members of the company on tour to Fredericton and Calais. For the rest of the summer and fall, the splendid theatre stood empty most of the time, in use only sporadically for concerts and readings, with the result that the Academy of Music Company ran deeply into debt. This culminated in a fracas on September 27 and 28, 1872.

On the afternoon of Friday the 27th, a gang of men under the direction of Messrs. Lordly, Howe & Co. (who had upholstered the opera chairs in the parquet) and W. E. Everitt (who had manufactured them) went to the Academy of Music and proceeded to unscrew and remove the chairs, which they claimed were rented to the Company under specific conditions. Between ten and eleven o'-clock the same day, Alexander Christie and John Ferguson, who held a mortgage of $13,120 on the property,[22] learned what was going on and, accompanied by their lawyer G. R. Pugsley, went to the Academy and forbade the workmen to proceed, on the grounds that the furniture belonged to the building and was covered by the mortgage. Over half the furniture had by this time been removed and, as the men refused to stop, the police were called in and the order given that no more should be taken out during the night. Nevertheless, Messrs. Lordly, Howe, Everitt, and their men continued

103

to take up the chairs and pile them in the vestibule ready for removal. In the meantime, Christie and Ferguson had secured the assistance of another group of men to prevent the chairs from being removed, and the police were also present.

Early in the morning, while the two parties were still waiting and watching each other, Judge C. N. Skinner was taking the seven o'clock train to Quispamsis to obtain from Chief Justice Ritchie an injunction entirely without precedent in the judicial history of the province, enjoining Lordly, Howe & Co. and Mr. Everitt "under the penalty of one thousand pounds . . . and also of imprisonment to desist henceforth, altogether and absolutely from severing, unfastening from, or tearing up from, or removing . . . the seats of and belonging to the said Saint John Academy of Music . . . until order shall be made to the contrary".[23] At the same hour, Mr. Everitt brought such a large gang of fresh workers that it was hopeless to oppose them, and "two loaded teams were quickly moving triumphantly away", watched by the crowd of spectators gathered on the street. On trying to re-enter the building, however, Everitt's gang found that the Christie gang had outwitted them by closing the doors:

> Matters continued in this way for about two hours when some one managed to open the door leading to the galleries and with a yell the men sprang in, passed up the stairs, over the flies, down on the stage, and across the parquette to the vestibule where Christie's men were gathered. Pressing down all opposition they seized the chairs and fittings and passed them from hand to hand, from floor to roof and thence to the sidewalk, the work of clearance occupying but a few minutes. As the first pieces were passed out of the door a rush was made by that portion of the opposing factions outside, and for a moment it looked as if there would be bloody work, two or three men getting broken heads from the iron rounds in the hands of those removing them.[24]

But Mr. Pugsley called off his men lest more serious trouble arise, leaving the opposition free to collect its booty. Before Skinner could return with the injunction, the temporary victors had finished their task, moved away to resume their ordinary duties, "and outwardly the Academy of Music presented its usual appearance". Inside the parquet was bare but its floor undamaged, for the looters had so carefully removed the two screws which fastened each chair that not even a splinter was visible. Fortuitously, the Board of Directors now had the opportunity to make necessary alterations in the terracing without the cost of removing the chairs.

Opening of the Academy of Music. From a sketch by E. J. Russell.
(New Brunswick Museum)

In its next edition, the *New Dominion* made fun of the whole affair by printing the script of "a new, exciting and excessively Opr-oar Bouffe" just brought out at the Academy of Music. In five short acts of three scenes each, the drama, "novel in plot, rich in inci-dent", has as its *dramatis personae* the following:

LORDLY, ALBERT — *Chair-man of the Furniture Board*
JOAN-AS-KNOWS-HOW — *Vice-Chairman*
WILL EVER-AT-IT — *An iron man*
ALICK CROSS-TIE, B.B. — *Builder and Bondholder*
THREE-EYE SEAL-EYE — *A chair-y lawyer*
GILT PUG SLEY — *A mort (Latin for dead) gauge lawyer*
SEM'N ERSKINE — *A judge of wills and consciences*
JUDGE RICH EYE — *A man-dam-a-tory injunctor*
MARSHALL JOINER — *A peace warrior*
FRED THE DOORMAN — *A janitor*
Attendants, Officers, Sewing Girls, and Citizens[25]

Act V of the "Oproar Bouffe" indicates the outcome of the fracas:

The act closes with a court scene, which is most amusing, some of the loudest singers previously, now singing very small, and all agreeing that the best way to end all is by selling out the whole concern to aid in having it devoted to the purposes first intended, and enabling somebody to earn money whereby the debts contracted may be paid. All is amicably arranged and happy matches are made between the retainers and the sewing girls, who witnessed their bravery from the windows of the fac-tory in front of the theatre.[26]

While the elegant Academy of Music was floundering, the other more modest hall erected by Otis Small on Dock Street was prospering. On September 3, 1870, Small, a prime mover in the building of the Victoria Hotel and president of the Victoria Hotel Company, had entered into an agreement with builders James Quinton and Charles F. Tilley concerning the construction of "a Building for Stores, Warerooms, Lecture Hall in Dock Street".[27] December 1, 1871, was the target date set for completion. Equal to four storeys in height and 83 feet across the front, the structure, de-signed by architect Matthew Stead, had gothic windows and was finished with mastic. The lower floor was occupied by stores and of-fices, including the head office of Small and Hathaway's Union Line Bay and River Steamers. The upper portion was given over to a high and spacious hall, whose roof was supported by arches rest-ing on columns which also supported the galleries stretching around the walls. The stage was deep and "admirably adapted for popular entertainments".[28] Seats on an inclined floor were meant to accommodate approximately 1000 persons, and the general interior, with the exception of the stage, was said to resemble a well-modelled church. As a theatre, the facility must have been far less grand than the Academy, for the total expense to Small, if no changes were made from the architect's specifications, was set in the agreement with Quinton and Tilley at $8,900.

Small's Hall was available for occupation when Bishop's Serenaders played in the Mechanics' Institute for a week in April 1872. Their variety entertainments of burlesques, songs, and dances delighted overflowing audiences; the aisles and every available corner where a chair could be placed were occupied, and many people had to be turned away. Obviously motivated by the overwhelming response and the opportunity to capitalize on it, Major George Bishop, the Serenaders' proprietor and manager, leased the hall from Small for an indefinite period and announced in the press his intention of making his headquarters in Saint John.

On May 6, the same day as the opening of the Academy of Music, the Serenaders officially opened the hall they renamed Bishop's Opera House. By that time they had completed certain renovations designed to make the hall more pleasing to its patrons. The orchestra portion of the main floor and the aisles had been covered with a rich Brussels carpet. Settees sufficient to seat comfortably about 150 people had been put in place in the front of the auditorium; seating in the rear portion of the auditorium and in the galleries was less "elegant" but supposedly equally comfortable. The walls had been newly panelled and the rest of the interior freshly painted. Windows were covered with closely patterned curtains, while the new gas fixtures provided excellent light. The stage and stage rooms were "conveniently and tastefully arranged", and the proscenium had a drop curtain made in Saint John. All scenery "necessary for entertainments of this kind" had been acquired. As an additional, aesthetic touch, four lamps had been added to the outside, making the building more attractive from Dock Street.[29]

If Major Bishop's own publicity can be believed, his company had "a glorious reception" on its opening night. The house, he said, was crowded to its utmost capacity with entertainment seekers who paid either .25, .35, or .50 for admission. The *New Dominion*, less prejudiced than Bishop, said only that the size of the audience was "respectable" and complained that the performances had degenerated from those in the Institute.[30] In any case, there followed a series of nightly variety shows and Saturday matinees intended to appeal to those who wanted their amusement kept light and humorous. Pete Lee and Harry Talbot made a hit with their negro sketches, as did the Freeman sisters with their character songs, and Charley Brown on his banjo. On one occasion tight-rope artist Harry Leslie, in a bid to attract an audience, created a sensation when he walked his rope successfully from the Mechanics' Institute to the Calvin Church across the street. Sketches like "Teeth Extracted Without Great Pain" brought laughter, as did farces like *Robert Macaire* and *Solon Shingle* and burlesques like Offenbach's *Grande Duchess*. Guest artist Jennie Kimball starred in the pantomime *Jack and Jill* with "new and Matchless Scenery, Tricks, Mechanical Effects and wonderful changes", and in the "Romantic, Sensational and Thrilling Drama" *Thirst for Gold*.

Variety and minstrel entertainments had become increasingly popular in Saint John, especially since the formation of the amateur Home Circle Minstrels in 1864. Numerous professional troupes had visited and found a following: Morris' Minstrels (1864), Christy's Minstrels and Brass Band and Charley Shay's Quincuplexal (1865), Burgess, Prendergast, and LaRue Minstrels (1865 and 1866), Skiff and Gaylord's Minstrels (1867), Georgia Minstrels (1868), Leavitt's Minstrels (1866-1868), Cool Burgess Minstrels and Rollin Howard's Opera Bouffe Company (1869), Tommy and Cohan's Australian Combination (1871), and others. Local amateur troupes, including Scribner Brothers Burlesque Opera Troupe and Daly and Friar's Combination Minstrel Troupe, had sprung up. Thus, the success of Bishop's Serenaders is not surprising.

While the Academy of Music had been brought into being by the professional and merchant elite of the city and looked to it for continuing support, Bishop's Opera House immediately catered to a wider segment of the population. Its ticket prices were much more within reach of the working man than were those for the Musical Convention, and the type of entertainment it offered demanded no intellectual predisposition. In a city whose 1871 census showed that the largest occupational group was labourers (many of them poorly educated Irish Roman Catholics), and whose property owners mostly belonged to a small group of Anglican merchants and lawyers, who also dominated the social scale,[31] a market for mass entertainment was readily at hand. No doubt many of those who regularly attended Lanergan's Dramatic Lyceum would also have laughed with enjoyment at the pleasures available in Bishop's Opera House, but many of those who frequented Bishop's would not have been comfortable in the more elegant Academy of Music.

The attendance at Bishop's Opera House fluctuated throughout the summer. In September the Major took a portion of the company on tour "up the line of the railway" to Moncton, Shediac, and Amherst, leaving behind a company sufficient to operate the Dock Street Opera House. Then, despite advertisements that his premises would be open all the year round, he closed his Opera House at the end of October.

During most of this time the Dramatic Lyceum was forsaken. It stood empty until mid-August when Hogan and Mudge's Minstrels and Burlesque Troupe played there until early in September. Flora Myers' Company then came with pantomimist and danseuse Marietta Ravel as star for five nights late in September, and Buckley's and Sharpley's Minstrels arrived at the end of October. Flora Myers returned, following a tour of Maine, to present three weeks of performances between November 25 and December 16 starring, in turn, J. W. Lanergan, John Matthews, and Dollie Bidwell. Because of the cold weather, special heating had been installed in the theatre.

No professional company established itself in Saint John in the winter of 1872-73. During the dreary dark months theatre-goers had to rely, as they often had before, on scattered entertainments provided by amateurs. Saint John owed a great deal to its part-time thespians, who had played such a vital cultural role in the early days, and who, since the entrenchment of Lanergan, provided support to the professional theatre and were in turn stimulated by it to greater activity. Numerous dramatic societies, in addition to the minstrel and variety companies, had sprung up in the mid 1860's. Some of these involved military personnel. The CELER ET AUDAX Amateur Dramatic Club of the 60th Rifles performed melodramas in their own theatre on the Barracks Grounds or else in the Lyceum; the Eureka Band of Tragedians, Comedians and Dramatists used No. 5 Engine Room on Germain Street; the Quid Est Club for juveniles acted Irish dramas in No. 6 Engine House; and the Garrison Amateur Dramatic Club and Sergeants Amateur Dramatic Club of the 15th Regiment performed in the Mechanics' Institute. Chief among civilian dramatic groups were the St. John Dramatic Club and the Carleton Dramatic Club; but active also were the St. John Literary Club and the Provincial Dramatic Society as well as Catholic and Temperance clubs such as the St. Joseph Literary Club and the Father Mathew Association. These groups generally performed familiar melodramas, comedies, farces, or temperance dramas in the Lyceum, the Institute, or the City Hall in Carleton, or in assorted halls like the Portland Temperance Hall or St. Malachi's Hall. As in earlier years, their productions were frequently for the benefit of some charity.

Within the amateur tradition may be included the penchant of some members of the literary elite to voice their political opinions in dramatic form. "M.....g of C......l", for instance, published in the *Morning Freeman* on May 1 and 3, 1860, presents a meeting of ten council members behind locked doors. A lively one-act farce which is a vehicle for a round of songs, the consumption of alcohol, and petty arguments based on personality conflicts, it satirizes a government more concerned with maintaining the power of Smasherdom[32] and with personal gain than with public good:

> No, my colleagues, — we've ignored
> All the people's wants and wishes,
> Satisfied if they afford
> Enough for us of loaves and fishes.

In the six years preceding the opening of Small's Hall and the Academy of Music, the columns of the *New Dominion and True Humorist* carried several of these political satires, most of them scurrilous in the bluntness of their attack. The pieces vary greatly in length and in quality, and not all are complete. Only four of the thirteen sections of the "Government in Session" survive (Dec. 13 & 30, 1865, Jan. 6 & April 7, 1866), but these are sufficient to disclose its purpose as a direct exposé of alleged corruption in the anti-confederate government of New Brunswick under the leadership of Albert Smith. Entirely lacking in subtlety, its author makes no attempt to disguise the participants in crime against the public: Hathnoway is obvious as G. L. Hatheway, postmaster general; Hutchinbum is clearly Richard Hutchinson, member of the Miramichi lumbering firm of Gilmour, Rankin and Company; Botsfurd is Bliss Botsford, surveyor general; and so on. The short "Scene in the Bar Room of the Barker House" (Nov. 4, 1866) treats the defeat of candidate Geo. L. Hath-no-pay (Hathaway) and Billy Nerdy (William H. Needham) with crude jokes.[33] Only four scenes of the five-act drama "Northumbria" are known to be extant (March 13 — April 10, 1869). This play and its farcical afterpiece, "A Trip to Frederictonia and back for $12", hit out specifically at election practices in Northumberland County and the "Imperial City" of Fredericton.

Complete, and a more interesting political satire in nine scenes, is "Measure by Measure, or the Coalition in Secret Session" (Feb. 25 — April 8, 1871). Full of Shakespearean quotations, it begins with a travesty of *Richard II*:

> Now is the Winter of our discontent
> Made glorious Summer by this son of *York*,
> And all the clouds that lower'd upon our *House*
> Scattered forever by this Coalition.
> Now may Gough's brow wrinkle with heavy frowns,

Georgell and Stephey stand as monuments
Of hateful treachery. What do we reck —
'Twas neck or nothing, and we chose the neck.

In mock heroic tones it discloses a government whose members
spend their time playing games of 'Muggins', promise never-to-be-
delivered money to the Board of Health in order to appear to be
working, and are occupied above all with the controversial School
Bill.[34] The much shorter "The Fall of the King-Lie Die-nasty"
(March 3, 1871), dealing with the same government, consists almost
entirely of corruptions of Shakespearean quotations in a format
suitable for choral reading. Complete also is the four-act "Sidewalks of Saint John" (July 2 — August 13, 1870) in which the edi-
tors of the *News*, *Globe*, and *Freeman* meet together, burying their
old rivalries, and plan the establishment of a joint paper to be called
The Reformer, which they intend to outstrip the rival *Telegraph*.[35]

A refreshing change from the perils of the political arena is
provided by three short pieces. In six brief acts "The New Fire Brigade" (Dec. 1864), which was prompted by a conflagration in Indiantown, ridicules the inefficiency of the Fire Brigade.[36] "A Local
Farce in One Act" (April 18, 1870) is set in the elegantly furnished
parlour of Madame Severity's boarding school to which Mr. Foppy-
law, "a young sprig of the law", and some other young gentlemen
have come to join the lady pupils in a *soirée dansant*.[37] "The Lost
Half-Penny, or the Pea-nut Boy's Revenge" (June 20, 1866), called
grandly "a drama in three acts", although it occupies only two columns, is an amusing spoof of the plot of some melodramas; in it the
swaggering hero-villain Biler, the peanut boy, rejected in love, pur-
sues and kills his rival out of revenge.

In 1876, four years after the opening of the Academy of Music,
William Murdoch, then theatre critic for the *Daily News*, published
"A Fireside Drama", the first play written in Saint John to be published outside of newspapers. The verse drama in three acts is included in a volume of poems and songs composed by Murdoch, entitled *Discursory Ruminations, A Fireside Drama, &c., &c.*, and
published by H. Chubb & Co., Saint John. A writer for the *Saint
Croix-Courier* found it "quite neat — a pretty little volume . . .
really a credit to the publishers", and its contents "also in some
measure a credit to their author, but not always".[38] The "Fireside
Drama', he said, "though sometimes unnatural in that it makes the
part represented talk to and answer each other in verse, is carried
on with considerable spirit and a good deal of pathos sometimes;
and the songs in it are good".

The play reveals many deficiencies — the singing collie in the almost wholly sung first act strains credulity considerably, the verse bears out Murdoch's own claim that he is "just a rhymer", and a sound knowledge of what is actable is lacking — yet the whole is, withal, charming. Though Murdoch had immigrated from his native Scotland in 1854, he remained a thorough Scotsman.[39] His play is written in the Scottish dialect of Robert Burns and is permeated with good natured Scottish humour. From its title and its opening setting in which John, his "guidwife", and their collie dog are sheltered cosily in front of their fire against a stormy night, the script expresses the Scot's strong love of home as it works sentimentally towards the mending of broken relationships and the cementing of new ones in the final wedding celebration.

From this digression on the amateur and literary dramatic tradition, it is now necessary to return to the professional theatre. Following the quiet winter of 1872-73, variety entertainment began once more in the Opera House on Dock Street in April. At that time Pete Lee, a former member of Major Bishop's Serenaders, took over the lease of the hall from him, renamed it Lee's Opera House, and hired as his agent G. B. Betts, formerly agent of the Home Circle Minstrels. Under Lee's management the company rapidly increased in popularity, receiving repeated encomiums from the press. Because it produced "pieces free from vulgarity or anything that might give offense to those of the most delicate taste", and because it brought forth new acts rapidly and with dramatic ability of "high order", it was "fast becoming an institution".[40] Pete Lee himself and the Ed Chrissies were the backbone of the small company which regularly added to its number with guest stars like the LaVerde children, Harry Talbot, and the Carroll family. Lee did well enough to keep the Opera House open to the end of the year, except for a week in August when he toured to Eastport and Calais while his theatre underwent renovation and for an interval in the middle of December.

On June 5, Mr. Lanergan opened his eighteenth season in Saint John with "the ladies' favorite drama", *The Lady of Lyons*. He had been too ill during the winter months to do more than give a few evenings of dramatic readings in Saint John, Carleton, and Fredericton, but by spring had recovered sufficiently to make his annual trip to New York to recruit a summer company. For the 1873 season he preferred to return to his own familiar Dramatic Lyceum, forsaking the Academy.[41] As usual, his programme was designed to appeal to a wide spectrum of taste within, of course, the bounds of decorum, but the *New Dominion*, as the organ of polite society, was anxious to stress its 'respectability'. Once more it commended Lanergan for "breaking down the rude barrier which kept the *elite* and better portion of our population from attending the theatre" and noted that "the popular manager had gradually seen his trees bearing good fruit, and now everybody goes to the Lyceum, and enjoys and appreciates the acting".[42] The paper's own elitist preferences are clear in its praise of Frederic Robinson, tragedian of the legitimate drama, and its scorn of Fanny Herring, whose loud slangy New York style it considered too lacking in refinement for Saint John. Other stars this season included Dollie Bidwell who, only in March, had been so seriously ill in New Hampshire that her recovery was doubted, Dominick Murray who attracted standing-room only crowds, Oliver Doud Byron whose *Across the Continent* continued to draw though the *New Dominion* did not approve of it, tragedian J. W. Albaugh, character actor J. M. Ward with Winetta Montague, and Mrs. Thomas Barry whose *A Bold Stroke for a Husband* on June 24 was "literally packed" by the visiting Knights Templar of Portland, Bangor, and Saint John. Mrs. Lanergan returned to the stage as leading lady, and W. H. Daly was stage manager. Included in the company was a young New York man, E. A. McDowell, who rapidly became a favourite for his ability, although the *New Dominion* took him to task for the carelessness of his make-up and inattention to details of dress. Lanergan closed the Lyceum early in August after a short but prosperous season and went to the north shore of the province on a fishing trip.

The Academy of Music, meanwhile, was struggling for survival. A total indebtedness of $39,000, including the mortgage of $13,120 held by A. Christie & Co., was threatening its life. Following the furniture fracas and amidst bitter letters to the newspapers condemning the inefficiency of the directors (one to the *Tribune* calling the whole Academy venture "a shattering, bungled concern, a fit emblem of the stupidity of man"), a series of stockholders' meetings made ready a scheme to rescue the theatre from the auctioneers' block. Four grand concerts were planned for May 1873, to which 16,000 tickets were to be sold at $5 and 11 for $50 and at which $30,000 in cash would be given away. William Nannary and William Olive were named managers of the ambitious undertaking which set up ticket agencies in New York, Boston, Bangor, Toronto, Montreal, Ottawa, Halifax, as well as in most towns of New Brunswick, Nova Scotia, and Prince Edward Island. Fortunately, the enterprise was successful, for it reduced the debt by $21,000. The first concert, postponed to June 16, was held in a full Academy, and the rest in the Victoria Skating Rink when the Academy was deemed too small. A 25 to 30 foot stage had been erected there, immediately in front of which were a thousand chairs. Behind a barricade were seats for 1500 persons more and ample stand-

113

ing room. By seven o'clock on the 17th, a procession of people "literally reaching from King Square to the City Road, was crowding in that direction. At the door the jam was dangerous to life and limb, and many turned away rather than trust themselves in that crowd. Once within the Rink everything was perfect order".[43]

The Academy's life having been thus prolonged, it remained to solve the problem of its use. Its transformation into a ballroom on the occasion of the Ball given to Lord and Lady Dufferin by the people of Saint John and Portland on August 22 was glorious but not permanently helpful. For one night, the whole of the auditorium and part of the stage were floored to create "a capacious and elegant ballroom" decorated to resemble an oriental palace; flags and draperies festooned the walls and galleries, rare flowers bloomed in the private boxes, tiny warblers sang from gallery tops and centre pieces, and gas jets emblazoned with WELCOME greeted each guest as he entered. More to the point was its lease for four days at the end of August to William Nannary, for this would have lasting repercussions. Using as a core some of Lanergan's actors, with assistance from the Garrison Amateurs, Nannary had formed a company he called the Grand Comedy Combination and opened in Halifax on April 11 under the patronage of the Countess of Dufferin. On August 19, the *Daily News* reported they were doing so well in Halifax that they had decided to delay coming to Saint John for a few days, but in due course their August 26 opening at the Academy of Music in Harris and Falconer's comedy *Rose of Castile* was well received. Misses Savory and Conway were seen as particularly strong assets to the company. Lennox was funny and familiar enough to warrant no special mention, but E. A. McDowell was singled out as "a fine and excellent actor" who "always plays with naturalness and never slights his work". The association at this time of McDowell and Nannary was significant in that it was the beginning of a collaboration that would flower in 1874.

William Nannary was proof that a lower class Irishman could be successful in Saint John if he had the right combination of talent and ambition. The eldest of four children of Patrick and Bridget Nannary (or Nannery), immigrants from Ireland, he had grown up on Protection Street in Carleton. His father was a labourer. The census of 1871 gives William's age as thirty-two and his occupation as dry-goods clerk. He was married to Anne, then aged twenty-seven, and they had three children — Mary Agnes, William, and Ann Genevieve who were, respectively, five, three, and eleven months. Later he would father a fourth child, Edward. From its beginning, William was an active member of the St. John Dramatic Club and, for several years, its manager. Perhaps because of him, this club

114

Lee's Opera House, a playbill
(Harvard Theatre Collection)

Benefit of Gertrude Kellogs
(New Brunswick Museum)

115

was frequently associated with Lanergan and his Lyceum. In 1866 Nannary played Antonio in Lanergan's production of *The Merchant of Venice*. In 1867 Lizzie Anderson, one of Lanergan's actresses, was featured in Dramatic Club productions. In 1869 two more of Lanergan's company, Rachel Noah and H. R. Lampee, donated their talents in a complimentary benefit the Dramatic Club tendered to Nannary. In 1870 he tried professional management briefly when, following the close of the Lyceum, he took some of its actors, including Rachel Noah and the J. H. Brownes, to the Mechanics' Institute. Gradually Nannary's direct involvement with the professional theatre in Saint John increased, from business agent for the Lyceum to box-office agent of the Academy, editor of *Footlight Flashes*, manager of the gift-concert campaign, and now manager of a company at the Academy of Music whence, following in Lanergan's footsteps, he would begin a career in management himself. Later his brother Patrick joined him on the professional stage, and eventually three of his children — May(Mary), Genevieve, and Edward.

In 1874 Nannary, together with E. A. McDowell, managed the Star Company at the Academy of Music. That year, in which the Academy finally came into its own, was an exceedingly active one for theatre in Saint John. Three halls — Lee's Opera House, the Academy of Music, and the Dramatic Lyceum — were open at various times to provide dramatic entertainment the year round. In May and June the Lyceum and the Academy operated simultaneously; in December the Academy and Lee's Opera House did so. All three theatres were open six nights a week and also offered Saturday matinees, and all three had comparable prices ranging from .25 to .50, with reserved tickets .25 extra. The Star Company occupied the Academy from May 7 to June 13, then moved to the Temperance Hall in Halifax, returning on July 18 until August 18. At that time Nannary and McDowell dissolved their partnership; McDowell went with a company of his own to Bangor, and Nannary remained in Saint John. From October 24 to December 29 Nannary managed a season alone at the Academy. Lanergan kept his Lyceum open a shorter time, from May 18 to July 18 only, although he had been in Saint John since January; during the winter he had given readings in the Mechanics' Institute, been a candidate for the civic office of alderman in Queen's Ward and been defeated, even though the *New Dominion* had viewed him as the favourite with the electorate. Pete Lee's Opera House was open longest, from January 1 to May 4, again from August 17 to October 24, and from December 1 to January 20, 1875.

In February 1874, "in its tenth month of reign", Lee's Opera

116

House was the scene of a benefit performance tendered to Pete Lee by citizens of Saint John who showed their appreciation tangibly in the presentation of a gold watch and chain. The Opera House was crowded to standing capacity. Not surprisingly, in March Lee renewed the lease from Small for a further twelve months. On April 25 the *New Dominion* fondly expressed the sentiments of Saint Johners toward his place of amusement: "The cosy little Opera House is as pleasant to us as the flowers in May, and the carrolling warblers of the leafy month of June". Lee's programme in 1874 consisted of the proven mix of dramatic sketches, gymnastics, song and dance. Some of the sketches, like "Streets of St. John" and "Sketches of St. John's Old Time's Rocks", were burlesques of local situations.

Although in 1874 Nannary and McDowell's Star Company produced some of the favourites of the Lanergan years, like *Money*, *Ingomar*, *The Hunchback*, and *The Corsican Brothers* (which introduced for novelty a live hen in the first act), they concentrated on introducing new plays. For their opening on May 7 they chose Boucicault's *Led Astray* (1873), "an emotional comedy in five acts and six tableaux".[44] The Academy was reportedly crowded to its utmost capacity with a brilliant and fashionable audience. W. S. Gilbert's *Charity* (1874), which had had a run of eight weeks in New York, was "simply munificent and magnificent. The scenery, appointments and what-not being especially deserving of mention, while the acting was perfection itself".[45] G. F. Rowe's *Geneva Cross* (1874) was more popular yet, while Augustin Daly's slightly older (1871) "5th Avenue Society Sensational", *Divorce*, was billed as the climax of the season. Wilkie Collins' *The New Magdalen* (1873) and Mcdermott's adaptation of Dickens' *The Mystery of Edwin Drood* (1872) were two other well-received plays new to Saint John. Lanergan, on the other hand, relied heavily on productions that had succeeded previously, such as *Ticket-of-Leave Man*, *Camille*, *Under the Gaslight*, and *Lost at Sea*. The repertoires of the two theatres were different except for *Macbeth*, *Hamlet*, *Richard III*, and *Romeo and Juliet*, and for *East Lynne*, *The New Magdalen*, and *Charity* (Lanergan produced the latter two after their success at the Academy).

Lanergan followed his usual custom of bringing a bevy of stars, and it was with these that he introduced new scripts, though nothing of consequence (for example, *Olive; or the Mysterious Murder* dramatized for Lillie Eldridge and *Deceit* written for Ada Gray). Yankee Locke appeared in his American specialties, Fred Robinson made his by now habituary visit, Mr. and Mrs. C. M. Walcot were newcomers in one of the newest legitimate plays of the Lyceum's season, Gilbert's *Pygmalion and Galatea* (1871), and in the last week Lanergan covered himself with glory in the engagement of Carlotta Leclercq, "the most magnificent actress of the century, the queen of tragedy and the goddess of comedy".[46] Nannary and McDowell brought no stars, apart from Miss Leclercq after her engagement with Lanergan, preferring to risk all on the merits of their leading players, Neil Warner and Grace Kellogg. It was a risk well taken. The press spoke in nothing but superlatives of both; Miss Kellogg's power as an actress, for instance, had "rarely, if ever, been seen in this part of the world".[47] Though these two were considered far superior to other members of the company, they did in fact have reasonable support from McDowell, Charles Loveday, Mrs. Frank Murdoch, Carrie Jameson, Messrs. Bebus, Hague, O. H. Barr, and Young.

The Star Company had at least one advantage over the Lyceum company, namely, the greater opportunity the Academy's more modern facilities offered for scenery (coupled with the very considerable talents of its scenic artist, Richard Farren). Repeatedly, reviews comment with pleasure on the excellence of scenic effects, costumes, and stage paraphernalia in Academy productions.

Some of the scripts produced by Nannary, McDowell, and Lanergan in 1874 were, of course, deemed trash, one even a "mass of conglomerated bosh", but the only play that entirely enraged some critics was presented by a travelling company that visited the Academy in September. This was *The Black Crook*, a spectacular extravaganza combining gorgeous scenery with music, song, and dance performed by lightly-clad girls belonging to Howard and Carle's Combination.[48] Tickets, at .75, .50, and .25 ($1.00 reserved), were more expensive than usual in order to pay for the transportation and maintainance of the dramatic company of forty-three people, a full ballet troupe, and "AN ENTIRE NEW YORK COMPLETE GRAND ORCHESTRA". In August 1867, when the piece had played in a jammed Mechanics' Institute, the *Morning News* had preferred not to comment, leaving the public to form its own opinion, and the *New Dominion* wrote a satirical review of the "Black Crook Menagerie", calling it "*leg*-itimate Drama" on a "*gal*-a night" of which "ye gods" had full charge.[49] In 1874 the advance publicity included favourable reviews from Montreal and Bangor in an attempt to overcome earlier censure on moral grounds in the New York press. The *Telegraph*, in summing up the opening night, on September 8 wrote: "To those who have been accustomed to ballet dancing and admire 'naked art', there is nothing in the play that they would deem objectionable, while persons to whom such exhibitions are an entire novelty and a surprise, may demure to the scantiness of female dress and the freedom of the principal dancers". A great many male Saint Johners did, it seems, admire 'naked art' for, even before the doors were opened, Germain Street "was packed with a crowd of men and boys loudly demanding admittance; and by the time the performance opened the parquet, both galleries and all the boxes were filled with a crowd that probably did not include more than twenty or thirty of the fair sex, though those of them who were present were highly respectable". The crowd was decidedly mixed, containing representation from "all the professions, trades, and other divisions of society". The *Telegraph* printed letters pro and con the show, and by the end of the week was expressing concern that its reporting had been misinterpreted as support; the *New Dominion* of September 12 was more detached, judging the entertainment a "wonderful piece, abounding in every species of variety business, gorgeous scenery, dazzling transformations, spider dances, ballets, songs, hornpipes, curious dogs and aerial acts" but, it added, hardly "an elevating performance". Following a week of controversy and profit, the Howard and Carle Combination proceeded to play to more packed houses in Halifax before completing their tour in Eastport, Calais, and Oldtown.

When William Nannary decided to open the Academy under his own management for the last two months of 1874, theatre-goers of Saint John were thrilled, for Nannary, whose reputation, the *Telegraph* said on October 19, "is so firmly established with all the theatre-goers", was "about to establish what exists in every city of any importance in England and the United States — a fall and winter season". With Neil Warner and Jennie Parker as his leading actors (the former back from touring with McDowell's company and the latter just free from an engagement at the Grand Opera House, New York), and the best company he had been able to recruit in New York, Nannary worked diligently to win the approval of his audiences, in part by announcing his intention to produce "the triumphs of the London and New York stage, in a style equal to the best theatre in America". His announcement was perhaps just a little misleading, for some of the 'triumphs' were not brand new; Byron's London comedy *War to the Knife* had been written in 1865, and *Lonely Man of the Ocean* was not only not new in Saint John (Lanergan had produced it), but it had been written in 1847, even though the audiences were most pleased with its sensations. Nannary did, however, introduce Saint Johners to some relatively new and significant drama including Halliday's *Checkmate* (1869), "one of the prettiest and loveliest of sterling English comedies", and Lewis' drama about a Polish Jew, *The Bells* (1871), and with Tom Taylor's *Clancarty* he was certainly up to the mark. That play had already been produced in England, had been played in San Francisco in September and later in Philadelphia and New Orleans, but Saint John would be seeing it in advance of New York and Boston. Nannary had, for $500, purchased the sole right of the play for Saint John and Halifax for one year. The *Telegraph* was proud of him, especially since McDowell had had a similar coup with *Geneva Cross* in the summer: "It is worthy of note that a young manager of this city has had the enterprise and pluck to produce pieces at considerable cost in advance of the large cities. The Geneva Cross was produced in London for the first time about two weeks ago, although it was played here last season; and now we have Clancarty ahead of New York and Boston".[50]

As a tribute to the efficacy of Nannary's management from those most intimately involved with it, a letter appeared in the December 26 issue of the *Telegraph* tendering the services of eighteen members of the company and orchestra for a benefit performance. Above this letter appeared another with twenty signatures of prominent citizens affixed:

Wm. Nannary, Esq.
DEAR SIR: The undersigned feel so much gratified at your successful management in catering for their amusement during the past year, that it affords them much pleasure to tender you a complimentary testimonial, and if agreeable you will please name the night.

The names which follow, when matched with their occupations, provide a record of many of the influential backers of the theatre in this period. They were A. Chipman Smith, mayor and druggist; Allan M. Ring, James T. Stevens, and Thomas Carritte, physicians; James R. Macshane, barrister; James I. Fellows, manufacturing chemist; John Guthrie, proprietor of Waverley House; John A. Edwards, manager of the Victoria Hotel and John M. Gibbs, its chief clerk; Lawton Brothers, druggists; John McMillan, stationer; Fred E. Scammell of Scammell Brothers; James G. Forbes and W. Herbert Sinnott of Forbes & Sinnott; Christopher Murray, grocer; Thomas B. Buxton, liquors; Henry R. Ranney, insurance agent; Hugh W. Chisholm, agent for the International Steamship Company; Hugh S. Gregory, stevedore; and T. & R. Coughlan.[51] *The Hunchback* and the afterpiece, *The Merry Cobbler*, formed the programme for the benefit performance on December 29. Nannary appeared before the curtain to thank the audience for turning out *en masse* and to accept the good wishes of his friends in his next endeavour, a full January season in Halifax. The citizens of Halifax

Frank Roche (Theatre Department, Metropolitan Toronto Library)

E. A. McDowell as Jack Desmond
(New York Public Library)

were just as pleased with him and tendered him a similar complimentary benefit at the conclusion of his stay among them.

Despite the strong ending to 1874, there were soon signs of trouble ahead. Lee's Opera House was open for variety entertainment during the first twenty days of 1875, and again from April 21 to May 1 and July 1 to 13, but then Pete Lee allowed his lease to lapse.[52] The reason for his action is clear from a review in the *New Dominion* on May 1 which absolves Lee from blame that the Opera House had not been filled during the preceding week, for "times are so hard and money so particularly scarce that people save their quarters and stay at home".

Saint John was once more feeling the effects of a world-wide depression. This is undoubtedly the reason why Lanergan and Nannary decided to consolidate their efforts by entering into partnership, leasing the Academy and offering a summer season jointly, in contrast to the direct competition of the previous year. Reflecting the policies of Nannary and McDowell's Star Company and of Mr. Lanergan, a balanced programme was planned which would combine the best of the legitimate drama with the "great novelties of the London and New York Theatres". With a company that included some of Lanergan's old standbys and members of the Star Company, the managers were off to an auspicious start with the production of Robertson's three-act comedy *Home* (1869 but new to Saint John) on May 20, that saw the entrance to the Academy crowded and a jam at the doors long before curtain time. From this date they performed seven times weekly until July 13, moved the company to the Temperance Hall in Halifax for July 15 to August 18, and were back in the Academy again from August 20 to September 15. Lanergan was dramatic manager of the company and Nannary the business manager, J. B. Fuller stage manager, and F. A. Muller leader of the orchestra. Regular members included the Fiske family, J. H. Browne, James Meade, Ida Campbell, and Patrick Nannary. Toward the end of the season in Halifax and for the last week at the Academy in September, Neil Warner and newcomer Sophie Miles were the leading actors. From August 23 to 28, E. A. McDowell starred in the title role of Boucicault's *Shaughraun* to which he had purchased exclusive Canadian rights, and for a week from August 30 to September 4, Kate Fisher galloped over rocks and precipices lashed to the back of the "horse-wonder" Mazeppa in a novelty corrupted from Byron's *Childe Harolde*.

The partners had, at considerable expense, procured exclusive Saint John and Halifax rights to Augustin Daly's New York success, *The Big Bonanza*, a clever satire of Wall Street brokers which was still running at Daly's Fifth Avenue Theatre when it made its Maritime première on June 28. The critics had a difficult time deciding which of the new plays was best. On May 31 Lester Wallack's romantic drama *Rosedale* (1874) was the "greatest dramatic treat that has been offered to the citizens of St. John for years", but by June 16 J. Oxenford's "sad, dreamy poem" *Two Orphans* (1874) was considered decidedly the best of the season. Both drew admiration for well constructed, exciting yet tender plots, gorgeous scenery, and magnificent tableaux. Admired also were two American plays, Bronson Howard's society comedy *Saratoga* which, on June 7, drew the largest house to date and proved to be as big a hit as his *Divorce*, and also Charles Morton's new society drama *Women of the Day* whose advertising was reminiscent of the advent of *The Ticket-of-Leave Man*: "Every young wife should see it. Every mother-in-law should witness it. Every roué should profit by it, and every maiden should take warning by it. It should run at least a week".[53] With these was a liberal sprinkling of familiar pieces including *Lucretia Borgia*, *Pizarro*, *The Marble Heart*, *Camille*, *Colleen Bawn*, and, of course, Shakespeare. A review of *Jack Cade* indicates the degree of success achieved by mid-July:

> The times have been hard, money has been scarcer among all classes than for many years past, and yet the average attendance at the Academy has been very good, while on some occasions the house has been filled to its utmost capacity. . . . The company will compare favorably with that of any American theatre. . . . The plays have been of a good class. . . . In a city such as St. John, where no play can have a run of more than two or three nights, and a constant variety is required, it is no light undertaking to produce a new and elaborate piece, and on this account the efforts of the managers are all the more commendable and worthy of recognition.[54]

At the end of September 1875 Nannary and Sophie Miles, with a small company, put on "two very pleasant entertainments" in the Academy, *Checkmate* and *Rip Van Winkle*, but Nannary's attention was particularly drawn towards Halifax that fall. That city had made several unsuccessful attempts to initiate a scheme to build an Academy of Music of its own. In 1873 one project that the *Acadian Recorder* had expected to succeed collapsed with no explanation. Now, in the fall of 1875, William Nannary, encouraged by the strength of his reception in Halifax, determined to revive the campaign for an adequate theatre. He established his presence in the city firmly with a stock company featuring Neil Warner and Sophie Miles in a season that lasted from October 14 to November 24, interrupted only by four days in Saint John and one in Moncton. Late in October, he proposed a wooden building just outside the brick district on the corner of Lockman Street and Poplar Grove at an estimated cost of $10,000. Although that proposal was rejected, it had served its purpose and, in December, announcement was made that another scheme for an Academy was underway. The *Halifax Herald*, reporting on Nannary's benefit, gave the credit to him: "Mr. Nannary has done so much to make theatre-going popular, to increase the public stock of harmless amusement, that he well deserves a bumper house. If we ever have a decent theatre here, it will be owing entirely to his enterprise and energy, and the good taste for public amusements which he has encouraged here".[55] To finish off his season, Nannary returned to Saint John for two days at the end of November, performed for a few days early in December in Pike's Opera House, Calais, and finally, filling a vacancy created by the Boston Comedy Company's cancellation, provided two days of entertainment in his hometown at Christmas.

Even with Nannary's preoccupation with Halifax, the Academy of Music was in regular use until the end of the year. McGill and Strong's Mirror of Ireland and Emeralda Minstrels and Comedy Combination were there following a tour of Nova Scotia and Prince Edward Island. Maggie Mitchell, the "pearl of the American stage", starred in *Fanchon*, *Barefoot*, and *Jane Eyre* with her own company. There were lecture series, concerts, and readings by persons of such varying stature as local amateur John March and the famed Sarah Siddons. Dora Wiley's Boston English Opera Company, the Caroline Richings Bernard Opera Company, and the Redpath Opera Company sang *Maritana*, *Rose of Tyrol*, and *Martha*, their visits reflecting the increasing attraction of opera to theatregoers. By the end of December the decoration of the Academy, left unfinished at its opening in 1872, had been completed. The intricacies of the gold leaf, delicate scrollwork, and heraldic designs which beautified the ceiling, the careful co-ordination of the colour scheme, emphasizing graduated shades of carmine and a new tint of lavender known as ashes of roses, with accents of deep blue and Naples yellow, and with bronze and gold for the pillars of dress circle and gallery, had all been executed under the superintendence of Professor Ashburn of London, an eminent fresco painter and professional decorator whose work could be seen in the Drury Lane Theatre and St. James' Hall. From the top of the proscenium arch a small gilded bust of Shakespeare watched over the thespians below, and each of two triangular panels just below the cornice contained a lyre, symbolic of the purposes for which the building had been erected, and two more panels near the top of the arch held the coats of arms of the Dominion of Canada and the city of Saint John. The

Telegraph, justly proud, proclaimed the Academy's "richness and artistic beauty unsurpassed in any similar building in the Dominion".[56]

The report of the annual meeting of the stockholders on May 1, 1876, confirms that the Academy was doing well.[57] The directors reported that, "notwithstanding the world-wide depression that has existed in commercial circles during the past year", the Academy was almost free of financial encumbrance. That is to say, at the annual meeting early in 1873, indebtedness was close to $39,000. Of this $21,000 was paid off by the receipts of the concert scheme and nearly $5,000 had been paid since the concerts out of the earnings of the building, leaving just over $13,000 in liabilities which were so well secured as to give the directors no alarm. In 1875 the total income from all sources was $4,705.50, of which $3,496.75 came from rental of the hall. Payments for running expenses amounted to $2,786.53, on former indebtedness $319.57, for laying a sewer and putting in a window $75.03, and for decoration of the interior $901.00, leaving a balance of $623.37. The directors were optimistic about the coming year, for the stores were rented, the Knights of Pythias had rented the hall on the third floor, William Nannary had taken out a lease for part of the summer, and "responsible parties" were negotiating for its occupancy otherwise.

The short season (April 26 to May 8, 1976) of E. A. McDowell's Company from the Theatre Royal, Montreal, was part of the positive trend. Excellent reviews and good houses rewarded McDowell for his introduction to Saint John of the English comedy *Our Boys*, the opera bouffe *Giroflé-Girofla* whose gorgeous costumes alone cost $1000, Daly's "beautiful emotional drama" *Alixe*, produced in an "elegant manner" with Sophie Miles as star, and *Rose Michel*, the "reigning sensation in Paris, New York and Boston the past Season", for which McDowell had bought exclusive Canadian rights. Equally appreciated were his magnificent productions of *Two Orphans* for which William Gill had painted three new and beautiful scenes, *Field of the Cloth of Gold* featuring American prima donna Clara Fisher, and *Rosedale* which used a detachment of the 62nd Regiment in its Gipsy-Dell scene and for which the curtain was rung up three times.

William Nannary's longer season from May 18 to July 8 did not fare so well. Houses, on the whole, were not good, and for the first time Nannary was in deep disfavour with some critics. He had employed Frank Roche as his leading man and Mrs. D. R. Allen as leading lady and proceeded to produce the old pieces in which those two had played at the Lyceum years before. The problem was that he had, at the beginning of the season, announced his intention to produce "all the great novelties", raising expectations that he would continue his and McDowell's practice of introducing new plays. When he failed to do so, the *Watchman* attacked him vehemently for his parsimony and ignorance as well as for his failure to keep his promises. In addition, the *Watchman* focused its attack on Frank Roche and on the stage management. Roche, it alleged, roared like a lion and, moreover, could play but one character, Frank Roche: "Romeo, Hamlet, Melnotte, Dazzle, Marlow or Surface is only Mr. Roche clad in a different suit of clothes. He plays them all like".[58] The wreck in "that silly piece of nonsense" *The Overland Route* was the most terrible burlesque seen in Saint John: "The ship reminded the spectator of a shady omnibus, and it had a mast and some rigging on it, carefully misplaced. The nautical gentleman who furnished Mr. Nannary with the design of this marvellous ocean steamship, must have been either an arrant knave out for a lark, or one of those sailors who exists only in the imagination. The like of it was surely never seen, and no one save the manager himself could have been deceived by it".[59] The prompter and scene shifter, the sarcastic critic accused, often did most of the play between them. The music was vile, and *Romeo and Juliet* was produced in a garbled *six* act version. Waits between acts were insufferably long, extending the evenings until nearly midnight. Nannary was accused of reserving half the house when only a dozen or so seats had been purchased, in order to wring an extra quarter from the spectators when he could, and he supposedly abused the benefit system. He was pronounced unfit to manage a theatre and deserving of the small houses of seventy-five to one hundred and fifty people that were quite common. The *Daily News* was loyal to the end, although it was eventually reporting small houses of fewer than eighty people. It did not care for Roche's conception of Hamlet and thought the murder-filled *Chamber of Death* a very bad play, but otherwise it was satisfied. The *New Dominion* put the *Watchman*'s harsh criticism down to "personal hatred and ill-will toward the performers" and prejudice against a native (because it extolled McDowell in comparison). Mr. Nannary, the *New Dominion* believed, honestly deserved credit "for his efforts to keep up in this city and to naturalize among us a taste for good plays".[60]

Even if Nannary was feeling the economic pinch, there does seem to be some truth in the *Watchman*'s unkind remarks and some attempt by the other papers to gloss over the situation. Nannary appears to have miscalculated what the citizens of his native city would accept. The large houses which all papers acknowledge during the two week-long visits of Kate Putnam seem to indicate that Saint John was demanding stars and that it was not prepared to settle for a rerun of the past. Certain plays had always been favourites, but even in the Dramatic Lyceum these had been mixed with carefully chosen new ones, and seldom did James Lanergan dare to rely only on his stock company for a whole season.

Mr. Lanergan had not operated his Dramatic Lyceum since 1874. Late in June 1876 he came to Saint John after completing a tour through New England with the George Honey Troupe. With his wife, he gave readings in Digby in August and then returned to the United States for an engagement at the Boston Globe. On September 22 he advertised his Dramatic Lyceum for sale, "together with the Dwelling House, Stores, &c., belonging thereto".[61] On October 8 the Irish Friendly Society purchased it for $2,000.[62] Lanergan had demonstrated in 1873 and 1874 that he preferred his cosy Lyceum to the larger, more elegant Academy; yet his collaboration with Nannary in the Academy indicates that, given the times, he could not compete and had no desire to do so. Ironically, he had encouraged theatre so successfully that he now found himself closed out of the market he had created, and he could no longer 'coin money' in Saint John.

With the closure of Lee's Opera House in July 1875 and its transformation soon thereafter into a ballroom for winter quadrille assemblies, and now with the sale of the Dramatic Lyceum, Saint John was left with only one proper theatre that, in comparison with the activity of the past years, was grossly underused. In the winter and spring of 1876 and 1877, lecture series went on as usual, both in the Academy and Mechanics' Institute; McGill and Strong's Minstrels and Frank Hussey with his performing dog Topsy made brief visits to the Academy, a few amateur organizations performed plays in various halls around the city, but the only serious professional entertainment was provided by the Boston Philharmonic Club and by W. J. Lemoyne's Evening with Dickens Combination.

Fortunately, William Nannary, undaunted by the *Watchman*'s adverse criticism, came back again to the Academy of Music in April 1877. Since his closure there on July 8, 1876, he had been very busy in Halifax. In fact, he had begun his 1876 summer season in Halifax even before he closed in Saint John, taking Kate Putnam and some supporting players there with him and leaving only a small company to carry on in the Academy; thus he gave the *Watchman* more cause for complaint. He kept Halifax's Temperance Hall open until August 25, while keeping his eye on the new theatre arising on Pleasant (now Barrington) Street. Then, on January 16, 1877, his company's production of Percival's *Clouds* was the first dramatic performance in the new Halifax Academy of Music. That was the beginning of a lengthy occupation of the Halifax

Academy that year, a term which was to go on until August 4 with only a brief intermission between March 24 and April 23. In that interval he brought his company to Saint John, producing in its Academy his successful Halifax repertoire: *Clouds*, *Pique*, *Flying Scud*, *The Shaughraun*, *Under the Gaslight*, and one new play, *The Great Divorce* (1876). His success this time was more obvious, even allowing for the prejudice of the *Daily News*.

Nannary's ambition now was to maintain companies in Saint John and Halifax simultaneously. Accordingly, while his present company returned to Halifax at the end of April, he went to New York to recruit a second company for a Saint John summer season and to engage stars W. H. Lytell, Kate Putnam, and Louise Pomeroy to play first in Saint John and then in Halifax. On May 21 his Saint John stock company, with R. Fulton Russell and Isabella Waldron (wife of the stage manager) as leading actors, opened in the Germain Street Academy with *Diavilo or Hunted Down*, while the Halifax stock company with guest star Helen Tracy was making a hit in *Magnolia*.

Audience response in the ensuing season was like a thermometer indicating changes that had taken place in popular expectations since 1870. Houses were initially thin; many people, the *Daily News* thought, were waiting for the coming stars: "A good stock business cannot be done anywhere when stars have been billed, and the sooner the latter begin to arrive the better".[63] By far the biggest attraction was the four night run of the "most gorgeous spectacle ever presented on a St. John stage", *Around the World in 80 Days*, starring W. H. Lytell, in preparation for which the theatre had to be closed a whole day while fifty hastily recruited volunteers, accepted from one hundred and fifty applicants, rehearsed with the twenty member company. The spectators, who nearly exhausted the seating capacity, were agog at the panoramic scenery depicting the route around the world, at the dresses imported from New York and at the splendid mechanical effects, especially the illusion of the sinking of the steamship. Much less successful in terms of audience size, although not in terms of audience enthusiasm was Louise Pomeroy's repertoire of *As You Like It* and *Romeo and Juliet*: "There never before was more enthusiasm in so small a house".[64] The Shakespearean productions drew out only those members of the intellectual elite who appreciated and understood the bard, but had no general appeal, for Shakespeare was no longer in fashion. In fashion instead were the increasingly realistic spectacular works, some of which Nannary and McDowell had introduced to Saint John's theatre-goers in 1874 and for which they had been hungry ever since.

Still, if it was not a popular one, Miss Pomeroy's performance of *Romeo and Juliet* on June 19, 1877, was at least an historic one, for it was the last in the five-year-old Academy of Music. On the 20th, when *As You Like It* was scheduled for repetition at the Academy and Madame Rentz' Minstrels were to make their second appearance at the Lyceum, much of Saint John was consumed by fire in the worst disaster of the city's history. The Academy of Music was nearly levelled, its side walls having had no support except wooden beams. The actors and actresses lost most of their wardrobes either in the fire or to thieves, and all the scenery and properties were destroyed. Gone too were the Dramatic Lyceum and Small's Hall. Two days later the *Saint John News* painted the grim picture of desolation but ended, like a Shakespearean tragedy, on a note of hope and determination:

> We do not despair of St. John because two-thirds of her surface has been burned over. St. John is more than lumber. . . . St. John is a growing city, a city that exists not because it has been built but because it has work to do, a mission to fulfill, a destiny to achieve, and it will increase in wealth and population in spite of the scourging it has received.

The Great Fire at St. John, N.B., June 20, 1877. Currier & Ives, 1877. Public Archives of Canada.

V
After the Fire: the Mechanics' Institute

After the Great Fire of June 1877, the resident stock company virtually disappeared from Saint John, and theatrical productions were, to the end of the century, furnished mostly by travelling professional companies or local amateur companies. The fire was not in itself the cause of the transition; it simply came at the time when touring companies were coming into their own. Rather than staying in one location for an entire season, mastering an extensive repertoire, and importing stars, companies began instead to move the scenery and properties of one play or a limited repertoire from place to place, varying the length of their stay in any one location according to the size of the population and the number of plays they were prepared to offer in rotation. The transition was occurring all over North America. Until 1870 most plays were produced by resident stock companies, of which Lanergan's company at the Dramatic Lyceum was Saint John's best example. In 1870 fifty permanent companies were playing in cities across the United States, but by 1878 the number had dropped to twenty, by 1880 to eight, and by 1887 to only four.

In 1918 Ida Van Cortland, who was juvenile lady and then leading lady with William Nannary's company in the 1870's, reminisced about what it had been like to be part of stock:

A stock company was a complete company of actors resident at a theatre, and playing there night after night throughout the season. They had their regular repertoire, built and painted their own scenery, constructed their own properties; lighting and mechanical effects were conceived within their own staff. . . . and every actor was expected to have the part corresponding to his line of business at his tongue's end in most of the standard pieces . . . for actors were seldom chosen to suit

131

the part, but had to adapt themselves to it, and were expected to present a creditable performance in tragedy, comedy, or broad farce at a moment's notice.[1]

Into these associations of players came, increasingly as the nineteenth century progressed, a succession of visiting stars, support of whom tested the versatility of the resident actors to the utmost. In time these stars, whom the public demanded, contributed in large measure to the decline in quality of the very stock system that supported them. They seldom arrived in time for adequate rehearsals, expecting the local company simply to dispose itself around them; their enormous salary demands depleted the manager's profits, forcing him to cut expenses in other areas and yet leaving him trapped, for the public insisted on novelties. When to these problems were added in the 1870's vast improvements in the railway system that made feasible transportation of both personnel and scenery, the days of the resident stock company were numbered. Some stars had already been taking one or two key actors with them rather than relying altogether on the readiness of the local company, and from this practice it was but a step to the formation and rehearsal of a whole company in a central place, usually New York, in preparation for a tour of the country. By the season of 1876 and 1877, as the number of resident stock companies shrank rapidly, there were nearly 100 travelling or combination companies on the road, in 1886 there were 282, and by 1900 the number had increased to 392. With the change, the old actor-manager who had chosen the plays, hired the actors and directed rehearsals, and who had often, like Lanergan, even owned the theatre, disappeared. In his place came managers who were merely landlords of theatres, required to book touring entertainments into their facilities through increasingly tightly controlled theatrical syndicates in New York.

It was fortunate for the cultural life of Saint John at this time that the Mechanics' Institute, whose directors had at one time discouraged theatrical entertainments within its walls, was not destroyed in the Great Fire. The longest lasting social and cultural centre in the city, it had been opened on December 9, 1840, and would finish out its life as a movie house called the Nickel before fire destroyed it in 1914. In 1877 it was in financial difficulty, and its directors readily welcomed the increased rentals which in the nine months after the Fire reduced the debt by $389.09.[2]

In 1840, apart from a lecture hall on the second storey, the three storey Mechanics' Institute had room for a museum and a day school on the ground floor, as well as one other large as yet undesignated space, and four large rooms on the top floor, of which one was to be the library. The lecture hall, reached by a double stair-way, was 55 feet square with a 23 foot ceiling. Banners of various trades hung on its walls, and seats arranged in an amphitheatre style could provide accommodation for approximately 800 persons.[3] In 1856 the lecture hall was enlarged to 95 by 60 feet at a cost of nearly £1000. Architect John J. Munroe raised the platform, enlarged the doors, and built another entrance so that the room could be emptied in ten minutes. Two stoves were put in place about midway down the hall on either side to provide heat, and attempts were made to improve the ventilation. The old seats remained as they were, in a semi-circular form upon an inclined plane in the front and along the sides, while additional seats were added behind them on the level floor. They were still hard, unpadded benches, but with arm rails added in order to prevent (unsuccessfully as it turned out) persons from taking up more room than they were entitled to. A gallery of benches above tended to be "the resort of ill-mannerly persons and such as may happen to be under the influence of liquor".[4]

It is hardly surprising that once the lecture hall in the Institute became Saint John's major cultural facility, another renovation was deemed necessary. In May 1881 the directors announced "the Re-o-pening of this Popular Place of Amusement, which has been thoroughly re-modelled, decorated and furnished, and is now one of the most pleasant and comfortable halls in Canada".[5] The remodelling included taking out benches and installing opera chairs, except in the gallery which, though it was lengthened, still kept its benches. The seats were better arranged on the lower floor, and the capacity increased slightly. Partitions up to the ceiling divided the gallery from the balconies, which ran the entire length of the two side walls and were entered by separate stairways on each side of the building. There was accommodation in the hall for approximately 900 patrons,[6] many of whom thought the greatest improvement of the renovations was in the new grand staircase: "Every citizen of Saint John knows how difficult it was to get into the hall. By the new arrangement the long tedious waiting and the jostling of the crowd one against the other in the narrow aisles will be avoided. . . . The old landing has been torn away and in its place a new staircase nine feet wide and having a straight run from the hall to the street has been erected. . . . A portico has been built out nearly to the line of the street, giving protection to patrons in case of rain".[7] In addition, the Institute's windows now had shutters, and two outside doors entered onto the stage so that the hall could be run independently of other parts of the building. Unfortunately, the 33 by 54 foot stage itself was not improved. The removal of the rickety cot-

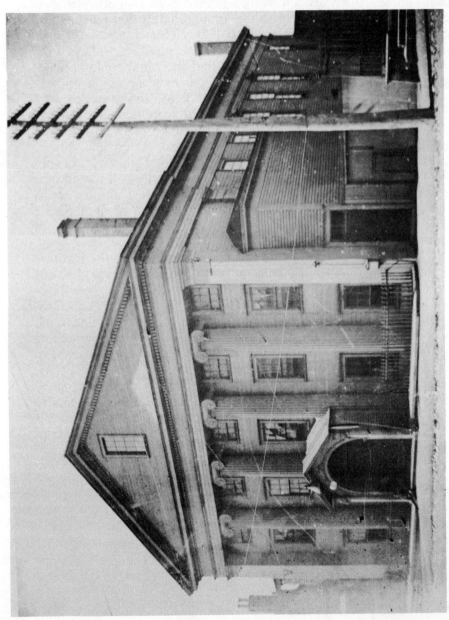

Mechanics' Institute (New Brunswick Museum)

ton proscenium screens and the building of a strong partition which could divide the stage from the auditorium did nothing to aid the performers, nor, appreciably, did the two new scenes designed by William Gill for the opening.

Six years later, in 1887, further attempt was made to provide for the comfort of the audience when the directors installed a new furnace. Since the two stoves installed in the 1856 enlargement had never been adequate, the building was at times "as cold as a barn, and the ladies were obliged to gather their shawls and wraps about them as if in the street".[8] The latest endeavour to regulate temperature cannot have been successful either, and was simply indicative of the impossibility of rendering satisfactory a building that had not been constructed with its present purposes in mind. A comment in *Progress* on June 30, 1888, expresses the general feeling of dissatisfaction: "I never went to the Institute yet in the winter season but I caught a cold. The place is full of draughts and a delicate lady cannot with safety to herself attend a performance held there. . . . Look at the walls, the ceilings! Black with the dust of decades! The stage is small and cramped, and the seats uncomfortable".

In addition to the Mechanics' Institute, a number of other halls in the city were pressed into service as theatres when required. Berryman's Hall was temporarily renamed the "New Academy of Music" and opened on March 19, 1881, by Lindley's Comedy Company for a very short season of drama before it reverted to its previous name and became once more a hall used for amateur performances and variety shows. The Victoria Rink on City Road (also known as the Exhibition Building) was used occasionally for elaborate productions, and in 1888 the Lansdowne Rink on Charlotte Street became a theatre. The most frequently used alternate theatre, however, was Dockrill's Hall on Union Street, renovated in June 1878 by the expansion of the stage to 20 by 22 feet, by improvements to the lighting of the stage, and by the provision of seating for 750 persons. Unfortunately, the building was damaged by fire in September, but it was refitted, used for a time as a roller skating rink, and then renamed in turn the Bijou Opera House, the Royal Museum, and the Royal Dime Museum to house variety shows. The Mechanics' Institute, inadequate as it was, was the best Saint John could offer to the numerous companies that included the city in their eastern tours.

It was in the Mechanics' Institute that Kit Carson Jr. and his company, the first entertainers to visit Saint John after the Great Fire, received a warm welcome in August 1877. As the *Daily News* explained in announcing him: "As everybody has been feeling pretty blue since the fire and few have either found time or oppor-

135

tunity to enjoy a laugh, the arrival of this company will be hailed with considerable delight".[9] People were in need of a laugh. The city presented a bleak appearance. A wilderness of chimneys and fragments of walls still stood forlornly where densely packed houses and bustling businesses had once been. Even the paths of King Square were filled with the temporary shanties that had been erected to enable business to continue. Architects had designed brick buildings, without the "frivolous" but stylish ornamentation of earlier ones, to restore Prince William Street, Market Square, and a portion of King Street to their former splendour, and many persons were engaged in what the *New Dominion* termed the dangerous madness of erecting more wooden buildings. The paper felt a responsibility to encourage amusements for the men "who are laboring here in such large numbers upon our new buildings".[10] Human nature, it pointed out, craves relaxation, "and the greater and more constant the strain put upon our energies while we must work, the more ready and eager are we to seek relief and refreshment in some kind of mere amusement".[11] For this kind of escapism, Kit Carson's border drama *The Wild Hunter*, stocked with such unintellectual treats as shooting a potato from the head, a pipe from the mouth, and snuffing a candle, proved ideal.

Despite the serious economic situation in the city consequent on the fire, which took place at the height of a business recession, and the lack of suitable facilities for theatre, dramatic entertainment was, in August 1877, commencing an active and satisfying year. John Murray and Grace Cartland arrived on August 27 with their Metropolitan Company and performed old staples like *Rip Van Winkle*, *Ticket-of-Leave Man* and *Fanchon the Cricket* nightly until September 22; they were then joined for a further two weeks by McEvoy's New Hibernica and Healy's Irish Comedy Company. For the first of the Irish plays every seat was occupied long before curtain time, and people overflowed into the aisles "until packed as closely as sardines in a box. The doors had to be shut to keep people out, fully five hundred persons being turned away".[12] These companies were followed in October by principal members of the Anna Granger Dow Opera Company who had just created "a regular *furore* of admiration in Halifax",[13] in November by the Boston English Opera Company in performances of *Martha*, *Bohemian Girl*, *Doctor of Alcantara*, and *Rose of Castile*, and at Christmas time by a week of the Boston Minstrels.

Only a handful of entertainments was available during the winter months, but whatever disappointment the winter may have brought was more than compensated for by two weeks of grand opera in late April and early May 1878. This was the event through which the Irish Friendly Society hoped to recoup the loss of its building and library in the Great Fire and for which it had appointed William Nannary manager of a lottery scheme similar to the one which had saved the Academy of Music from the auctioneer's block. Eight thousand tickets at $5 and eleven at $50 entitled their holders to a chance at cash gifts totalling $16,000, and as the deadline drew near, the rush for tickets was so overwhelming that Mr. Nannary was obliged to keep his office open in the evening to accommodate it. Artistically, as well as financially, the feast brought by William T. Carleton's English Opera Company, starring Marie Stone and Adelaide Randall, was highly satisfactory, if one can judge from the excellent reviews of *Martha, Il Travatore, Faust*, and other operas.

No sooner was Carleton finished than the always popular E. A. McDowell and his Boston Comedy Company, with a "complete Corps de Ballet and Orchestra from the principal Theatres of Boston", commenced a four week season of "drama, comedy, burlesque, ballet and spectacle" designed to appeal to all tastes. As the *Morning Freeman* observed on May 4, "We have had our season of opera, and now are to be treated to a series of dramatic performances. . . . All the latest stage novelties will be produced during the season". McDowell introduced to Saint John the "reigning sensation" *Pink Dominoes* (1877), which pleased its audience exceedingly well though it belonged to a class of play that the *Morning Freeman* hoped would never be very popular in the city. He advertised the first Canadian production of *A Celebrated Case*, an emotional drama by the authors of *Two Orphans*, which was then in its sixth month at Union Square Theatre, New York. People had to be turned away from his new version of *Uncle Tom's Cabin*, one strong attraction of which was music provided by the Jubilee Singers, a group of fifty singers from the local black community under the direction of Professor Washington. The "Grand Romantic, Operatic, Spectacular Drama" *The Naiad Queen* was produced in "brilliant style" with "New Magnificent Scenery, Gorgeous Costumes and Armours, New Mechanical Effects, Songs, Ballets, Character Dances and Specialities . . . making the most magnificent spectacle ever presented in St. John".[14] These, with the society drama *Divorce*, Irish drama *Eileen Ogue* and *The Shaugraun*, the "fairy extravaganza" *Beauty and the Beast*, and the old (but new to Saint John) spectacular play *Angel of Midnight* made a season to attract and keep attention.

Since the Irish Friendly Society opera series, William Nannary had been acting as manager of the Mechanics' Institute. Following his return from his own first tour as far west as Montreal and Otta-

Shanties on King Square c.1877 (New Brunswick Museum)

King Street, c. 1879 (New Brunswick Museum)

wa, and even before McDowell left for the Halifax Academy of Music at the beginning of June, he had made arrangements to bring the May Howard Company which had been in Halifax since late April. For two weeks in June, May Howard featured guest star George Fawcett Rowe, a British actor and the author of a hundred plays, in his own comedies and in impersonations of Dickens' character Micawber. A two week gap was then all there was between the departure of May Howard and the arrival of Charlotte Thompson in the newly renovated Dockrill's Hall. An emotional actress born in Yorkshire, England, in 1843, Miss Thompson had brought the South to her feet with her stirring performance of plays like *East Lynne* and had made many starring tours across the United States as Jane Eyre. In private life she was the wife of her business agent, Major Loraine Rogers, and the devoted mother of an unappreciative son. The quality of the marriage was such that those who knew the couple marvelled, but the separation of the family necessitated by a life of touring pulled on the mother's heart strings so that it was not unusual for her women friends to find her sobbing on her dressing-room table with a letter from her son in hand.[15] In Saint John, far removed from her Alabama home, she performed for a month the plays in which she had made her reputation — *East Lynne, Jane Eyre, Camille, Miss Multon, Sea of Ice*, and, not so much in character, *Romeo and Juliet* — interrupting the pattern only for three days in Fredericton during which C. H. (Funny) Clarke marked his first visit to Saint John in six years by a production of *Uncle Tom's Cabin* at Dockrill's. During the same period, the Hess Opera Company held forth at the Institute, followed by McDowell, this time with Neil Warner as his leading man, in a repertoire of Shakespearean and other verse drama.

The August 5-15 engagement of the Lingard Comedy Company came next, and then the city would have a wait of two months before J. W. Lanergan brought a company of new faces from Boston to do his old standbys, including *Still Waters Run Deep, Othello*, and *The Octoroon*. The Lingards were advertised as the only dramatic organization that had played nine consecutive years in New York. Their strength lay in the husband/wife team of William Horace and Alice Dunning Lingard and his sister Dickie Lingard. His career had begun in the English music hall; his wife, a woman of extraordinary beauty, played first in burlesque and later grew into emotional roles; his effervescent younger sister captured hearts with her vivacity. The company's forte, of course, was comedy, and in one of its specialties, "Lingard Sketches", Mr. Lingard presented impersonations of public personalities such as the Prince of Wales, the Czar of Russia, and the Sultan of Turkey. The touring pattern was becoming firmly established in these days; Charlotte Thompson went on to Halifax for nearly two weeks and Lanergan for one, while the Lingards were returning to the United States after stops in Prince Edward Island, Halifax, and Moncton.

During 1879 the Mechanics' Institute was without a manager, for no one replaced William Nannary when he went to Halifax in January. In complete contrast to the busy months following the Great Fire, the managerless months were exceedingly slack. After one performance of *Il Travatore* in December 1878, there was no professional dramatic event of any significance until late April, when the Boston Pinafore Company arrived to give the first Saint John performances of the operetta which became the most popular work of the decade. In the rest of the year, a week-long visit in August by Nannary's company from the Halifax Academy of Music, as part of a tour that included Charlottetown, Moncton, Amherst, and Yarmouth, and two days each in November of Grace Egerton and of the Boston Gaiety Opera Company, the latter with more *Pinafore*, comprised all the professional theatre there was, unless one counts scattered popular entertainers like the diminutive General Tom Thumb.

In Halifax and St. John's, Newfoundland, Nannary was learning by experience that the days of the old stock companies were over and that the bulk of the theatre-going public (who at that time included people from most walks of life) demanded novelty and comedy. At first the Haligonians were delighted with him, for his presence meant they did not have to be dependent upon "amateur managers, and snap companies" for entertainment, but, in a difficult summer season, he discovered at the box-office that the citizens of Halifax, like everyone else, wanted sensations rather than legitimate theatre. He then paid the fares of his company to St. John's where, without a comedian, first because his agent had been unable to procure one and then because Harry Lindley reneged on an engagement, he was unable to play a repertoire which might have drawn patrons in greater numbers into the Total Abstinence Hall. For six weeks he lost an average of $200 a week and was thus unable to pay his actors, but he had apparently reached an agreement with them to close the season early, after providing a benefit for each. Directly following the initial benefit, however, ten members of the company refused to play any longer under his management, and Nannary was forced to resign. In a dignified letter to the St. John's *Evening Telegram* announcing his resignation and dated November 15, 1879, he explained the facts of the situation at length, concluding with a defence of his reputation:

140

I have managed successfully for a number of years the largest operatic and dramatic companies ever in Canada. I have paid as high as $4,700 per week in salaries, and have had over 100 people employed in various theatres at one time; but in 10 years, with the exception of last summer, I have had no trouble like the present. I write this letter reluctantly and with no hostile feeling to any one member of the company.[16]

For thirty-seven evening performances and seven matinees in Newfoundland, he had paid Frank Roche $370, C. G. Craig $200, leading lady Ida Van Cortland $192.50, and the others in decreasing amounts according to their position in the company.

Wounded and nearly defeated by his misadventures, Nannary in the spring of 1880 shared management of the Lindley Comedy and Opera Company as it toured, arriving in Saint John on June 14 for a two week stay. Catering to the tastes of the times, the company offered sensational dramas like *Buffalo Bill* and *The Streets of New York*, finding their greatest success with tragedian E. T. Stetson in the four-act drama *Kentuck*, "illustrating life in the blue grass region". In mid-July they were back again briefly as part of another tour that took them on to Charlottetown and then by sea to Chatham. After this Nannary was never again associated with theatre in Saint John, although to 1887 his companies occasionally appeared in other Maritime centres. Finally he removed his family to California to seek his fortune there.

Significant for the promotion and continuance of theatre in Saint John during the 1880's was the formation, in June 1880, of the Micawber Club. An association of gentlemen whose purpose was to bring to Saint John first-class dramatic and musical organizations, the Club was organized on the same principles as a Club in Bangor that had been instrumental in bringing quality performances to that city, and under its sponsorship some of the best known stars of the theatrical world would play in the Mechanics' Institute.

The association's initial project was, however, from one point of view, disappointing. Fred Stinson's Ideal Opera Company of Boston came in July with burlesque extravaganzas: *Babes in the Wood*, *Evangeline*, *Chilparic*, and *The Maid with the Milking Pail*. The reviewers seem to have enjoyed them but, ironically, in light of the Micawber Club's avowed intention to present nothing but first-class art, the company must have been in trouble, for less than a month later manager Stinson was reported to be living in Machias, Maine, under the assumed name of Bragton. An engagement of much more significance was that of Kate Claxton with her own company in late August in performances of *Two Orphans*, *Frou*

Frou, and *The Double Marriage*. The part of Louise in *Two Orphans* had been Miss Claxton's earliest emotional role and the part with which she became identified. In 1877 she purchased the play and all rights of production to it, undertook to supervise her own ventures, and became a star. With her husband Charles A. Stevenson as her chief support, she earned a fortune touring the United States and Canada as Louise (with just a few other roles to extend her repertoire) and in the process managed to find time to give birth to six sons, all of whom predeceased her.[17] She began her visit to the Maritime provinces in Halifax, and performed for two nights in Fredericton before coming to Saint John. Her company, which included in its membership her sister Margaret Cone (Kate's real name was Catherine Cone), was particularly praised by the *Telegraph* because it "was not, as is the usual case, one in which there was a wide range between the leading people and the support".[18] Neither Miss Claxton nor Fred Stinson stayed in Saint John as long as a week; the longest single engagement by any troupe in 1880 was that of Shelby's Constable Hook Company headed by the same John Murray and Grace Cartland who had provided such welcome entertainment shortly after the fire.

Under the Micawber Club's lesseeship of the Mechanics' Institute, a fondness for light opera which was clearly evident in 1880 was well nourished in 1881. The fashion for opera was at its height in these years, for at no other time in the 1880's was there such a concentration. Three opera troupes visited the city in the first half of 1880, of which the week-and-a-half engagement of the Corinne Opera Troupe with *Pinafore*, *Cinderella*, and the operatic burlesque *The Magic Slipper* was the longest. Little Corinne, the star of that troupe, was the adopted daughter of shrewd manageress Mrs. Jennie Kimball who, immediately after the death through illness of her own young actress-daughter named Corinne, had found her new star in a New Orleans concert hall and silently substituted her for her own child;[19] the Saint John *Telegraph* pronounced the seven-year-old youngster a "wonder". Corinne was followed in April by E. A. McDowell, prior to his western tour to Winnipeg with *H. M. S. Parliament; or the Lady Who Loved a Government Clerk*. Fuller's Montreal-written burlesque of *Pinafore* was of particular interest to Saint Johners because one of its characters, Sir Samuel Snifter, the elderly and portly minister of finance to whom Captain Mac. A. would marry his daughter if he could, was "Up from St. John, N. B.".[20] In May the Ninon Duclos Folly Company repeated *Magic Slipper*.

The most frequently sung operas in 1881 (and in the rest of the decade) were *Chimes of Normandy*, *Martha*, *Fatinitza*, *Olivette*,

142

W. H. Lytell as Shylock
(New York Public Library)

CHARLOTTE THOMPSON.

Charlotte Thompson
(New York Public Library)

John T. Raymond as Col. Mulberry Sellers
(New York Public Library)

Giroflé-Girofla and, of course, operas by Gilbert and Sullivan. Manager George Jones of Mrs. H. E. Carter's English Opera Company, which held the stage at the Mechanics' Institute through most of February 1881, following a brief appearance the previous November, had purchased exclusive rights from Gilbert and Sullivan for the first production of *Pirates of Penzance* in New Brunswick and Nova Scotia and had secured Sullivan's original orchestration of the opera together with "the entire wardrobe imported from England by D'Oyly Carte for the production of the piece in New York".[21] The audience on opening night "filled every part of the Institute", and Mrs. Carter was "in fine voice" at the head of the company of thirty-five.[22] Dora Wiley's Boston English Opera Company included *Pirates* and *Pinafore* in their repertoire in May, and in June that company's production of *Billee Taylor* introduced Saint John to yet another "reigning New York sensation". In July children of the Bennett & Moulton Juvenile Opera Company delighted audiences with still another *Pinafore*, and the Holman Opera Company sang burlesque operas. Mrs. Kimball returned with Little Corinne's Merrie Makers in September. After a reorganized Boston English Opera Company, without Dora Wiley, sang Gilbert and Sullivan's *Patience* and Audan's *Mascotte* in February 1882, the sounds of light opera were not heard in the Institute for a year, and apart from three days of grand opera with the Tagliapiatra Grand Italian Opera Company in the fall of 1880 and two performances of *Il Travatore* by the Brignoli Opera Company in October 1882, the great classical operas were entirely absent from the Institute's stage. Gilbert and Sullivan could generally draw, but everything else competed with difficulty against the straight drama.

The much-observed fondness of audiences for novelty and sensation in the theatre was gratified in 1881 by Snyder and Lytell's Fifth Avenue Theatre which came for a short summer season to present "the latest and most successful plays produced in New York during the past season",[23] including *The Banker's Daughter* (Union Square Theatre), *Hazel Kirke* (Madison Square Theatre), and *The Guv'nor* (Wallack's Theatre). Particularly well received was the company's production of *The World*, which the newspaper advertisements described in superlatives as "The Greatest Production of the Nineteenth Century. Produced by Manager Lytell at an expense of fully One Thousand Dollars. The most wonderful Scenic Sensation ever Presented". The reviewer for the *Telegraph* commented on August 2:

> No doubt many care more for the wonderful pictures of the setting than the play. Never, before, has the boundary of any

144

stage in this city been so completely removed from sight as in the raft scene — the artistic triumph of the play. The curtain goes up here to reveal a limitless expanse of rolling waves, that, apparently, stretch for miles and miles. . . . The appearance of the full-rigged, rescuing ship, hull down, upon this waste of angry waters produces a genuine sensation among the spectators.

The scene of the explosion aboard ship which caused flames to burst through the deck was also singled out as especially realistic and effective, as was the elevator down whose pit the villain finally leapt to his death. In a different vein, when the company returned for a few days in October, it introduced excellent houses to Joaquin Miller's poetic drama *The Danites*, about the society formed among the Mormans to avenge the murder of Joseph Smith. As well, Lytell, "his face ever beaming with fun and frolic . . . and with a 'beautiful brogue' and wonderful expressions",[24] amused audiences as Conn in *The Shaughraun*.

W. H. Lytell was one of the century's successful managers, playing at least as late as 1916 when the Minneapolis *Journal* says he was performing comedy sketches in that city.[25] He had tried retirement, but the theatre was too much in his blood and, as the Cleveland *Plain Dealer* of June 8, 1910 notes, he had been lured back. A skilled actor of farce who could nevertheless portray tenderness and pathos, he had come to the theatre in consequence of a broken arm received while working as top man in double bareback riding in a circus. He played at Daly's, Wallack's, and other New York theatres, rating as one of the best actors of various companies, and for fifteen years his name was linked with the role of Passepartout in *Around the World in Eighty Days*; he played it in Saint John in 1883.

In 1882 Lytell fitted out the Victoria Rink/Exhibition Building as a theatre. At the beginning of July he moved from the Institute to the larger building to accommodate scenery for the "Grand Military Drama" *Youth*, written by the authors of *World*. He spent $1500 to renovate the building and paid $400 in royalties, but the 1200 to 1500 persons who witnessed each of the eight performances in a single week more than rewarded him for his outlay. Especially admired were the fight of the Zulus, for which members of the city's black population had been employed, and the departure of the troop ship, which required a detachment of Fusiliers to march on board headed by a band.[26] In the same summer, with what he claimed to be the largest dramatic company ever in Saint John, he introduced Atlantic Canada to *Michael Strogoff*, a five-act drama

Victoria Skating Rink/Exhibition Building (New Brunswick Museum)

Victoria Skating Rink, interior (New Brunswick Museum)

with prologue closely modelled on Jules Verne's book, but found the Mechanics' Institute an unsatisfactory facility in which to stage it. Accordingly, after his return from Halifax at the end of July, he staged it in the Exhibition Building where there was room for all the "mechanical effects, horses, auxiliaries and drum corps necessary",[27] and with the same scenery employed in New York.

That year Lytell was part of a motley collection of visiting entertainers which included celebrities like playwright Oscar Wilde, who lectured twice in October on interior decoration, and Toronto-born Cool Burgess, the highest paid American comedian, author of the popular 'coon' song "Shoo, fly", a clever dancer, and the originator of comic monologue, who performed for two nights in December. Eugenie LeGrand, a pretender to celebrity status, ended the year with uninspired renditions of *Lady of Lyons*, *Camille*, and *New Magdalen*. Though she claimed to have an illustrious French background, the New York *Spirit of the Times* first heard of her as an actress in Australia, then as Camille in Jersey City; next it followed her to Canada with George Fawcett Rowe and eventually pronounced her New York debut in May 1882 a dismal failure. Returning artists included Kate Claxton in August with her 1878 repertoire and the F. S. Chanfraus, favourites from the Dramatic Lyceum days, for three weeks in May/June, immediately following a brief visit of the Mrs. Partington Comedy Company. Mrs. Chanfrau had scope for her emotional talents in a specially adapted version of *East Lynne* and in *Camille*, while Mr. Chanfrau shone in *Sam* and especially as Kit, the Arkansas traveller, the role with which, after Mose, he had become identified, and which he had already played over 3000 times. The couple would pay one more visit to Saint John, in 1883, before Mr. Chanfrau died suddenly over dinner the next year, leaving his widow $300,000 as a result of the popularity of his characters Mose and Kit.

After a two year absence from Saint John, McDowell's Star Company began a week's engagement on New Year's Day, 1883, with standard pieces, including *Our Boys*, *Rosedale*, *Pygmalion and Galatea* and, for the first time in Saint John, *Diplomacy*, adapted from Sardou. They were followed at the end of the month by C. H. Smith's Furnished Rooms Company. A week of mostly Gilbert and Sullivan by the Egleston English Opera Company in February started with large audiences and ended with small ones, and at the last brought the verdict that the company was "unable to the task" of Von Suppe's *Boccaccio*.[28] Said the *Sun* of February 12: "The less said about the performance the better. Every member of the audience went away in a state of perfect bewilderment, as to what was supposed to be the end of the plot, the piece being most clumsily cut short in the second act". March was devoid of professional entertainment, but mid-April brought W. S. Harkins' newly formed New York Windsor Theatre Company for a week. Though the visit of this company was made difficult by the death of Harkins' wife Leonora Bigelow just over a week before and by his own illness, the productions of the "romantic spectacular" *Passion's Slave*, for which Harkins enlisted the help of the local Jubilee Singers, and of *A Russian Romance*, in which the 62nd Fusiliers' Band assisted, were well received. Less so were the productions of *Olivette*, *Billee Taylor*, and *Patience* by Rennie's Bijou Opera Company that followed immediately and prompted a warning in the press: "Unless good companies are better supported here than this has been, St. John will get a bad name in the theatrical world, and deservedly have to be content with second rate performances".[26]

By far the most exciting event of 1883 was the two-day visit in June of the celebrated 'Jersey Lily', actress Lily Langtry, society belle and 'friend' of the Prince of Wales.[30] In preparation for her June 5 arrival, the Institute had made arrangements for special trains from Moncton, and city merchants advertised Langtry "frizzies", waves, and hairpins, and a special ice cream made from the milk of Jersey cows. Despite the fact that ticket prices had been set exorbitantly high at $2.00, $1.50, and $1.00 (normally .75, .50, and .25 or less), the populace displayed its eagerness to see the famous actress-beauty for themselves by packing the hall for her opening performance as Hester in *An Unequal Match*, so that the amount taken in tickets was the largest ever known in Saint John for a single performance. At that point, half the seats for the next evening's production of *She Stoops to Conquer*, in which Mrs. Langtry played Kate Hardcastle, were already sold. The Wednesday matinee of *Pygmalion and Galatea* was less well patronized. The critics, fearful of reports of amateurish acting that had reached them from England, were agreeably surprised; they found her acting easy and graceful, showing promise of success in the "highest spheres", even though her voice lacked power to express deep emotion.[31] Her beauty, as always, worked its magic. The Lily triumphed in Saint John as elsewhere, surviving a last minute strike for higher wages by ushers of the Institute. She left as she had come, by rail, in her specially-fitted coach, and travelled to Halifax by way of Moncton to complete her North American tour with two days in the Academy of Music. It might have been expected that Herne's Hearts of Oak Company, which occupied the Institute the very next day, would have palled by comparison, but this was not the case; company member 'Funny' Clarke could always bring down the house.

Two weeks of Lytell's Dramatic Combination at the end of

June and again at the end of July, with a week of W. J. D. Leavitt's Standard English Opera Company in between, made for a reasonably rich early summer season, though August was entirely empty. As before, Lytell specialized in spectacular effects such as a rain storm using real water in *The White Slave*, and elaborate scenery like that painted by Mr. Neville from the Union Square Theatre to illuminate "The Great London Bridge Scene; St. John's Park", and "Blackfriars by Night" for *The Lights o'London*. Two particularly appreciated pieces this time were *Esmeralda*, whose leading male role was taken by the actor who had created it at the Madison Square Theatre, and *The St. John Fireman* (properly *The New York Fireman*), a benefit for the Fireman's Relief Association, which the firemen attended in uniform.

Young actors Albert Tavernier[32] and Ida Van Cortland, who came to Saint John with their own New York Comedy Company for a total of three weeks in September and October 1883, are, with W. S. Harkins whose New York Windsor Theatre Company had played in the Institute in April, examples of the changes taking place with the disappearance of the resident stock companies. Miss Van Cortland and Harkins had both been with Mrs. Morrison's Stock Company in Ontario. She probably met Tavernier when both played under William Nannary's management in the fall of 1879, and both left the company in Newfoundland during the dissension over salaries. They were together again in the spring of 1880 when Nannary and Lindley joined forces, and married that summer in New York. As juvenile lady of the Halifax Academy of Music Company in 1879, Miss Van Cortland was more popular with the public than leading lady Phosa McAllister. Said the *Halifax Recorder*, "Miss Van Cortland is the favorite lady of the company. Her voice, accent and delivery are faultless, and she withal seems to be intelligent. . . . She is young, handsome, and invariably succeeds in whatever character she undertakes".[33] Her talent was evident, and the experience with Nannary, she said many years later, had given her the confidence, in 1882, to form with her husband a company of which he was manager and she was leading lady. It was the only alternative the young couple could see if they were to perform a variety of the kinds of plays they liked and if they were to succeed professionally in an age when the one-play company had come to stay and when the run of *Pinafore* had glutted the stage with amateurs.[34] In 1883 they came to Saint John through Maine from Boston, continued on to Halifax and then retraced their steps. Miss Van Cortland was "attractive and bright" as Lillian Westbrook in *The Banker's Daughter* and drew tears as Billy Piper in *The Danites*.[35] The company's repertoire (which generally included twelve to fifteen

149

scripts a season, enough to change bills nightly during a two week stop) ranged from these to the romance of *Two Nights in Rome*, to the gimmickry of the live donkey used on stage in *Arabian Nights*, to the satisfying familiarity of *Camille, Ticket-of-Leave Man*, and *Under the Gaslight*. The next year the Taverniers had only four days in April to spend in Saint John, during which they introduced the American comedy *The Mighty Dollar* and then moved on to Chatham, Newcastle, Moncton, Sackville, Amherst, Halifax, and Charlottetown. After that they neglected the east in favour of Ontario and the United States.

W. S. Harkins followed much the same route of decision. He had toured with Louise Pomeroy in 1877 and played under Nannary's management then and in 1878 and 1879, and in 1881 he had been in Saint John with Lytell. Dissatisfied with membership in the companies available to him, he formed his own company in 1883. In 1884 he shared management with William Morris and William A. Whitecar, who had been with Lytell in 1883. Together they produced plays new to Saint John — *Confusion*, the "funniest play now on the stage", *Partners for Life*, and the drama *Moths* — in a style that caused the critics to comment on the high quality of the management, stage setting, and acting. In an interview with the *Telegraph* printed on May 31, Harkins made comments concerning his choice of repertoire which are revealing of the tastes and attitudes of the Saint John populace: "I have avoided getting anything thoroughly American and have tried to secure only English successes, believing that the taste of the people of the provinces would be better satisfied by plays which met with the approval of the English public than with those that are essentially American". When Harkins came to Saint John next, in late June 1886, he was with the King Hedley Company. In the next decade his own firmly established company would be a familiar favourite in Saint John.

Until the arrival of Harkins, Morris, and Whitecar in June 1884, there had been no more than a dozen days of theatre in the Institute since Frank Mayo played Davy Crockett at the end of the previous October. The anticipated season of English-born actress Katherine Rogers in March, following her tour of Halifax, Moncton, Fredericton, and Houlton, Maine, had been aborted after the second performance. Patrons arriving for the play on the third night found the doors locked, the result of a quarrel over financial arrangements among Miss Rogers, her manager Mr. Parker, leading man William Burroughs, and the managers of the Mechanics' Institute. No company that year stayed longer than four consecutive days, except for the Lytell Fifth Avenue Company's two one-week periods in August. Catering to the taste for the spectacular again,

150

Albert Tavernier in Two
Nights in Rome
(Theatre Department,
Metropolitan Toronto Library

*Ida van Cortland as Billy
Piper* (Theatre Department,
Metropolican Toronto Library)

151

Lytell treated the Saint John public to five performances of "the new realistic spectacular melo-drama" *The Silver King*, "By kind permission of Mr. Harry Miner of the People's Theatre, New York", and with "spectacular scenery painted by Mr. Wm. Gill".[36] On this occasion too, there was an instance of company rivalry, for Lytell decided to produce *Uncle Tom's Cabin* at the end of his season, surely knowing that C. E. Marshall's New York Mastoden Dramatic Company was booked to perform it the whole of the week following. Lytell played to full houses, and Marshall, left with small ones, closed his production after three nights. Nothing is known about either Lytell's or Marshall's production, but productions of *Uncle Tom's Cabin*, of which these were the latest in a series, were in general becoming increasingly complicated and dangerous. Companies were now usually double, with two Topsys and two lawyer Marks, and as realistic as possible. In 1881 C. H. Smith's Mammoth Double Uncle Tom's Cabin Company had demonstrated the hazards of using trained bloodhounds in the thrilling pursuit of Eliza when two men stationed in the wings to catch the animals were bitten by them, one in the hand and the other more seriously.[37]

By far the greatest praise of 1884 was that heaped on sixteen members of the Boston Museum Company, one of America's leading companies, who played Sheridan's *The Rivals*, Gilbert's *Sweethearts*, Boucicault's *London Assurance*, and Conquest's *Angel of Midnight* on four evenings in November. Casting aspersions by implication on all other visiting companies, the *Telegraph* called the company "an oasis in the desert of ordinary dramatic companies" and hailed its advent as the beginning of a "new era in dramatic events for St. John". Patrons packed the balconies and galleries of the Mechanics' Institute to witness acting whose quality, allegedly, had "rarely, if ever" been seen before. They did not pay the same tribute to the Boston English Opera Company later the same month, nor had they to John Murray's Constable Hook Company or William Stafford and Evelyn Foster's Shakespearean productions in September.

James West Lanergan, Saint John's best known representative of the old school of actor-managers, brought a company to the city for the last time in 1884. The years since the closing of the Dramatic Lyceum had not been good to him. Failing health deprived him of the vigour he once enjoyed, yet he had not given up initiating new enterprises. In 1881 and 1882 he conducted long seasons in a new theatre in Lawrence, Massachusetts, but the strain of this prevented him from undertaking seasons in Saint John, so he only visited friends on holiday, as he did nearly every year. In February 1883 he announced plans to erect an inexpensive new Academy of Music on a 100 foot square lot he had secured between Charlotte and Germain Streets, but the project is not heard of again. His very brief season from June 30 to July 5, 1884, was a reminiscence of the old days. Supported by his wife, H. R. Lampee of the old Lyceum company, and emotional actress Edith Stanmore from his Massachusetts company, he performed once more *Still Waters Run Deep*, *Don Caesar*, *Lady of Lyons*, and *Therese*, then crossed the Bay of Fundy to Yarmouth. Two years later he died in his home in Boston, leaving his widow in such a precarious situation that friends in Boston and Saint John thought it necessary to raise a fund on her behalf.

The Irving Club, rather than the Micawber Club, was lessee of the Mechanics' Institute in 1885, an extremely poor year for theatre. In mid-April Joseph Proctor's three days of *Richelieu*, *Virginius*, and *Damon and Pythias*, plays which belonged to the early 1860's when he had last played in Saint John, were indifferently received. Late in the same month McDowell arrived with the "great New York and London Laughing Success", *The Private Secretary*, for which he was said to have paid an exorbitant price to produce in Canada, but he remained only three days before going to Fredericton and Moncton, never returning to Saint John as he had intended. In late May comedian John T. Raymond, the only real celebrity of the year, brought his own company to support him as General Josiah Limber in the satire on American politics *For Congress*, as Major Bob Belter in *In Paradise*, and especially as Colonel Mulberry Sellers in the adaptation by that name from Mark Twain. It was as Colonel Sellers that Raymond had burst forth into stardom and prompted some to rank him as one of America's most distinguished actors, with Forrest, Booth, Hackett, Jefferson, E. L. Davenport, Wallack, and others. So profitable was the play that Twain "employed a representative to travel with Raymond, to assist in the management and in the division of spoils".[38] It attracted "fine houses" in Saint John but caused no real excitement. W. H. Lytell's company, now called simply "Comedy Company", came for the last time, and for only three days, at the end of June. July and August, for the first time since the fire, were silent. English actor William Redmond and American Mrs. Thomas Barry pleased "large" audiences for two days in September, as did Irish comedian and vocalist J. S. Murphy and Miss Ida Burrows. Atkinson's Comedy Company provided a brief spurt of interest in October with *Peck's Bad Boy* and *The Electric Shock*, comedies admittedly without plot whose sole purpose was to make people laugh. Price Webber attracted good houses to three days of performances by his Boston Comedy Company in November (a day more than he had given the year before). After tours as agent for Flora Myers, Marietta Ravel, and John Murray, Webber had been called to management of the Boston Comedy Company on the death of its manager E. M. Leslie. The rather old-fashioned repertoire of *Hidden Hand*, *Gipsy Queen*, *Kathleen Mavourneen*, and *Under the Gaslight*, featuring Webber's wife Edwina Grey, somehow pleased, despite an assessment that the company made no pretence to histrionic ability but put its plays on in an "agreeable manner". It was left to the Wilbur Comic Opera Company of New York to finish out the year with a week of *Mikado* and other popular operas early in December.

The Micawber Club was again lessee of the Mechanics' Institute in 1886. That year performances began in February, and there was something each month after that, with the greatest amount of activity in August and October. It was a year of colourful personalities, beginning and ending with preacher-turned-actor George Miln. A powerful orator as a preacher, who in 1882 had been offered a salary of $10,000 a year if he would retain his ministerial charge, he carried over into the theatre his rhetorical skills. As large crowds had come to hear his pulpit oratory, so they flocked to hear him declaim from the stage. Taking Edwin Booth's advice that he should pursue the great Shakespearean roles in his new career, he adopted Hamlet as his first part, a suitable choice for, in the words of one of his agents: "His face is such as any idealist would place upon Hamlet's shoulders. Pale, thoughtful, dreamy, lapsing into romantic preoccupation, and again lit up into wonderful animation by a pair of the most expressive eyes".[39] He travelled widely in Canada and the United States and then, near the end of the 1880's went to Australia, England, India, China, and Japan where he was the first actor to give a complete representation of a Shakespeare play. In February 1886 he came to Saint John from Halifax where, in a reversal of the usual pulpit denunciation of the theatre, the rector of the Church of the Redeemer had preached a sermon on the theatre's potency for good. Although his performances in the Institute were "a revelation to lovers of the legitimate, who have had . . . an awakening when hardly expected",[40] his engagement was financially unrewarding because he had to cancel two performances when snowbound in Fredericton. The *Telegraph* and the *Sun* disputed whether he was superior as Bertuccio in *The Fool's Revenge* or as Cardinal Richelieu. His Othello, the role some said was his strongest, was "a painstaking interpretation". His Hamlet, the *Sun* thought, made more noise than the Hamlet Shakespeare had in mind, but his Richard III "was taken in a manner never before seen in this city"; in it Miln's powerful voice was used to advantage and

154

he did not, as so many actors did, overdo "the deformity business".[41]

Very different was Lilly Clay whose all female Gaiety Company was the subject of a short-lived scandal in July. "This sylph-like daughter from the Rockies", with her "lightsome, graceful, lovely blue eyes, long golden locks hanging down and clustering around her intellectual and shapely head",[42] had won the admiration of thousands of New Yorkers who needed only to hear the rapture in her voice to be enthralled. The same was true in Saint John of the large audience composed entirely of men and boys who gathered to witness her company's *New Adamless Eve*, but the press was not equally enthralled. This guardian of the public ethic found the burlesque catered to "depraved rather than to moral tastes" and was pleased to note that it was banned in Halifax on account of the scanty dress of the women.

Much more elevated in tone, and therefore more popular with the press and with a large "fashionable" audience, was the week-long engagement of Brussels-born Mme. Rhea. One of those ladies whose age is difficult to determine, she had decided to study for the stage while receiving her education at the Ursuline Convent in Paris. Following her first professional appearance in Brussels, she toured in France, and then settled for five years in Russia, where she might have remained had not the assassination of the Czar motivated her to remove to England. She learned her English through the lines of Beatrice in *Much Ado About Nothing* and, one month after her arrival in London, was playing the part at a Gaiety matinee.[43] Discovering that her accent was part of her charm, she was shrewd enough never to learn English better.

Her Saint John engagement illustrates the secrets of her success. She paid careful attention to the elegance and richness of her own costumes; the heavily decorated one for *Frou-Frou* was originally designed for the Queen of Holland. Music for *Pygmalion and Galatea* was specially arranged by Jesse Williams of the Casino in New York, the properties made by Siebbe of Wallack's Theatre, lighting effects and stage mechanism precisely worked out under the direction of Mr. Teal, and the cast chosen for its ability to support Mme. Rhea in excellent style. In addition, the star's ability to establish an instant rapport with an audience was successfully at work from her opening performance in Sardou's *A Dangerous Game*:

> Her stage presence is enchanting: She takes one into her confidence and makes friends at once. Her bright face, her sunny smile, her sparkling eyes seem to bring happiness everywhere,

155

and add to that the graces of her person, her natural magnet-ism, her versatile talent, all combine to make M'lle Rhea the most accomplished actress that St. John ever beheld.[44]

The confidence and the praise lasted for the whole week; in fact, the *Telegraph*, commenting on her engagement after it finished, ob-served: "It requires an artiste of undoubted merit to hold the inter-est of our theatre-goers for a week, and that there has been no di-minution in the size of the audiences speaks well for her".[45] Prices were a little higher than usual at $1.00, .75, .50, and .25, but the pa-per claimed that the box-office receipts for her last matinee, on Sat-urday, August 28, were the largest ever received in the Institute, presumably thus even surpassing Lily Langtry's.

Several other actors came with their own supporting compa-nies during 1886. In April petite and girlish Lizzie Evans, who was nicknamed 'The Electric Battery', did her "celebrated impersona-tion" of Chip the ferrygirl in *Fogg's Ferry*. In October the "Peerless Emotional Actress, and the most famous of Stage Beauties, Pauline Markham (the Magnificent)" was a huge success in several old fa-vourites of the Lyceum era, and immediately afterward Irish come-dian Charles Verner entertained overflowing houses with Irish plays. There were a number of other companies as well. Day's In-ternational Theatre Company announced a three-week run in May of "the Latest London and New York successes" at popular prices of .10, .25, and .35. The critics were "agreeably disappointed" at the excellent productions of *Under the Gaslight*, *The Octoroon*, and *The Banker's Daughter* (hardly the latest successes), after the ad-vertised low prices had made them fearful. Still, the company must have lost money, because they terminated their engagement after ten days. An announcement that the first company ever to visit Saint John from the "celebrated" Madison Square Theatre would arrive in the city by steamer for an August 2 opening sounded rather grand, except that the list of the company, headed by E. A. McDowell and his wife Fanny Reeves, was so familiar. They stayed only three days, long enough to draw loud bursts of laughter with *The Private Secretary* and did not return as announced; instead McDowell came in October with his own Comedy Company. The highlight of that visit was a revival for three nights of the production of *The Geneva Cross* that McDowell had given at the Academy of Music before the Great Fire. William Gill designed the scenery that the *Telegraph* described in its advance publicity on September 29:

The view of the exterior and courtyard of Pierre LeBrunn's gunfactory at Auxerre, in France. This consists of a very hand-some drop in perspective, and set pieces and boxing flats re-

Mme. Rhea
(New York Public Library)

Madame Janauschek
(New York Public Library)

presenting the main entrance of the factory, the porter's lodge, and the lodge gate at the whole estate . . .

an elaborate garden and marquee set, used in the birthday fête scene of the second act. This consists of back perspective and two cut drops . . .

the underground fortifications — a vast range of massive vaults and pillars of solid masonry lighted here and there by a lurid flash. This forms the prison where some of the characters are confined, and the thunder of artillery outside, the explosion of a mine, the falling walls, and the pouring in over the broken fragments of the retiring forces all combine to make this one of the most effective tableaux ever presented.

The year had the usual sprinkling of comic operas. Through the "engaging music and handsome toilets" of *Three Black Crooks*, the forty strong Wilbur Opera Company amply compensated for arriving an hour late at the theatre on August 11. The rest of their repertoire was only indifferently received, however, as was the limited repertoire of the Maritana Opera Company of Boston in November.

In 1887 a severe blow was dealt to theatre in Saint John when new American railway legislation made it expensive for American actors to include the eastern Canadian city in their tours.[46] There were only two extended periods of theatre in the Mechanics' Institute that year, from April 18 to May 14 and from June 30 to August 12, and the rest of the year was spotty, with February, March, September, and November having no professional drama at all. English actress Claire Scott began the period of drama in April, followed after a five day interval by comedian Sol Smith Russell and, after a further two weeks interlude, by opera singer Clara Louise Kellogg and then by Abbey's Double Mammoth Uncle Tom's Cabin Company. Since the advance publicity for Miss Scott had commended her as a first-rate Lucretia Borgia and Mary Stuart, the *Telegraph* was surprised to find that there was in her acting "an inartistic and unnatural straining for effect", that her "manner was sometimes hard and unsympathetic, and she did not always resist the temptation to rant".[47] By the time she left, expecting to return, the paper was sympathetic towards her. Unfortunately, she became seriously ill with diptheria in Charlottetown and, when finally able to travel in August, she simply passed through Saint John enroute to rejoin her company in Eastport, whence she began a tour to Calais, Houlton, Woodstock, Fredericton, Moncton, Chatham, Quebec, Montreal, Toronto, Winnipeg, and San Francisco. Sol Smith Russell made a hit in his new comedy *PA*, enroute to Moncton and Halifax on his penultimate Maritime tour prior to leaving the stage. By the time he came back with *Edgwood Folks* in July for a last farewell, he had already moved his family from Boston to Minneapolis and made arrangements to set himself up in business there. When Clara Kellogg sang scenes from *Il Travatore* and *Faust* in mid-May, the citizens of Saint John considered themselves extraordinarily fortunate to be able to hear one of the leading prima donnas of the day even though, according to Odell's *Annals of the New York Stage*, her star had set a decade ago.[48] The Templeton Opera Company's productions of *Mikado*, *Pinafore*, *Mascotte*, and *Olivette*, which the *Sun* on July 1 termed "an instantaneous success", began the second period of drama. Then Thomas Keene, billed as "America's greatest tragedian", held audiences spellbound with his Hamlet, Richard III, and Iago. The period finished with four days of the Redmond-Barry Company's "exciting" production of *René* and their "amusing" *Cure for the Blues*.

The reduction in the number of entertainers visiting the city in 1887 meant a corresponding reduction in revenue from rentals, which the Institute could ill afford. Throughout the decade, after the Micawber Club had responded to the decision of the 1880 annual meeting to rent the hall on a yearly basis, setting aside only fifteen nights for lectures and annual meetings, the directors had been relying on income received from theatrical entertainments to keep their organization alive, as it had been experiencing serious difficulties for years. Membership had declined from 552 in 1869 to around 300 in the 1870's and had continued to fall steadily through the 1880's. The lecture course, which had once provided a substantial portion of the annual revenue, became instead a drain on the budget during the mid-1870's when the expensive visiting lecturers, whom the directors had hoped would stimulate interest, failed to attract attention, and by 1885 the lecturers had to be volunteers, since there was no money to pay them. During the period other societies and institutions emerged to fulfill functions that formerly had belonged to the Mechanics' Institute; the Saint John Public Library opened its doors in 1883 (the same year as the Natural History Society's incorporation), and churches of various denominations sponsored lecture series. Moreover, increasing interest in athletic societies signalled a change in taste. When to these facts was added an inability to meet their debts in 1887, the directors decided the Institute could no longer continue. Accordingly, the annual meeting on January 17, 1888, authorized them to take the necessary steps to dispose of the property and assets, and an Act of the Legislature passed on April 6 empowered them to sell the property in whole or in part or, failing that, to donate it to any public body or

159

corporation.[49] The building was then put up for sale, first by tender and then by private sale, but as the decade closed, it had not yet found a buyer, and plans were being made to remodel it — despite the fact that public opinion was opposed to the expenditure of more money to prolong the uncertain existence of a structure which was "felt to belong wholly to the past".[50]

So deep was the gloom at the beginning of 1888 that the *Telegraph* predicted darkly on January 13: "It is more than probable that the theatre-goers of St. John have seen the last 'show' that will ever be given in the hall of the Mechanics Institute". Fortunately this was not to be the case, and, in fact, the drama made its presence felt strongly quite early in the year, for from January 24 to February 21 Price Webber's Boston Comedy Company played a season that was a huge success in terms of both critical and popular response. The four-week season was a throw-back to the days of regular double bills, for unless, as in the case of *Under the Gaslight*, the mainpiece was too long, Webber followed it with an afterpiece in which he used his knowledge of the city to devise local hits which brought down the house each time. Press and people warmed to Webber and Edwina Grey, and the tone of the reviews is affectionate. With each performance the size of the audience seemed to increase even if sometimes cold winds, snow, or rain that made the walking dangerous could have their effect. The performances were obviously a bargain at .15, .25, and .35.

There was nothing else, however, until the Gilbert Opera Company in April presented a week of *Mikado*, *Boccaccio*, and *Chimes of Normandy*, which a letter in *Progress* on June 2 said were not nearly so good as the amateur productions Saint John was used to seeing. Tragedian W. A. Whitecar, who had last been in Saint John with Harkins and Morris in 1884, arrived on May 14 for a week, with a company under the direction of George Edeson. Houses were small to start with, even though the press urged encouragement of such a faithful and versatile actor, but increased for his *Othello*, and especially for *Fool's Revenge* on the last night. Definite hits, on the other hand, were *A Night Off* and *Nancy & Co.*, recent successes from Daly's Theatre in New York brought to the Atlantic provinces in early June by twenty-six year old Arthur Rehan, younger brother of Daly's leading lady Ada Rehan. In its strength the Company of Comedians was compared favourably with the Boston Museum Company, and it was appreciated particularly for its evenness, there being no one star round which was grouped a number of inferior satellites. *Progress* enjoyed the King Hedley Company's *Dr. Jekyll and Mr. Hyde* on June 5. Irish comedian and playwright Dan'l Sully drew overflowing houses to two of his own

160

plays, and the Huebner-Holmes Company was satisfactory but not exciting during three days of *Saratoga*, *Baby*, and *Led Astray*. In July the only professional performance was the Ince Comedy Company's *Fun in a Boarding School*, and August saw only two performances of James A. Herne's splendidly mounted *Hearts of Oak*.

What ought to have been the theatrical event of the year was the visit to Saint John in September of "the greatest living actress", Prague-born Mme. Janauschek. As popular off the stage as on, she was made a social lion wherever she went. Then fifty-eight, a woman of imposing presence, with noble features, though not physically beautiful, she was known for her "lustrous dark eyes that smouldered with emotion", her sweeping gestures, and her rich, thrilling voice.[51] On September 10, at the first of four performances at the Mechanics' Institute, the house waited restlessly for her initial appearance in the third act of *Meg Merrilies*, and then "an electric thrill passed through the audience followed by a burst of applause".[52]

Though there was never any question as to the talent of the star, her visit to Saint John was far from a complete success. *Progress* indicated this in a criticism of Saint John it quoted from the Halifax *Mail*: "The receipts of the artiste's *three* nights in St. John just about came up to her *first* night's money in this city. It is so with nearly all high class shows. Halifax almost invariably gives first-class actors a substantial welcome, while it takes an entertainment like *Peck's Bad Boy* to draw a crowd in St. John".[53] Even if there may be some truth below this expression of the traditional rivalry between the two cities, it appears that Saint John may have been more demanding of Mme. Janauschek than the Haligonians were, because a review in *Progress* on September 15 gives an insight into the reasons behind the small attendance at her performances and at the same time shows the besetting weakness of the star system. The reviewer is commenting on the performance of *Macbeth* and praises Mme. Janauschek's Lady Macbeth as "almost diabolical at times in its intensity", never departing from "the ideal of a determinedly wicked woman". The strength of the star, however, contrasted noticeably with the incredibly weak performance given by the rest of the company: "Macbeth and Lady Macbeth had the stage virtually to themselves. Most of those who saw the play had seen it put on the boards in infinitely better shape in St. John theatres". This failure to recruit adequate support was not untypical of Mme. Janauschek's judgment. Lacking in common sense as she grew older, she would tour with weak companies and sometimes even in "the most absolutely impossible dramas by aspiring playwrights with which it was ever the ill fortune of a genius to be associated".[54]

As the fate of the Mechanics' Institute continued to hang in the balance, there were only scattered engagements in 1889. Of these, the lengthiest was the Wood-St. John Company's visit for eight nights in May and nine in December. The company, featuring George M. Wood and Marguerite St. John offered a mixed repertoire including new society plays such as Grove's *As In a Looking Glass*, Pinero's *The Magistrate*, and, on their last night in December, Ibsen's *A Doll's House*, but most popular with the ladies at least was *David Garrick*, for it was their choice as the programme for a Saturday matinee in May. The company had good houses, especially in May, though they drew criticism for not being evenly balanced. The People's Theatre Company was guilty of "some disgusting vulgarisms" in February, and Arthur Rehan's "gilt-edged" Company of Comedians provided three evenings of merriment in early June. Atkinson's Comedy Company drew only fair houses to *Peck's Bad Boy* on July 1 and 2, while Maloney's Irish Comedy Company discovered on August 1 that Irish plays were as popular as ever. There was yet another *Uncle Tom's Cabin* — the Boston Ideal Uncle Tom's Cabin Company advertised in December for fifty coloured people for the Southern scene and, as an incentive to attendance, offered each child at the matinee a Christmas present. Price Webber's Boston Comedy Company from December 23 to 28 helped to make the holiday season festive, initiating a practice which would become part of Saint John's Christmas celebrations for many years.

In the fall of 1888 and during 1889, because of the uncertainty surrounding the Mechanics' Institute, the Micawber Club wisely turned its attention to the development of alternate facilities for theatre. In October 1888 it transformed the Lansdowne Rink into a "commodious theatre" by fitting it with electric lights, raised seats, a new act drop by William Gill, and a stage "thoroughly equipped with handsome and appropriate scenery".[55] The new theatre's first occupants were the thirty-seven member Bennett-Moulton Company with familiar operas such as *Boccaccio*, *The Bohemian Girl*, and *Black Hussar*, followed on November 1 by the Levy Operatic Concert Company in *Martha*.

In June 1889 the Club developed the space further and, in a bold step, engaged E. A. McDowell to head a stock company there for an indefinite season, hiring H. Price Webber as business agent. The company, an exceptionally strong and efficient one, included among its members Fanny Reeves, Julia Arthur, Percy Haswell, Mary Hampton, Violet Campbell, Lee Jarvis, Timothy Frawley,

162

LANSDOWNE
THEATRE!

MICAWBER CLUB, ... LESSEES
E. A. McDOWELL....... ...... MANAGER

WILL OPEN

Monday, June 17th,

WITH A CAREFULLY SELECTED

STOCK COMPANY.

MONDAY, TUESDAY, AND WEDNESDAY, | June 17, 18 & 19,

DAVID BELASCO'S BEAUTIFUL COMEDY DRAMA:

MAY BLOSSOM!

Or, Between Two Loves.

CAST:

Steve Harland, a Young Fisherman..... Mr. George Fawcett
Richard Ashcroft, Boss of the Fishermen. Mr. T. D. Frawley
Tom Blossom, Father of May............ Mr. Ferd. Hight
Uncle Bartlett, the Village Preacher. Mr. Eugene A. McDowell
Owen Hathaway, Fisherman............. Mr. John Bunney
Eph, a Negro Devoted to Richard......... Mr. Ernest Sterner
Capt. Drummond, of the U. S. A........... Mr. Chas. Edson
Hiram Sloan, } Fishermen Friends of Tom | Mr. D. R. Whipple
Hank Bluster, } Blossom. { Mr. Wm. B. Hagan
May Blossom, the Pet of the Fisheries..... Miss Percy Haswell
Deborah, May's Aunt................... Miss Bessie Hunter
Millie, Servant to the Blossoms........... Miss Helen Mowat
Little May,............................ Dot Clarendon
Yank,............................... Georgie Mack
Children, Fishermen, Soldiers, Neighbors, etc.

TIME AND PLACE:—Hampton Village, Virginia, during the War. A lapse of Six Years between Acts III. and IV.

SYNOPSIS OF SCENERY:

ACT I. The home of May Blossom by the sea. Steve's Oath "Poor boy, the girl's broken his heart."

ACT II.—(Two years later), the home of Steve Harland. The presentiment.—The son has given up it's dead." Face to Face. (NO INTERMISSION HERE.)

ACT III.—(Same as act II.) The surprise party. Uncle Bartlett's blessing "It is like tearing out my heart, but I must go."

ACT IV.—(Six years later), Cherry Dell Autumn. Mother and Child "Don't let this false idea of wrong forever come between you." The Children's procession. Steve's return. Burial of the Bird. Little May and her playmates "Tell us a story." "Steve, husband, can you forgive me?"

👉 **NEXT PRODUCTION, Thursday, JUNE 20,**

◀ MOTHS! ▶

In which Miss CARRY JAMIESON and Miss MARY HAMPTON will appear.

Director of Amusements, ... Eugene A. McDowell
Business Management, ... Micawber Club
Stage Manager, ... Ernest Sterner
Leader of Orchestra, ... Morton L. Harrison
Master of Properties, ... Wm. B. Hagan
Master Carpenter, ... Edward James

☞ **OTHER NOVELTIES WILL FOLLOW IN RAPID SUCCESSION.** ☜

General Admission,............. 25 cents.
Reserved Seats,......35 cts. and 50 cts.

☞ Seats may be Secured in Advance at the Bookstore of ALFRED MORRISEY, KING STREET.

TELEGRAPH JOB PRINT

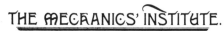

THE MECHANICS' INSTITUTE.

LESSEES AND MANAGERS
MICAWBER CLUB

●—DOMINION DAY, JULY 1ST:—●

THE GREAT

KING HEDLEY Co

—AND—

WILLIAM S. HARKINS

IN DION BOUCICAULT'S GREAT SENSATIONAL DRAMA

AFTER DARK

CAST OF CHARACTERS.

GORDON CHUMLEY (Light Dragoons), WM. S. HARKINS
"OLD TOM,"........................KING HEDLEY
CHANDOS BELLINGHAM,................WM. BEACH
SIR GEORGE MEDHURST,.......... BYRON DOUGLAS
(Under the Assumed Name of Hayward.)
DICEY MORRIS,................... J. H. STUART
(Keeper of a Low Gaming House and Proprietor of the "Elysium" Music Hall.)
POINTER (a Policeman),.............JOSEPH BRENNAN
CRUMPETS,........................E. C. COYLE
AREA JACK (a Night Bird),..................ELSIE GREY
WAITER,............................ W. B. DAILY
ELIZA,.... .... ELEANOR MORETTI
(Once a Barmaid at the "Elysium," now Sir George's Wife.)
ROSE EGERTON,................ LEONORE HARKINS
(An Heiress, Sir George's Cousin.)

SYNOPSIS.

ACT I.—SCENE I—Victoria Station and Grosvenor Hotel. SCENE II.—No. 5½ Little Compton Mews. SCENE III—Silver Hall. SCENE IV.—No.—Rupert Street. SCENE V—Blackfriar's Bridge. The Suicide. OLD TOM TO THE RESCUE!

ACT II.—SCENE I.—Dry Arches under Victoria Bridge. SCENE II—The Lilacs exterior. SCENE III—Garden Gate. SCENE IV.—The Lilacs interior. "WHO THEN IS THIS?" "MY WIFE!"

ACT III.—SCENE I—Elysium Music Hall. Not so Drunk as he looked. "Safer in mine!"

ACT IV.—The Lilacs. "THE GATES OF JUSTICE!"

☞ The Incidental Music to the Drama under the direction of Mr. FRED. LYSTER.

BETWEEN THE ACTS THE

CLUB'S NEW ENLARGED ORCHESTRA

Under the Leadership of Mr. Morton L. Harrison,
WILL PERFORM A CHOICE SELECTION OF NEW MUSIC.

TO-MORROW, THE POWERFUL DRAMA:

IN HIS POWER

MATINEE, SATURDAY, 2.30.

Doors Open at 7.15. Overture at 8. Seats secured in Advance at A. C. SMITH & CO'S.

Ellis, Robertson & Co., Printers, "Globe" Press, St. John, N. B.

(New Brunswick Museum)

163

George Fawcett, Thomas Wise, John Bunny, and Ernest Sterner, several of whom returned to Saint John in the 1890's. If the press reviews may be believed, the venture triumphed with the public. The opening performance, on June 17, of David Belasco's *May Blossom*, saw every seat taken, and from this point on compliments flowed. The second play, H. Hamilton's romantic drama *Moths*, was said to be "admirably cast", each player interpreting his character in such a way as to "completely fill the idea of the dramatist".[56] Of the next, the military comedy *Our Regiment*, the *Telegraph* enthused: "St. John has never seen a finer play. . . . The house was crowded. . . . It is a comedy in every sense of the word, and has not a 'stick' part in it. Every one is good and it is doubtful if a more satisfactory interpretation could be had anywhere than was given by the ten who comprised the cast".[57] Costumes, of the richest and most elaborate description, were singled out as a strong feature of *Two Orphans*. A mail carriage and a pair of horses contributed to the reality of the courier's murder in the Henry Irving version of *The Lyons Mail*, as did the immense body of real water to the lake and cave scenes in *Colleen Bawn*. The success of the latter was so phenomenal that the practice of changing the programme twice weekly was waived. The *Colleen Bawn* ran for seven consecutive nights before overflowing houses excited especially by the scenery and special effects: "The scene where Eily is thrown into the lake, with the plunge by Myles, and where Danny is shot and drops into the same body of water were most thrilling and the spectators fairly lifted the roof with their plaudits".[58] Although the *Sun* unhesitatingly termed this production "the biggest theatrical hit of the season",[59] the *Telegraph* preferred to reserve that title for *School for Scandal*, which celebrated the arrival of Fanny Reeves as leading lady of the final two weeks. The seating capacity of the house was regularly strained. Standing room was at a premium for *School for Scandal* and for the *Shaughaun*, and many had to be turned away from *Colleen Bawn*.

Despite an exuberant audience response, the season could not provide its backers with financial profit. H. Price Webber, as business agent for the Micawber Club, was in the best position to understand the reasons for this:

I stayed five weeks, and I saw very plainly that the admission rates would not furnish enough funds to carry on the enterprise, as the people in the company being exceptionally fine performers and high salaried artists demanded a great deal more patronage than could be looked for, and so I told the gentleman who furnished the money for the company that it was utterly impossible to put it on a paying basis. In fact, I said to him:

"The whole outfit is superb. However, you cannot pay Broadway, New York, salaries with St. John, New Brunswick, receipts."[60]

Here, in a nutshell, is set forth one of the chief obstacles to the presentation of first class artists in Saint John, or indeed any provincial centre, and one of the major reasons for the increasing centralization of the theatre business in the more heavily populated cities.

After Mr. Webber's departure and despite his pessimistic outlook, the season continued a further three and one-half weeks, making a total of eight and one-half weeks. It finished on August 15 with *My Uncle's Will* and *Engaged*, and there would not be another season like it for ten years. By the 16th of August most members of the company were on board the Boston steamer enroute to new engagements with an assortment of American companies. The exception was Fanny Reeves, who was returning to a Winnipeg stock company; her husband had accepted an invitation to tour with Clara Morris.[61]

It would not be appropriate to leave the narrative of the post-fire years without reference to the amateur dramatic societies that were active then. The majority of amateur companies belonged to temperance societies or to church organizations, almost all of which were Roman Catholic. In addition there were secular companies, notably the Carleton Dramatic Company and the Saint John Opera Company. There were also groups of various names gathered by musicians of the city. Professor Washington supplied "Jubilee Singers" for most of the visiting performances of *Uncle Tom's Cabin* and directed various amateur productions as well. Professor Max Sterne gathered amateur groups for light opera, and Signor Ronconi and his pupils put on scenes from *Faust, Norma, Lucia,* and *The Barber of Seville.* Members of the military establishment frequently assisted at professional productions and occasionally offered an evening's entertainment themselves. Perhaps the most interesting instance of Regimental Theatricals was the presentation by the 62nd Fusiliers, in June 1887, of T. W. Robertson's military drama *Ours.* According to the programme, the production offered "Grand Spectacular and Military Effects . . . By the Officers, Non-Commissioned Officers and Men of the Regiment, and a detachment of the Garrison Artillery, with guns".[62] It is easy to see why it was necessary, as the *Telegraph* reported on June 17, for the stage to occupy one-half of the Exhibition Building. In the cast were Captain H. J. A. Godard, and Mrs. Godard, who in 1889 would leave for New York to undertake professional study for the stage. She received especial commendation: "To a graceful charm of manner she added a naturalness that is rarely met on the amateur stage, and throughout was so unaffected as to invest her part with all the attractiveness that seemed capable of being drawn from it".[63]

The most popular scripts for amateurs were *H. M. S. Pinafore* and other Gilbert and Sullivan operas. As early as July 1879, at least eleven amateur and professional performances of *Pinafore* had been given in the city, and the influence of the opera was so profound that the Fife and Drum Band of Portland renamed itself 'The Pinafore' and adopted uniforms similar to those worn on H. M. S. Pinafore. Before long, burlesque operas began to appear. The first was Professor Washington's *His Mud Skow Pinafore* in December 1879, peopled with such characters as "Sir Joseph Sporter, Black Commander of Zulus, First Lord of Mudskow Squadron", "Dick Deadhead, Able C Dog", and "Little Buttertub". Not surprisingly, the *Globe* was able to report on December 10 that the Mechanics' Institute "was too small for the crowd", and the *Daily News* the same day noted that "the appearance of each performer was the signal for loud applause and much laughter". In November of the next year, Washington and his "Colored Juvenile Pinafore Troupe" again put on a burlesque *Pinafore*, but apparently not the same one, for the characters had the usual *Pinafore* names this time. (In 1885, Professor Washington's "Colored Troubadors" performed a burlesque of *Uncle Tom's Cabin* entitled *Uncle Pete's Cabin; or Life on the Old Plantation*.)

Professor Max Sterne's Juvenile Pinafore Company, assisted by the Philharmonic Orchestra, mounted a straightforward version of *Pinafore* in the spring of 1880. In its review on April 3, the *Telegraph* noted that the part of Buttercup was taken by Ethel Mollison, "a little girl only six years old" who "fairly took the house by storm by the excellence of her acting". The result, the paper claimed, "proved that in her St. John has a child who would be quite equal to Little Corinne in this part had she but a little more stage experience". The *Telegraph* was discerning in its judgment, for Ethel Mollison was to acquire considerably more stage experience and become a professional actress in the next decade. In Sterne's *Pinafore* she was one of a company of children who had "never faced an audience before" and whose performance, on that account, had to be styled "simply wonderful".

As other Gilbert and Sullivan operas were popularized by professional companies, these too were performed by amateurs. The Amherst Amateur Company's production of *Patience* in January 1882 received a good review in the *Telegraph*. In June 1886 the

Bangor Opera Company brought *Mikado*. Saint John's own Amateur Opera Company under the direction of E. E. Gubb, organist at Trinity Church, filled the Institute in the same month with *The Sorcerer* and in 1887 with *Pirates of Penzance*, although the latter was judged to have needed more study. Two years after, in early March 1889, the Saint John Amateur Minstrels performed a burlesque of *Pirates*, entitled *Pirates of the Bay of Fundy*, "a new and original burlesque" by Saint John author H. G. Mills. Pronounced "quite laughable . . . with local hits aimed at the police", it was nonetheless disappointing, for patrons "had been led by the title to believe that the action would take place on board the steamer *Dorcas*, and it was hoped that the *finale* would represent her descending to the infernal regions, having been scuttled by the bugs. Still, it was a good show".[64]

More of the plays performed by amateurs were written locally. W. Henri Wilkins' "new and original nautical drama", *The Turn of the Tide; or Wrecked in Port* was produced on January 27 and 28 and February 16, 1886, and repeated on July 9, 1890, by the Siron Amateur Dramatic Club. *All for Gold*, "a new and original drama" by James J. Power, was produced for the first time at the Mechanics' Institute on February 2, 1886, by the Young Men's Society of St. Joseph Dramatic Club with the author in the cast, and repeated in January 1887. Most popular of the locally written plays, however, were John L. Carleton's *In One Night* and *More Sinned Against Than Sinning*. The first was a temperance play and the second an Irish drama, the two most common categories of stage play produced by amateur societies in this period, not surprisingly, given the large number of temperance societies in the city and the large number of Irish Roman Catholics. *In One Night* was a three-act drama written for performance by the Father Mathew Association Dramatic Club,[65] and its text, like those of Mills, Wilkins, and Power, has been lost. Only a list of the *dramatis personae* given in the *Telegraph* of November 17, 1886, remains: Arthur Hardy, Gerald Montgomery, Counsellor Bloatface, Harry St. Leonard, Augusta Littlebrain, Barney Murphy, Tom Watts, Willie, Napoleon Tenderfoot, Bob Buttons, and Slideback Silkhat. John Carleton was in the cast that played to a bumper house at the Institute on November 16. In December, the Children of Mary of the Convent of the Sacred Heart, assisted by members of the Father Mathew Association, gave the play a second performance. *More Sinned Against Than Sinning* was first performed by the Father Mathew Association Dramatic Club on March 17 and 19, 1884. Its cast, most of whom were making their debut before the footlights, though it could not "be claimed for them that they followed Hamlet's advice to the players, or that they were able to avoid mannerisms of which even professionals do not always succeed in divesting themselves",[66] succeeded in pleasing probably the largest audience ever to have assembled in St. Malachi's Hall. For the next three years the play was an annual St. Patrick's Day event. The *Telegraph* of March 18, 1885, reported that the Mechanics' Institute was "crowded to the outer doors, and there many had to be turned away". The next year the building was "literally packed" again, and the author, "as the hero of the piece . . . was greeted with an ovation on his appearance, and his acting deserved the applause given".[67]

More Sinned Against Than Sinning survives in published, if rather inaccessible form. A three-act drama with prologue, set in Killarney, Ireland, it was published as Number 312 of DeWitt's Acting Plays, with "A description of the Costumes — Synopsis of the Piece — Cast of the Characters — Entrances and Exits — Relative Positions of the Performers on the stage, and the Whole of the Stage Business".[68] A publicity note in a Butte, Montana, newspaper of June 22, 1899, indicates that it had fairly extensive performance: "The citizens of Butte have a rich dramatic treat in store for them this week in the presentation of the popular Irish melodrama, More Sinned Against Than Sinning. The author of this play is a brilliant young Canadian lawyer residing in St. John, N. B. Mr. Carleton wrote the drama during his leisure moments and it was purchased by a New York publisher and was afterwards produced at many of the leading theatres in the United States and Canada".[69]

In its review of the opening night in Saint John, the *Weekly Freeman* described the script as "a recital of events of continuous occurrence in Ireland — events of which many in the audience still retain very vivid recollections, and with which the public of other nationalities have become more or less familiar through the newspaper press".[70] The play's message of the need for social and political reform is explicitly stated in the final sentimental exchange between Squire Hilton and his son Marmaduke, popularly known as "the Duke":

SQUIRE. No! no! you were more sinned against than sinning. My eyes have been opened to the injustice of my treatment, not only of you, but of my tenants, and the rest of my life shall be devoted to repairing those wrongs. You shall manage everything; and your humane and generous treatment of my tenantry will make them love you, and, I trust, forgive your father.
DUKE. My dear father, the past shall be retrieved. Would that all who hold my country in thrall might, like you, come to

168

see and acknowledge her wrongs, and accord her the rights for which she has so long waited. Then she could assume her proper position and sit a queen among the other nations, with just pride; and of her, too, it might be truly said, "She was more sinned against than sinning."

Saint John's best known playwright, Carleton was born on October 1, 1861, the son of William Carleton and the former Bridget O'Connor. After completion of his education at Public School and the School of the Christian Brothers, he studied law and was admitted to the Bar as an Attorney in 1882 and a Barrister in 1883.[71] An advertisement in the *City Directory 1883-4* lists him as "Barrister-at-Law, Solicitor in Equity, Notary Public, Conveyancer, &c." with an office in Palmer's Chambers, Princess Street. Married in 1886, he was widowed in 1908 and remarried in 1911. In 1892 he unsuccessfully contested Saint John City for the House of Assembly as a Liberal, and in 1899 was appointed Queen's Counsellor. When, on February 26, 1904, he was appointed County Court Judge for Carleton, Victoria, and Madawaska, he moved his residence to Woodstock. Ill health finally forced his retirement in February 1930, and death followed on May 28, 1936.

During his residence in Saint John, Carleton wrote at least two plays after *More Sinned Against Than Sinning* and *In One Night*, and from Woodstock he published three others. His one-act drama *The Convict's Daughter* was performed first on October 23, 1893, in St. Patrick's Hall, Carleton, and again on November 23 in the Mechanics' Institute, with Carleton as the ex-convict John Lispenard. Kate Donovan took the title role of Jess Lispenard, and other characters were Cribbie Cribbler of the P. D. A., Billy the Crook (wanted), Dick Chambers, a lover, and Mother Jefferey, an injured huckster. His "clean" one-act "domestic drama" *Love Was True to Me* was staged in the Opera House on July 13, 1894. Carleton was cool and calm in the title role of Uncle Seth Hulbert, and spoke his lines with clarity. The production was given a boost by the appearance in it of professional actors Mr. and Mrs. Sidney Drew, who were loud in their praise of the piece. Carleton had written it for the Chicago ledger competition, from which he received honourable mention.[72] *Coom-na-goppel*, a five-act Irish drama, was published in 1906, and *A Medieval Hun*, a five-act historical drama about Henry IV of Germany, was published in 1921. *The Crimson Wing*, published but not now extant, was winner of the first prize in the Canadian Play competition in 1918.[73]

A sympathetic obituary summed up the attributes of the man: "Possessed of rare gifts of literary ability and oratory, Judge Carle-

169

ton . . . had the fine courtesy, ready wit and genial manner that are characteristic of the Irish race".[74] In him, Irish influence for the encouragement and perpetuation of drama in Saint John reached a peak. Carleton supported the drama in all its aspects — as a playwright, as an actor with the Father Mathew Association and the Carleton Dramatic Club, and as a director of the Saint John Opera House in the 1890's.

John Carleton
(New Brunswick Museum)

vi
A Dream Fulfilled: The Saint John Opera House

Almost as soon as the elegant and ornate Academy of Music had been devoured by flames, plans were set in motion to replace it. By the end of October 1878, architects W. P. Clarke and Harry W. Black had completed drawings for a new opera house to be erected on the site of the old Dockrill Hall on Union Street. The new structure was to be a remodelling and extension of the existing building, with an auditorium and gallery to seat approximately 850. A modest structure, its cost was estimated to be only $3500, exclusive of seating, and shares for stockholders were priced at $25. This endeavour was short-lived, passing completely away from public view after December, following the illness of one of the architects, even before a company could be formally set up to administer the project.[1]

Discussions, planning, and dreaming must have gone on over tea or over a pint of beer, but nothing more was newsworthy until a new set of drawings prepared by J. C. Dumaresque was inspected at a meeting of interested gentlemen in the Royal Hotel in November 1883. A subsequent meeting on December 6 drew up a prospectus and stock list for a new Academy of Music and appointed a committee of twelve to solicit subscriptions.[2] The formation of a Joint Stock Company was proposed, with capital of $40,000 divided into 8,000 shares of $5 each. The site chosen was again the Dockrill property, presumably as much because of the Dockrills' excellent offer as because of its suitability. Though the land and buildings required for the Academy had been appraised at $27,000, the Messrs. Dockrill agreed to put in the property at $20,000 and take half the net earnings of the house in payment, leaving only $20,000 to be subscribed for the erection of the building. The intent was to take steps to proceed as soon as the first $10,000 had been raised.

Plans called for the new theatre to be constructed of brick, with hollow walls, 62 by 101 feet exclusive of two vestibules (24 x 24 and 26 x 34), and a 37 by 38 foot wing for six dressing rooms.[3] It was to be set back about 68 feet from Union Street,[4] its main entrance a sixty-foot-long grand lobby entered through the front of the existing Dockrill store. The edifice was designed to take advantage of the natural slope of the site. Because of this, the horse-shoe-shaped auditorium was to be at street-level both front and rear; the balcony to be 12 feet high from the ground in front but in the rear only a step from Union Alley, and the gallery, while 24 feet from the ground in front, was to be only a six-foot flight of stairs above it in the rear. Altogether, the building was planned to provide seating for 1200 persons, with easy and safe ingress and egress to the street. The intention was that ladies should attend to their toilettes in comfortable dressing and cloak rooms on the auditorium floor, and that gentlemen could smoke contentedly in the waiting rooms provided. The actors would perform on a 58 foot wide by 35 foot deep stage whose proscenium opening was to be 35 feet across and 40 feet high (in fact, the proscenium arch in the completed building was only 29.6 by 29.6 and the stage area 60 by 40 feet).[5] For the comfort of all, the building would be lighted by electricity and heated by steam. The three storeys over the Dockrill store at the front were to be occupied by the Academy Company and fitted up as halls or restaurants as they chose.

Nearly eight years were to pass before Dumaresque's plans became reality, five before excavation of the site began — and on numerous occasions it looked as if the dream would remain just that. When, in late 1887, the company's activities temporarily ground to a halt, only $6,000 worth of stock had been subscribed.

It would be easy to blame social and economic conditions in Saint John for the delay, for the 1880's were not easy years. The Great Fire of 1877, which destroyed upwards of 1600 homes in the city's main peninsula, had only aggravated a downward trend that could not wholly be blamed on world-wide depression. The fire speeded up a migration of the population to Upper Canada and the United States that had begun earlier in the 1870's. As well, British immigration had fallen off by 1861. The large 24.5 percent in population increase that had occurred between 1851 and 1861 dropped to 6.5 percent in the next decade and to only .07 percent between 1871 and 1881. In the 1880's the inward migration of up-river people did not balance the exodus, so that the population actually decreased by 5.3 percent — a loss the city would not recover for forty years. The social and religious composition of the city was changing rapidly as hundreds of Irish Roman Catholics moved out and num-

172

bers of Baptists came in. Economically, the city was not prepared to cope well. The coming of the steam ship had rendered her once famous sailing vessels obsolete. For reasons that remain unclear, her shipbuilders were unable to convert to iron. The actualities of Confederation and of the eagerly anticipated railway connections with New England and the rest of Canada, moreover, were disappointing. Instead of increasing markets and thus saving the economy, the railway had so exposed the local industries to competition that they could not survive; the sailmaker and the small merchant vanished. Improvement came only after 1887 when the Board of Trade commenced a campaign to make Saint John the winter port for the federally subsidized mail steamers then using Portland, Maine. In 1890 the completion of the Canadian Pacific's 'Short Line' from Montreal gave Saint John more direct access to central Canada than before and shifted some business away from Portland, the previous eastern terminal. Then, in 1896, the federal government finally subsidized the Beaver Line for fortnightly service between Saint John and Liverpool, and the city became a winter port.[6]

While the problems of the 1880's were severe and must have influenced all plans for construction and redevelopment, the difficulties besetting the opera house scheme were more mundane, rooted in the quirks of human nature. The directors of the Opera House Company were ineffective and apathetic. The campaign for subscriptions to stock was undertaken neither energetically nor consistently. Perhaps even more serious, and a factor contributing to the directors' indecision, was public dispute over the appropriateness of the Union Street site and, in particular, the opposition of the Saint John Oratorio Society and the St. Cecilia Society, both of which had selected their own sites for an opera house. The St. Cecilia Society's choice, Chipman's Field, was ultimately out of the question because of its location, but the Oratorio Society was more persistent. Its choice was an interior lot between Charlotte and Germain Streets, the choice a few years earlier of J. W. Lanergan, and in the 1880's occupied only by the refuse deposited from the oyster saloon and bar-room in front of it on Charlotte Street. The site could be obtained cheaply, for its owner, Gideon Prescott, following the Dockrills' example, was willing to give the lot and right of way to it in exchange for only $1600 in paid-up stock. An architect designed a building to cost about $20,000, and an unnamed representative of a New York syndicate was found to lend his weight to the proposal.[7]

Vocal opposition to the Dockrill property seems to have focused on the poor reputation of Union Street: "Liquor saloons and worse hovels were too numerous, and the air of tidiness and cleanli-

173

ness . . . was absent".[8] It was not enough that Samuel Stockris of the New York *Mirror* noticed that it was the most populous and densely thronged street at night, "just as Broadway is in New York".[9] In the property's favour was chiefly its sloping ground which would provide insurance against loss of life through fire.

Ironically, a fire which started in the Christie Woodworking Company on nearby Peters Street, damaged the front of Dockrill's store, and destroyed several other wooden buildings on the block, simultaneously removed the opposition and stimulated interest in the proposed Union Street opera house. By August 25, 1888, six days after the fire, the subscriptions reached $8,500, in September eighty more subscribers were added to the list,[10] and by mid-October the directors had given out the excavation contract.

With the removal of the fire-hazards and eye-sores, the street's future importance as a business centre could be seen more clearly. For a few months the Oratorio Society pushed forward with its opposition scheme, but eventually this was abandoned and, from February 18, 1889, when the Union Street company reorganized its directors, the opera house on the Dockrill property made steady, if sometimes troubled, progress. Officers chosen to guide the project to completion were John F. Dockrill and Alfred O. Skinner, merchants; Richard F. Quigley and Charles N. Skinner, barristers-at-law; Adam H. Bell, tobacconist; George A. Hetherington, physician; Michael W. Maher, Inspector of Buildings; and Parke W. Melville, Associate Editor of the *Daily Telegraph*.

A mood of optimism prevailed as 1889 opened, for $13,000 of stock had been subscribed, leaving $7,000 more to be found. "There should be no trouble getting it", *Progress* proclaimed confidently on January 5. "Energetic men are in the company and failure isn't in their calendar for 1889." Although the lease for the land was not signed until October 1, 1890,[11] excavation had begun and by April 1889 had proceeded so well that tenders for building were received on the 6th. On September 10 A. O. Skinner and P. A. Melville, as President and Secretary of the Opera House Company, signed articles of agreement with John B. Morrison, John Sharp, and Richard Cassidy for the erection and finishing of the new building "at the north side of Union Street in the City of Saint John, N. B., to be known as the Saint John Opera House". Morrison was to do all the masonry for the sum of $10,620, while Cassidy and Sharp were to be responsible for "all the Carpenter work, Smith work, painting and glazing . . . and also to do the Lathing" in exchange for payment of $8000.[12] The company agreed to pay the builders ninety percent of the value of the work and materials actually performed and furnished on the ground as the work progressed, and to make

174

the last payment within three months after completion of the work "to the entire Satisfaction of the architect and Superintendent".

The enthusiasm persisted into the new year. At the stockholders' meeting on January 27, subscriptions were increased on the spot, and a sufficient sum was guaranteed to complete the building in time for a planned opening on Dominion Day 1891. By September 1890 the brick work had reached the second storey and the foundation pieces to support the balcony had been put in place, but at this point the directors found their hands tied, for too many people, apparently thinking that the walls could "be constructed of air and promises", had failed to make good their subscriptions. On October 17 the directors found it necessary to take out a $5000 mortgage[13] in order to ensure that the roof could be put on before the snow fell. At the same time, they arranged for a mammoth benefit concert at St. Andrew's Rink on October 21 to give the project a further boost, although this almost certainly did not raise the additional $10,000 which the *Telegram* of October 22 said was still required.

While the brick walls of the Opera House were rising in 1890, three other buildings were being refurbished as theatres. In the early months of that year, the Saint John Mechanics' Institute was formally dissolved and the building itself became the property of a new Mechanics' Institute Company which undertook to make the facility more suitable for public purposes. By the end of October the interior was completely remodelled. Downstairs, the museum was converted into a ballroom, ladies and gentlemen's retiring rooms, and a kitchen. Upstairs, the auditorium was freshly painted — its walls pale green and its ceilings buff — and new matting was laid down. The iron work beneath the balcony rail was coloured and the heavy portion dotted with gold. The panels skirting the ceiling were "prettily colored" and the reflectors on the ceiling made to "stand out prominently from a variety of shades of harmonizing tints". In appearance, the entire building looked "as bright as a new pin".[14] For comfort, the company installed two badly needed ventilators in the roof, introduced electric lighting, and replaced the inefficient stoves by steam heating.

October 22 marked the grand opening of a rejuvenated Palace Rink on Queen Square as the Palace Theatre, and November 4 of McCann's Lyceum Theatre, formerly "Jack's Old Hall" on Charlotte Street. The Palace had been provided "with a seating capacity equal to any place of amusement in the city".[15] A new stage was constructed, and "a perfect auditorium with sufficient heating appliances provided". After only four days of use in November, the Lyceum was closed for renovations. A new floor on raised tiers was

GROUND PLAN OF THE NEW OPERA HOUSE.

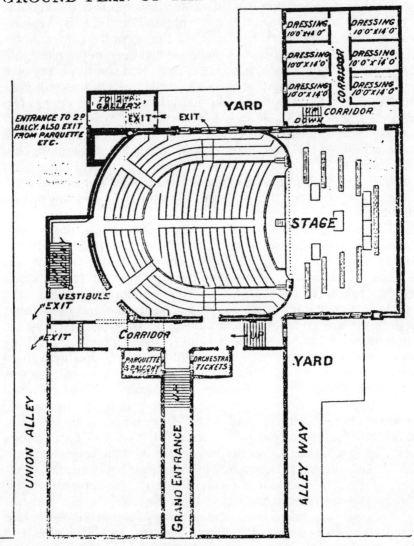

Ground Plan of the New Opera House (New Brunswick Museum)

laid, the usual "commodious" stage was erected, and "beautiful" scenery painted. In addition, the walls were kalsomined, the windows upholstered to keep out the light, and adequate heating installed, altogether making "a very cozy and beautiful place of resort" for 800 patrons.[16] When it reopened on December 12, its name was the New Lyceum, but by the 18th this had changed to the Bijou. Both these theatres aimed to be the "Family Resort of St. John" and to present good vaudeville entertainment all winter long. The Bijou appears to have done this at least to the end of March, though the Palace closed in December and did not become active again until Yamaski's Imperial Japanese Troupe arrived in June 1891.

To these theatre buildings was added in June 1891 a newly-converted St. Andrew's Rink, formerly the Lansdowne, situated across Charlotte Street from the Bijou. A large stage was put in place and the seats raised as they had been when E. A. McDowell played there with such success. The bare open spaces at the sides of the main body of the house which then had seemed so unattractive were now filled with booths for the Centuries Exhibitions and, to the ears of one pleased patron of Adelaide Randall's New York Bijou Opera Company, even the accoustics had improved. There was thus much going on in the way of amusement in the summer of 1891, even with the Opera House unfinished and the Bijou temporarily closed. Charlotte Street was the popular amusement centre; the crowds seemed to have formed the habit of walking in that direction, for the St. Andrew's Rink was an attractive place to spend the evening, in contrast to the close, hot air of the Institute where an unpopular management drew only indifferent business. The Palace was a little further away from the centre of town; even so, its variety entertainments drew steadily until well into the fall, until after the St. Andrew's Rink had closed once more and the Opera House had at last been opened.

In the summer of 1891 the interior of the Opera House was a beehive of industry as the directors pushed the work forward as quickly as possible to meet a revised opening date of Monday, September 21. Carpenters were busy in every part of the building, on the floors, in the balconies, in the lobbies, and on the stage. By September the rough work had been completed and the men were putting on finishing touches that would make the hall attractive. Some were making the large white frames for the scene painter's brush, while the scene painter himself, Sidney Chidley, toiled far up in the fly gallery, mid-way between the roof and the stage. To reach him, one had to climb a long, almost perpendicular stairway, and there, away from the hubbub below, in a large frame suspended from the roof and hoisted up and down by weights and a winch, were the scenes he was painting into life. Masons and plasterers stood on staging far up near the ceiling to put a moulding around the proscenium arch and smooth the walls with plaster and trowel. On the 15th the seats were placed in position. The boxes were completed just in time, and the iron street-gates hung in readiness on opening day. The permanent drop-curtain was still unfinished, some painting remained to be done, and the heating would not be installed until October, but these things, in the circumstances, seemed minor details.

With the opening imminent, the press expressed its enthusiasm about the fittings of the new theatre. The *Sun* concentrated on the modern lighting fixtures from Robert Mitchell and Company of Montreal:

> There are about 200 incandescent lamps in the building. The handsome electrolier which hangs a polished brass dome in the centre of the auditorium contains 50 incandescent 16-candle power lamps. Nearly 300 electrical connections had to be made on this fixture alone. The main floor has eight three-light brackets to match the electrolier. These lamps are wired for 32 candle power should more light be required at any time. The balcony has two 3 light and two 2 light brackets of the same pattern, also made to carry more power if needed. The gallery is lighted by the massive electrolier . . . Particular attention has been paid to the lights on the stage. There are 20 foot-lights, and three rows of border lights, 20 in a row, light up the scenery. They are placed on reflectors, and can be used at any height or on any angle required. The seven different circuits used in the house are all controlled from a switch board on the stage.[17]

On September 19 the *Globe* described the numbered chairs on the main floor and in the balcony, which had been supplied by the Canada Office and Desk Furniture Company of Preston, Ontario: "They are of quartered cut oak with crimson plush seats and arm rests. Each seat has a hat rack, and the backs are rounded and very comfortable". Although the arrangement of the seats resembled that of the Mechanics' Institute, audiences would have a less inhibited view of the stage, since each section of the building had been provided with a sloping floor. As the *Sun* of the 19th agreed: "The gallery gods will have as good a view of the entire stage as the occupants of chairs in the balcony or dress circle". In the orchestra 304 chairs stood ready to furnish comfort for the theatre's patrons, in the dress circle 258, and in the balcony 302, while the gallery had room for 400 spectators more.[18]

The raising of the curtain on the New York Stock Company's performance of *The Marble Heart* on September 21 was a triumph, and a tribute especially to the energy, courage, and determination of A. O. Skinner, promoter of the project from the outset and its staunchest supporter throughout:

> When the hour for opening came, there was an unwonted throng of the elite and commonalty of St. John gathered along both sides of Union Street, and pressing about the grand entrance to the new temple of the muses . . . The electric lights made bright the entrance hall and all within; it was a convenience to have one's wraps and umbrella taken in charge by polite attendants, and there were general expressions of approval on all hands as ushers conducted the host of patrons to their seats. Everything moved smoothly and with order and precision till the main auditorium, balcony and gallery — rising like Medea's gardens, terrace above terrace — were adorned with a multitude of happy, expectant faces and rich toilettes. Every one took a survey of the interior and its appointments, and during the process nods and smiles of recognition innumerable were exchanged. No one has yet an 'accustomed' seat and no one knew where to look for the familiar faces of friends or even of some *habitué* of the theatre who, upon a grand occasion, one expects to find in his own particular section. There was some apparent stock taking, too, in many minds and questionings as to which are the best locations for future evenings down the long vistas of pastimes which the imagination so readily pictures as in store for us in this new arena for enjoyment. While thus engaged, enjoying the comfortable sittings and their convenient appliances for the bestowal of extra incumbrances, the members of the orchestra filed into their places and were greeted with a rattling cheer in which the voices of the gods joined heartily with the hand clapping of ordinary mortals below. Then the opening strains of the national anthem rolled through the building and the loyal audience rose to their feet. Applause followed in no stinted measure.[19]

Sadly, the company that had been obtained through a supposedly reliable agent proved disappointing. Far from being a first-class company, as the directors had promised all companies engaged by them would be, the New York Stock Company was inadequate even to the old and popular *Ticket-of-Leave Man*. This, coupled with the fact that the entertainment-seeking public seemed to prefer the Kickaboo Indians at the Palace, Professor Skinner's mesmerism and magic at the St. Andrew's Rink, and the minstrels at the Mechanics' Institute to the standard plays available at the Opera House, meant that the opening weeks at the new theatre were a financial drain on the management, for houses fell off after the first night. So ill satisfied were the local managers that they settled with the company to terminate its four-week contract a week early. There was thus an unplanned quiet period until the more successful week-long engagement of Jane Coombs' company early in November.

Throughout the 1890's, and particularly in the first half of the decade, the directors of the Opera House had a difficult time keeping their operation afloat. With their limited means, the directors were not always able to obtain the performers they wanted; on the other hand, some companies did not live up to their advance publicity, while others cancelled. Poor business in Boston, New York, and on the New England circuit, brought about by a world-wide depression in 1893, reflected itself in Saint John.[20] In addition, railroading cost more in Canada than in the United States. Duties on theatrical scenery, costumes, properties, lithographs, and pictorial printing for advertising were such a heavy tax on managers of all Canadian theatres (as well as a reason why some American companies refused to cross the border) that the managers, through their representative Edward Varney, appeared before a Tarriff Commission in Montreal in January 1897 to argue for their removal. Even in the best of circumstances, the business was an unpredictable one. At their annual meeting in January 1893, the directors of the St. John Opera House Company were optimistic about the coming year. A $5000 liability had been paid off in 1892 in addition to running expenses,[21] and twenty weeks of 1893 had already been booked by allegedly first-class companies. By the next annual meeting the optimism was completely gone. 1893 had been a disastrous year; the company had lost about $800 on the Standard Opera Company, and the floating indebtedness had increased $1000 to about $12,000. The next year was somewhat better (the total receipts of $4,859.55 at least covering expenses), and 1895 saw the indebtedness reduced by a few hundred dollars even though the company failed to pay the city $125 for its licence either by the May 1 deadline or the August 1 extension. A similar pattern followed for the remainder of the decade with the annual reports of 1899 showing a small credit balance on the year's business.

Despite its difficulties, the Opera House was frequently filled to capacity, and some of the best known theatrical personalities performed on its boards — James O'Neill, Tyrone Power, Lewis

180

Morrison, and Mme. Rhea among others. A symbol and temple of culture, it was valued much by the professional and middle classes especially, and supported by their good will if not always with their money.

Tastes of theatre-goers, continuing the trend of the 1880's, were away from tragedy towards comedy and variety entertainments. This can easily be seen in the large number of troupes who included 'comedy' in their name and in the numerous variety, minstrel, and specialty companies — ranging from Norris Bros. Equine and Canine Paradox Company with its 100 educated dogs, ponies, and monkeys, to Turner's English Gaiety Girls, to Pawnee Bill's Historical Wild West Show. Shakespeare, not unnaturally, was all but absent from this assortment. In 1891 the Washington *Star* sarcastically indicated what would be necessary to make the content of even his *Romeo and Juliet* acceptable in present conditions:

> Mr Shakespeare should have had the opportunity of submitting his Romeo and Juliet to a modern manager, who says: "What the public wants is fun, see?" He would then have had the pleasure of rewriting his drama somewhat in accordance to the above idea. Romeo has just executed a song and dance, in which the Montagues and Capulets joined, making a scene of hilarity that was alone worth the price of admission. Romeo begins a serenade; enter the most intelligent trained dog in the profession today. Juliet, who is one of the handsomest ladies on the burlesque stage, and incidentally a queen of song and exponent of terpsichorean art, tries to rescue him, but he catches his waist-band on a nail in the porch and is suspended in statu quo or thereabouts, while the curtain goes down amidst the thundering plaudits of a delighted throng. There is no doubt that Shakespeare missed a great deal by being born too soon.[22]

The Shakespearean text and the Shakespearean tradition, even when assisted by the elaborate scenic effects with which the nineteenth century had tried to improve them, did not allow sufficiently for the passion for realism that was gripping the stage. The Elizabethan actors had "no races with real horses and a moving panorama, nor any saw mill, with a real buzz saw and real logs to fall back upon. The effect of the situation was not helped out by any real water and real ice floating on it, and realism as represented by live blood-hounds and reformed burglars and ex-convicts was unknown".[23] In contrast, during the performance of Hatti Bernard Chase's Uncles Darling Company in 1892, seals played tambourines and a drum, dogs tore the vellum to pieces, bears drank from a bot-

Germain Street 1899 — taken from book entitled "Art Work on City of Saint John" by William H. Oarre. (New Brunswick Museum)

Prince William Street, reproduced from N.B. postcard, c. 1887-1894
(New Brunswick Museum)

tle, and reindeer walked the stage without knocking over the iceberg. "It was realism with a big R", drawing howls of excitement from the gallery.[24] Even though the critics condemned the Chase Company as inferior and wished that actors could, like the Elizabethans, do more than merely recite their lines, the ticket-buying gods could do much to influence the choice of repertoire.

From November 1891 the Opera House was a showcase for the amateur talent of Saint John as well as for the professional troupes that passed through. The Saint John Oratorio Society, defeated in its ambition to possess its own theatre, performed there annually. In 1892 and 1893 the St. John Amateur Athletic Club Minstrels presented varied programmes, including an assortment of vocal solos, choral renditions, and dances; always concluding with a musical burlesque — "Mr. Mikado; or Japanese from Willow Grove", "King of the Cannibal Islands", or "Princess Tutti Frutti, the Lily". The first of these, whose *dramatis personae* were as follows, was particularly enjoyed for its local hits:

> Mr. Mikado, a Son of the Sod
> Nanki-Poo, a King St. Masher
> Ko-Ko, the Tonsorial Artist of St. John
> Poo-Bah, who holds all the Public Offices in St. John
> Pish-Tish, One of the Boys
> Katisha, an old Hot Corn Beauty
> Yum-Yum, Pitti-Sing, and Peep-Bo — Ladies from the Quaco Seminary
> The Imperial Japanese Band, Japanese Nobles, Colored Barbers, Almoned [sic]-eyed Beauties, Ward Workers and Local Politicians by the numerous multitude.[25]

In the latter part of the decade, the St. John Amateurs under the direction of J. S. Ford gave straightforward renditions of the still popular Gilbert and Sullivan operas. As in the 1880's, the amateur dramatic societies belonged predominently to Roman Catholic parishes and to temperance associations. In addition, there were groups from at least three Anglican parishes as well as assorted groups like the Amateur Snowflake Minstrels, the Cecilian Dramatic Union, and the St. John Proscenium Club. Most often they performed in the Opera House, but the Mechanics' Institute and various church and lodge halls were also used. Rather than reflecting the trends in the professional theatre, the repertoires of these groups consisted of Irish plays, temperance dramas, military and nautical dramas, melodramas, and even a cantata for children entitled "The Old Woman Who Lived in a Shoe; a Terrible Tale of a Dragon".

Only a few of the repertory companies who had played in Saint John during the 1880's returned in the 1890's. Harry Lindley, who had last visited the city in 1881, brought to the Mechanics' Institute a company which the advertisements said was endorsed by the Prince of Wales, the Marquis of Lorne, the Earl of Dufferin, and President Grant. They came for only four days in May 1890 and, despite their honourable endorsement, do not seem to have made much of a stir with their productions of *The Castaways* and *Zeppa, the Child of the Mines*. E. A. McDowell came in September, opening with *The Balloon*, a breezy comedy based on mistaken identities, for which he had purchased production rights at a high price. In a further successful bid for attention he brought actor Edward O. Lyons to perform the role of Bob Acres in *The Rivals* as he had played it at London's Globe Theatre and at Saddler's Wells. In December W. H. Lytell, basing his appeal as before on scenic effects, won the largest houses. Simms and Pettitt's *Harbour Lights* packed the Institute "from stage to doors, from cellar to garrett".[26] The vision of the guillotine was enthusiastically applauded in the thrilling romantic *Paul Kouvar*, and the raft scene in *The World* was as powerful as it had been on its introduction eight years earlier. Halifax reviews were used to underline the scenic attractions of *The Great Metropolis* — the discharge of a real cannon, flashing lights to aid the realistic representation of a storm from which a shipwrecked crew is fortuitously rescued, the interior of the lighthouse, and "a realistic scene on the river at night when an attempted murder is averted by one of the would-be perpetrators recognizing the body of his sister floating past in the water".[27] The audience found that not a moment dragged. The same was true of Pettitt's *Hands Across the Sea*, given with "Grand Revolving Scenic and Mechanical Effects" in February 1891. Less spectacular success was achieved by the Redmond-Barry Company on three days in May 1891, although the villain in the military drama *Herminie* was heartily hissed in a rousing tribute to virtue.

No matter how excellent the company, it could not generally succeed unless the type of programme offered appealed to the theatre-going public. This fact was learned to the distress of two companies who had done well in Saint John previously. It was not difficult for the *Sun* to predict accurately that the one-act drama *A Modern St. Anthony* and the two-act comedy *Santanella*, both of which had done poorly in Halifax, would not prove popular at the Opera House either, but Arthur Rehan brought them nevertheless in October 1893. A "classical drama of the French school of acting", as the New York *Sun* described *St. Anthony*, was simply not acceptable in the Atlantic provinces at this time. Oliver Doud Byron's play, the same actors performed for two weeks in November, was better received, but the only really well-attended play of the entire engagement was written by local author Ethel Knight Mollison, the same young lady who in 1880 had won so many hearts on her initial stage appearance as Buttercup. The news that Miss Mollison's society comedy, *The Mischievous Miss*, would indirectly portray many prominent citizens and that the authoress herself would play the title role was enough to fill the Opera House three times. The nineteen year old's excellent acting surprised everyone, but her script, which reportedly suffered from the common beginner's fault of too much dialogue and too little action, incurred the wrath of the *Sun* for its too obvious satire — wrath directed particularly against the Opera House management that permitted it.

More surprising, perhaps, than the failure of Arthur Rehan's company was that of the same Mme. Rhea who in 1884 had drawn even larger receipts at the box-office than Lily Langtry. In September 1894, when Rhea presented *Much Ado About Nothing*, *Camille*, *The Lady of Lyons*, *Pygmalion and Galatea*, and *The New Magdalen*, she was unable to pay her expenses. A measure of the distance theatre-patrons had moved away from the past came in the press-statement that much of her repertoire was unfamiliar in Saint John. The acting support was as good as before and the costumes as magnificent, but the accent that had formerly been so endearing was now seen as a liability. For the *Globe*, the lack of appreciation shown Mme. Rhea refuted the much touted notion that if the Opera House management would provide better players better attendance would follow. The truth was that only a minority of theatre-goers favoured the legitimate drama. As *Progress* pointed out on September 29, "the public will have what the public wants and there is no use fighting against it. If the public wants farce comedy then that is just the material that must be supplied. The fad will cure itself in due course".

By far the most frequent visitors to Saint John in the 1890's were H. Price Webber's Boston Comedy Company and W. S. Harkins' Company, both of which had built up a loyal following before the decade began. On New Year's Day 1890 Webber was in residence at the Mechanics' Institute, where he had been since Christmas Day 1889 on the first of several annual holiday engagements. Webber was the only manager who could consistently and successfully fly in the face of public demand for farcical comedy and novelty. Year after year he could draw bumper houses to his productions of old-time plays like *East Lynne*, *Under the Gaslight*, *Kathleen Mavourneen*, *Ten Nights in a Bar-room*, and *Lady of Lyons*. He packed whatever house was available. In 1890/1 this was the Palace because W. H. Lytell possessed the Mechanics' Institute, but as soon as Lytell moved to Moncton, having cancelled a performance on account of snow, Webber transferred his company to the Institute; neither snow nor rain could deter Webber or his audiences. On Christmas Day 1891 over 1100 people crowded into the Institute for a matinee, and as many came at night, bringing in over $600 at the box-office even with tickets priced "to suit the time" at 25¢. The next Christmas, for only the second time in the building's year-long history, every reserved seat in the Opera House was sold for the evening performance before the doors opened. Webber, moreover, was not deterred by adversity. When in June 1893 he lost all his uninsured scenery, wardrobe, and properties in a Truro fire, he ordered new scenery from L. J. Couch of Boston, was back on the road in mid-August, and at the Mechanics' Institute again for a profitable Christmas season, while the Standard Opera Company lost money at the Opera House. Mrs. Webber's surgery in Boston for the removal of a fibroid tumour, though successful, did force him to cancel his engagement for 1895. He did not return to Saint John until the holiday season in 1897 when, once more, the Opera House proved inadequate to the crowd who wanted to watch his revival of *The Stranger*. It was a matter of record, the *Sun* reported on December 20, 1898, that Webber had put more money into the Opera House treasury on each visit than any other dramatic organization that had catered to holiday business. "Critics may shake their heads," it observed, "but the general public who are presumed to know what they like, fill the seats everytime".

On December 29, 1894, *Progress* suggested some of the reasons for Webber's extraordinary success: "Webber is always honest to the people. He claims no more for his show than it is worth, his admission charge is in proportion, more than that he knows everybody and they know him. This is why, perhaps, he played in spite of the miserable weather on Christmas afternoon and evening to 694 matinee people and an audience of 1362 in the evening". At the end of each engagement, Webber would regularly appear before the curtain to thank the audience for its patronage, the press for its kindly notices, and Morton Harrison's orchestra for its assistance. Not to neglect the people of Carleton (who felt somewhat isolated from the mainstream on their western peninsula) he would, whenever possible, perform a night or two in the Carleton City Hall. His productions were always pleasing and tasteful; even if admittedly below par for a New York company, they were, by popular consensus, the best value for the money of any company that came to town.

Webber was a painstaking and energetic manager who personally looked after all the business and advertising of his company. Versatility and adaptability were essential for him as for other touring actor-managers. He had to be ready to change the bill at a moment's notice, as was the case in 1899 when his wife and leading lady, Edwina Grey, fell down the stairs on the *S. S. Prince Rupert* while crossing the Bay of Fundy, injuring her knee so badly that she was unable to appear at the opening of Yarmouth's Royal Opera House. During his career Webber was reputed to have appeared as an actor in 514 different plays and farces in a total of 11,000 performances and never to have missed a bill because of ill health.[28] He was a good comedian, clever, funny, and witty, whose local hits were always hillarious though never of a sort to wound any one's sensibilities. His wife was warmly admired as much for her personality as for her ability. A versatile actress, she was intense as Lady Isabel in *East Lynne*, equal to the emotional acting demanded by the role of Mrs. Haller in *The Stranger*, acted Capitola in *The Hidden Hand* with "dash and spirit", and was quite satisfactory in comedy; her shadow dance in *Fanchon* was always loudly applauded.

For forty years, to 1915, Price Webber's "husky locks and stage-like gait, his alert expression and ever-genial manner"[29] were familiar to theatre-goers in New England, Quebec, and the Maritime provinces. He visited regularly many small towns such as Houlton, Eastport, and Calais in Maine; Annapolis, Berwick, Amherst, and Hantsport in Nova Scotia; and Sackville, Moncton, Chatham, Newcastle, St. Stephen, and Milltown in New Brunswick, even performing on Grand Manan in November 1898, the same year he extended his tour for the first time to St. John's, Newfoundland. A review in the *Halifax Mail*, reprinted in *Progress* on December 12, 1891, sums up the general response to his company:

> Houses jammed to suffocation have been the rule since the popular Webber opened in the Lyceum . . . The company is good, reciting their lines intelligently, acting their characters correctly, and costuming them in a very superior manner. The leading lady, Edwina Grey, is an established Halifax favorite, and is undoubtedly one of the most versatile actresses that has ever visited us. Price Webber is an always welcome comedian, and he has the happy faculty of knowing when to leave well enough alone, and his fun is clean and wholesome, provoking laughter.

W. S. Harkins based his appeal to public favour on quite different ingredients from Webber. He attempted to secure the rights to the latest successes and to produce these efficiently and with fine scenic effects. His prices, even in the Institute, were higher than

Webber's at .35 and .25 with reserved seats as much as .50 and .75, but he too could draw full houses. In his 1890 and 1891 seasons he established the pattern his company would largely adhere to for the rest of the decade. The company arrived from New York after a leisurely voyage aboard the steamer *Valencia* and went straight into rehearsal. For the initial week-long May engagement in 1890, Harkins had chosen three plays new to Saint John, *The Golden Giant*, *The Unknown*, and *Jim the Penman*. The last, written in 1886, had run for over 200 nights at Madison Square Theatre and was, Harkins advertised, considered by New Yorkers one of the best of its class. Several members of Harkins' Fifth Avenue Company had belonged to the original company, and much of the original scenery had been brought on tour. Every seat at the Institute was full for its opening performance there. In his longer engagement from July 14 to August 21, Harkins concentrated particularly on efficiency of production. Because of short waits between the acts of Pettitt's *Black Flag*, he was able to bring down the curtain at 10:45, allowing people living out of town or in the west end to catch train or boat for home. Even better, Jefferson and Shewell's *Shadows of a Great City* was over by 10:35. His efforts did not go unnoticed or unappreciated, for curtain calls increased as the engagement proceeded, and the press found each play better than the last. Harkins must have been satisfied because, though he interrupted his Saint John tour for two nights in Moncton, he refused an offer to shorten it and move to the Halifax Academy of Music instead. Though he would later include Halifax regularly on his route, this time he simply went to Fredericton briefly after termination of his contract at the Institute and then returned directly to New York.

The sixteen member 1890 company had as leading ladies Grace Huntington and Julia Arthur and included also H. B. Bradley who, in July 1891, returned to Saint John with his own Bradley's Players headed by Grace Huntington. Miss Huntington was a New Brunswick girl whose real name was Lucy Hortense Cronkite. Though she still owned the family homestead above Fredericton, she lived in Boston. Then 22, she had already earned a reputation as a strong emotional actress. Since in her childhood she had often heard her father Hezekiah speak of Hon. S. L. Tilley, she wrote to him from Boston asking permission to visit him in Saint John during her few leisure moments between the long hard rehearsals each day and the evening performances, and also inviting him to be present at the theatre.[30] Saint John's theatre-goers, however, did not know Miss Huntingdon by any other name. They knew her only as a handsome, talented actress who held their attention firmly as Lady Ralston in *Jim the Penman*, whose denunciation of her husband as a

188

Grace Huntington
(New York Public Library)

Price Webber as Rip Van Winkle
(Fred Phillips)

W. S. Harkins (New York Public Library)

thief and forger was done with consummate skill, and whom they presented with a beautiful bouquet in reward. That reputation was her advertisement when she came next as Bradley's leading lady.

Harkins' penchant for spectacular scenic effects is clearly seen in his 1894 season. He and his company arrived by the *State of Maine* accompanied by two Arabian horses and a steam fire-engine for Arthur and Wheeler's "decidedly sensational melodrama", *Still Alarm*, that he intended to show May 16-19 before departing for Halifax and then Truro to open Gunn's new Opera House there. Several large theatre parties were planned, and on one evening the Saint John firemen witnessed the realism of "the well trained fire horses, the interior of the station, the firemen, the still alarm, the fire engine with its lighted fire".[31] All this, however, was insignificant beside the "mammoth scenic production of the great spectacular English military melodrama", *The Soudan*, produced July 2-7 by special arrangement with Jefferson, Klaw, and Erlanger, that "most prominent and enterprising theatrical firm, who control more theatres and plays than any other one interest in the world". For it Harkins had 18 complete sets, 28 people in the speaking cast, 125 auxiliaries, the 62nd Fusiliers' Band, a drum corps, horses, and "many tons of intricate and odd paraphernalia".[32] The whole evening's programme proceeded without intermission. Scene changes, for the first time, were made without lowering the curtain; the stage was darkened for a moment and, when the lights were turned up, a new picture stood in place. These "dark shifts" were a useful novelty, since they did away with the tiresome waits so common in scenic productions.

From 1890 Harkins' company came to Saint John annually for two one-or-two-week engagements (generally in late May and June with an engagement in Halifax between), performing always in the Opera House, once it had opened. The exception to the pattern was 1895, when he came for a single three-week period from June 17 to July 6. That year, which he opened with Belasco's *Lost Paradise*, showing the Knowlton iron mills in full blast, Ethel Mollison played a leading role in *Men and Women* and a smaller one in the five-act version of *Uncle Tom's Cabin*. After her considerable amateur experience in her native Saint John, Miss Mollison had made her professional debut in Olga Nethersole's company at the Chestnut Street Opera House, Philadelphia, in November 1894. She does not seem to have been a regular member of Harkins' company in 1895 but was probably in Saint John on holiday.

At least from 1895 — when his troupe's name was changed first to Metropolitan Company and then to W. S. Harkins' Dramatic (or Stock) Company or simply to W. S. Harkins' Company —

190

Harkins employed another manager. From 1897 he did not always travel with the company, although he was in New York early every May to attend to the recruitment of its members. On tour his agents made careful advance preparation; to advertise *The Soudan* in Saint John, they plastered billboards, fences, and rocks in the lower end of the city with brilliant lithographed paper. The store-windows all over town were filled with lithographs and printed announcements, and nearly 100 boards and canvas frames covered with attractive pictures were tied to telegraph poles. To avoid the confusion which sometimes saw companies arriving by train or boat just in time (or even late) for curtain time, his company and scenic effects came early. In part this was necessary because of the immense amount of scenery carried. Two days prior to the opening of the 1897 season, for instance, a season that would include Sutton Vane's melodramatic *Cotton King*, the allegedly realistic *A Bowery Girl*, and Harvey's domestic drama *Shall He Forgive Her?*, passers-by witnessed the unusual sight of not fewer than eight double loads of scenery and effects hauled to the Opera House.

Harkins acquired a reputation as a man who always aimed to please his patrons with the newest plays and capable talent, no matter how expensive, and also as a man who kept his promises whenever possible. Because he attempted to appeal to a wide range of taste, he kept his programme varied. No doubt understanding that good actors became more popular with increased exposure, he regularly brought many of the same faces with him, the presence of especial favourite Tom Wise and his "pleasant, happy looking wife", Gertrude Whitty, coming to be regarded as a matter of course.[33] The fact alone that Harkins returned to Saint John year after year indicates that he was successful financially as well as professionally. In 1896 the first night of a week-long run of his production about the blue-grass region, Dazey's *In Old Kentucky*, had the largest attendance and the third highest box-office receipts of any production at the Opera House that year. The 1467 individual tickets and 7 boxes amounted to a gross of $521.60 and indicate that more than 200 people must have been standing.[34] The house was not full on any other night, however, and by Saturday, habitually a poor theatre night in Saint John, receipts were only $139.05, of which the company received 70 percent and the house 30 percent. Harkins did not always take enough to justify the tremendous expense of his elaborate scenic effects; the papers frequently complained that he did not receive the patronage he deserved. Nevertheless, *Variety Fair* described him as parading Broadway "rich and rosy, and grown corpulent upon the profits of a stock company which he sends up through Nova Scotia and other British Canadian possessions".[35]

In 1898 Harkins completely reorganized his company, employing new actors and a new emphasis in his repertoire. Tom Wise was gone, furthering his ambitions by striking out on paths that would lead him to London in 1899. Harkins filled up the company with actors who had already won good names in their stage career, but whom he judged to be "fired with ambition to climb the ladder of fame still higher".[36] As leading lady he chose Mabel Eaton, "a young and remarkably handsome woman, with an ease of bearing and a vivacity that win every beholder,"[37] who came well qualified from three years of schooling in Augustin Daly's New York stock company. Also present was Ethel Mollison who had, since her last Saint John appearance, been with Daly's theatre as well as with the Girard Avenue Theatre in Philadelphia. Within a couple of years she too would rise to the position of leading lady in other companies, only to leave the stage to star in another field — in 1903, when playing leads during the tour of J. C. Williamson's company in Australia, she married a Melbourne gentleman whose yearly income was then $300,000. As Mrs. T. H. Kelly, Saint John's 'Little Buttercup' made her home for a time in India where she occupied a social position second to none, later becoming one of Sydney society's leading hostesses as well as that city's best-dressed woman.[38]

Although he kept to the principle of variety in his repertoire, Harkins in 1898 abandoned his emphasis on sensationalism for a focus on farcical comedy. The season opener, Broadhurst's year-old *What Happened to Jones?*, proved him wise. The result was a fire marshal's nightmare. According to the *Sun* of May 25, over 4000 persons witnessed two performances on Victoria Day. In the evening standing-room was at a premium past seven and, in order to accommodate the eager spectators, the orchestra eventually vacated their chairs, compelled, for the first time in the history of the Opera House, to play behind the scenes. The crowd, not disappointed, kept up a continuous roar of laughter from the rising of the curtain to the finish of the last act. Learning from this, Harkins concentrated exclusively on comedy in 1899, opening with a sumptuously mounted production of another new farce by Broadhurst, *Why Smith Left Home*, a piece even then playing at the Strand, London. This time the crush in the Opera House was so great that the orchestra had to be put on stage to make room for extra chairs, while hundreds of persons stood around the rear of the dress circle and balcony.

Well into the twentieth century, Harkins' popularity continued widespread and undiminished in eastern Canada: "No actor or the-

192

Ethel Wright Mollison (New York Public Library)

atrical managers with whom Halifax people have become acquainted ever held so firm a place, or was so solidly entrenched in their affections as is Mr. Harkins".[39] Citizens of Saint John would have wanted to share the honours with Price Webber and, in the past of course, with J. W. Lanergan.

Relatively few opera companies visited Saint John in the 1890's and of these only the Dora Wiley Company (1891) and the Gilbert English Opera Company (1893, 1895) had been there previously. Of the new companies, only the Grau Opera Company, whose name, the *Sun* said, stood at the head of operatic circles, achieved financial success. The crowded houses during its week-long engagement in December 1891 were a new experience to the frustrated directors of the Opera House. "What a remarkable run Grau's Opera Company has had!" the *Telegraph* exclaimed after the performers' departure for Quebec. "Who says that there are hard times in St. John when our people spend from $500 to $800 a night in attending operas?"[40] Grau had brought a large company of some forty people. He had spared no expense on wardrobe, specialties, or spectacular effects, including a pack of hounds for *Dorothy* and two costumes costing $4000 for *Queen's Lace Handkerchief*. The audience for *Said Pasha* on December 2, 1891, was the largest yet seen in the three-month old Opera House. During Grau's second visit in 1893, there was standing-room only for *New Boccaccio* on October 30 and for *Ship Ahoy*, whose receipts were $518 on November 4. The company's 1894 season began well with a packed house for *Amorita* on October 29 but then fell off. Increased costs had caused Grau to reduce his company, so that it was not up to what the Saint John public expected.

The New York Bijou Company (1891), Sargent Aborn's Comic Opera Company (1892), George A. Baker's Company (1892), the Standard Opera Company (1893), the Jaxon Opera Company (1898), and the Robinson Opera Company (1898, 1899) all offered similar repertoires of *Olivette, Chimes of Normandy, Bohemian Girl, Boccaccio, Robert Macaire, Said Pasha*, and *Fra Diavolo*, and all did only fair business regardless of merit. Even though Washington-born contralto Adelaide Randall had repeatedly received favourable notices in the New York *Spirit of the Times*,[41] and although her New York Bijou Company did the best business in Saint John in the summer of 1890, she still had difficulty paying salaries. Her chief problem was one that artists had experienced in Saint John before, namely, that the city was not large enough to give paying houses to two theatres. For the other opera companies, the problem lay as much in the nature of the competition. The unknown Standard Opera Company could not compete

194

with the popular Webber at Christmas 1893, nor could W. T. Carleton's Opera Company outdraw the Irish entertainment offered by Paddy Murphy in 1897. Another, probably lesser, problem is revealed in *Progress'* criticism of the Carleton Company: "What we are getting for opera this week, may be more correctly designated little more than dress rehearsals. What we lose in this, Halifax will gain, as the company is to appear in that city and there they will have the more finished work".[42] Press notices are difficult to evaluate, of course — although it is certainly true that several companies considered Halifax the better show town in these years, and consequently gave it preference. The *Sun*, in contrast to *Progress*, found Carleton's performances "worthy of metropolitan fame", of a general excellence rare in travelling companies, and took the public to task for its lack of encouragement, and it was supported in this by a letter to the editor. On another occasion, the *Sun*'s critic eagerly anticipated the American Grand English Opera Company's productions of *Faust* and *Il Travatore*, blithely assuming that others shared his enthusiasm: "Already St. John opera goers are furbishing up their neglected memories of the gems of the grand operas. And from the many pianos heard in an evening walk about town, it is noticeable that grand opera is being thought of".[43] The same critic, dismissing the inadequate patronage as the result of insufficient notice, would long remember the engagement as "a red letter day in the history of the Opera House". Although we do not know how well the company sang in Saint John when sober, in Halifax some of its members indulged in so much whisky that they were pronounced unfit to sing.

More than eighty dramatic companies new to Saint John (exclusive of opera and variety companies) came to the city for varying lengths of time in the 1890's. Most of these were repertory companies, but just over thirty were one-play companies who paid one or at the most two visits. Some of their plays were realistic comedies or melodramas relying for appeal on realistic or spectacular staging effects. *Uncle Hiram*, performed in May 1892, and *Joshua Simpkins*, in October 1894, were realistic rural comedies whose effects included operational saw mills that produced real sawdust in view of the audience. In *Joshua Simpkins* one of the characters was bound on a log and dragged within an inch or two of the circular saw's glittering teeth, to unbounded applause from the large audience. *Uncle Hiram*, in imitation of *Under the Gaslight*, had a railroad scene that "puts all others in the shade", in which a 200 foot train crossed the stage in 10 seconds. A ship scene was the focal point of *The Stowaway*, produced in 1895; its yacht was genuine, "complete in every appointment, with real mast, ropes, sails, spars, hatchways, brasses and a deck" upon which the actors walked.[44] From a box-office point of view, one of the most successful plays was Sutton Vane's melodramatic *Span of Life* in which, thirty feet above the stage, "the world's most famous acrobats" formed a human bridge over which three people nightly ran to safety. That production came to Saint John in 1899 from six weeks of successful touring in the United States, Great Britain, Australia, Germany, and France. In the same year *Darkest Russia*, besides its magnificent staging and especially the revolving scene in the last act, offered "something substantial in the way of theatrical diet"[45] in its well-constructed plot. Theatre-goers were sufficiently excited by the performances of Torontonian Herbert Fortier, his young leading lady Kathleen Willard, and their supporting cast that they attended in greater numbers on the second night than on the first, an occurrence rare in Saint John.

Other plays, like *A Social Season*, produced before a standing-room-only audience at the Mechanics' Institute in September 1890, and again at the Opera House in 1894, were intended "for Laughing Purposes only". *Doctor Bill* was received with "screams of laughter" on its first production in August 1893. Reportedly, some people nearly fainted from excessive laughter at *Town Topics* in June 1899, while *The Real Widow Browne* was "a long hearty laugh" in November. *Side Tracked*, illustrating the funny side of life on the rail, packed the Opera House "almost to suffocation" in May 1899, though Frank Tannehills' *Nancy Hanks*, an absurd piece about a man masquerading in female attire, drew only good houses in August 1898. All these plays are farce comedies with little plot, ludicrous situations, catchy music, and usually sensational effects. The *Sun*'s review of *Side Tracked* indicates those features most appreciated by its theatre critic: "The play's merits briefly stated are: The absence of horse play and vulgarity, the cleanness of its humor and the richness and abundance of its almost never-ceasing merriment . . . The songs, sketches, imitations, and specialty work generally were bright, cheerful, and for the most part new to St. John, the scenery was all that was called for, and the comedy went from start to finish with a delicious slam and abandon . . . Everybody who enjoys seeing and hearing pretty girls, funny comedians, and farce comedy with capable people in its cast should take in Side Tracked".[46]

Cole and Johnson's *A Trip to Coontown* in 1898 was full of clean, wholesome fun, and irresistibly funny. Arthur Moulton's A Baggage Check Company, on the other hand, needed to tone down its script a little to suit local taste; patronage was not what its management expected, and the *Sun* was not surprised when it was taken off the road after twelve weeks. The New York Trilby Company had poor houses, and was criticised for "indiscreet language". Charles Hoyt's earliest piece, *A Bunch of Keys*, was ill received in 1898. A "collection of incidents to teach no moral in particular", called a comedy "because comedy is the word used to describe almost everything put upon the stage at present", its cast "risked their limbs and reputation" in presenting it.[47] A far better reception was given Hoyt's best known work, *A Trip to Chinatown*, in 1896. That piece, a satire on hypocondriacs, whose chief character was Mr. Wellandstrong, was said to have earned $500,000 in its first five years and at the time of its author's death in 1900 to hold the record for the longest consecutive run in the annals of American drama. Described on one programme as "a musical trifle", it was popular for its songs, especially "Reuben, Reuben, I've been thinking", "After the Ball", and "The Bowery".[48] On September 4, 1896, its box-office receipts were $548.75, the second highest of the year at the Opera House.

A more sophisticated piece of this type, and one exceedingly well received was Yale's *The Evil Eye; or the Many Merry Mishaps of Nid and the Weird Wonderful Noddings of Nod*, produced in October 1899 at a cost reportedly greater than that of any show of the entire decade. The company arrived in Saint John with fifty people and two cars of scenery to delight very large audiences until past 11:00 with what the *Sun* described as "a trick pantomime, embellished with beautiful scenery, with costumes and pretty ballets".[49] More than a pantomime, the piece combined elements from grand opera, farce comedy, tragedy, melodrama, vaudeville, and ballet with mechanical marvels such as a human drawbridge, a human windmill, and a mammoth revolving stage. During the last act, dancers in an electric ballet were covered with tiny incandescent lamps that flashed and sparkled in a kaleidoscope of colour. In addition to all this, the *Evil Eye* was funny from beginning to end, incomparable with anything except Yale's own much earlier *Forever Devil's Auction*, which he had just revised for tour.

Of the repertory companies new to Saint John in the 1890's, Thomas Shea's came most frequently. Shea was a hardworking actor and playwright who toured the United States and Britain with his own stock company for more than half a century. At one of his London performances late in his career, he played before the monarchs of England, Belgium, and Spain, all of whom were present at once. In his thirties and nine years in the business when he first came to New Brunswick in 1892, he was respected as "an ordinary, normal, well-balanced individual" with no illusions about his profession. According to his own statement, he was in the profession

197

Fashion for the Theatre (New Brunswick Museum)

"for business reasons": "I try to be as artistic as I can, and a business man at the same time. . . . I give the popular price audiences the best I can in a serious vein".[50] Always conscious of the drama's influence on its audiences, he advertised on the front page of his programme: "I would not have a play in my Repertoire that any mother, any wife, or any daughter could not witness".[51] Criteria in keeping with his goals governed his selection of a new play: "My first search through a manuscript is for a moral that will be taught my hearers. Not a sermon, remember, but just a good suggestion for clean upright living. . . . If the moral is good, the scenes natural, then it remains to see if the play contains dramatic possibilities. That is, will the scenes lend themselves to the fine portrayal of emotions. Will the climaxes sustain the interest of the auditors and is there sufficient general interest in the subject portrayed to hold a big audience".[52]

Shea's repertoire in his first three seasons in Saint John was repetitive, emphasizing comedy. It included *Escaped From Sing Sing*, *Barred Out*, *Tangled Up*, *Mixed Up*, *The Eagle's Nest*, *Monte Cristo*, *Rip Van Winkle*, and *Dr. Jekyll and Mr. Hyde*. The company's engagements were brief, consisting of week-long periods in August or September on either end of a longer Halifax one. Even with popular ticket prices of .25, .35, and .50, the company rarely filled the Opera House's seating capacity. The trouble, according to the *Sun*, lay in inadequate support within the company for Shea's own strength and versatility as an actor. With his excellent stage presence, his full and resonant voice, and his abundant energy, he easily overshadowed other members of his company. The disparity was so great that in 1894 the *Sun* advised him not to return to Saint John until he had mended it. Seemingly heeding the paper's advice, Shea did not return until 1897 and 1898, at which time he came with a different repertoire and a stronger company than before. The favourite *Dr. Jekyll and Mr. Hyde* remained, but to it were added the thrilling dramas *Man O'Warsman*, *The Bells*, *Fire Patrol*, and *Slaves of Sin*.

Three members of Shea's 1892 company were, however, good enough or adventurous enough to start their own companies. Frankie Carpenter, his soubrette in 1892, advertised herself as "The Winsome Little Ray of Sunshine" when she came for a week in August 1894 at the conclusion of Shea's engagement. Jere McAuliffe, singer comedian, and Joseph Greene, character-actor and scene-painter, remained with Shea through 1894 but then returned to Saint John in 1896 with their own company. Their admission prices of .10, .20, and .30 and Frankie Carpenter's of .15, .25, and .35 indicate that neither company expected to rival Shea's in stature. Although the *Sun* awarded Miss Carpenter dubious praise when it judged her company good considering its low prices, *Progress* was unhappy with McAuliffe and Greene because it disputed their claim that their repertoire was new, written expressly for them; *My Boy Jack*, at least, had played in Saint John under another name. Greene occupied the Opera House himself for short periods in 1897 and 1898 with a repertoire that included *Plain Old Irishman*, *Condemned to Siberia*, Jones and Herman's *Silver King*, and Gillette's *Held by the Enemy*, and McAuliffe teamed with Maud Hillman to present *Fire Patrol*, *A Barrel of Money*, and *Cuban Spy* in April 1898. McAuliffe drew good houses because he could make people laugh, especially in his specialties. Joe Greene was no actor, but his popularity with the ladies made up for this, especially at matinees.

The other most frequent visitor to the Opera House in the 1890's was a more colourful figure than Shea. Lewis Morrison had embarked upon a stage career almost by accident, first when a friend in New Orleans invited him to fill a major role left vacant after a member of his stock company departed on account of some domestic trouble, and then when Edwin Booth invited him to replace an actor in his cast of *Richelieu* who had suddenly become ill. After an apprenticeship with established actors like Charlotte Cushman and Edwin Forrest, there followed three years of touring with James O'Neill, which terminated with O'Neill going on his own with *Monte Cristo* and Morisson travelling as Mephistopheles in his own five-act adaptation of Goethe's *Faust*. The first fifteen months on the road with *Faust* were disastrous. Morrison had invested $10,500 (every penny he had) in the project. Then the show lost money, the scenery burned, and he had to go deeply into debt to replace it. Finally, money derived from the sale of his house turned the tide. When he came to the Opera House in 1892 on the first of five visits there before 1900, he had already played Mephistopheles 2500 times and was well on his way to a fortune. Audiences never tired of seeing him as a "plausible and pleasing sort of devil."[53]

Although prices for his Opera House engagement were high at $1.00, .75, .50, .35, and .25, Morrison filled the theatre; the proceeds of $571.35 on a fine August evening in 1896 were the highest of the year.[54] He arrived in 1892 with twenty-five calcium lights, an electric plant, and two carloads of scenery to enable his "Sublime Scenic and Dramatic Production".[55] Particularly effective each year (1892, 1895, 1896, 1898, and 1899) were the garden scene in the second act, where 1000 irridescent bulbs glowed irresistibly, and the intricately weird witches' Brocken scene, which the *Sun* on November 17, 1899, described in some detail:

200

Owls hoot and flap their wings, vampire bats flit by in hideous silence, huge green slimy snakes float through space, monster dragons appear emitting fire from their dilated nostrils, myriads of scintillating fire flies illuminate the chasm, satyrs stir in stoical silence, sirens sing seductive ditties and goblins gyrate in demoniacal revelry. Mephisto in satanic majesty views with ghoulish glee this labyrinth of weirdness and from the summit of the 'Brocken', hurls thunderbolts at the poor mortals who have been banished to everlasting torment.

Finally, said the Brooklyn *Eagle*, "the shrieking, dancing witches and demons were swallowed up in a wonderful glare and downpour of electric rain, sulphurous, red flames, the rattling of thunder and the lightning darting hither and thither".[56] According to the *Sun*, it was "the most novel and imposing pyrotechnic display ever presented on any stage".

On three occasions during the 1890's, Josie Mills and Wallace Hopper brought companies to the Opera House. Miss Mills's company, managed by her twenty-nine-year-old husband Charles Haystead, came first in March 1892 via the Annapolis Valley, having only recently closed a six-week season in St. John's, Newfoundland, and prior to bookings in Moncton, Amherst, and Halifax. That year the company, whose repertoire included *Hazel Kirke*, *Under the Gaslight*, *Kathleen Mavourneen*, *Woman Against Woman*, and *Esmeralda*, was received cautiously. Those who chose the opening night performance of *The Galley Slave* over the other attractions in the city were not prepared to be easily captivated, but when their reserve dissolved during the second act, they responded generously with applause and curtain calls. From this point, the company gradually increased in favour until it packed the house at the opening of its return engagement in April 1893. This time the company came from Montreal and left for Fredericton, the Annapolis Valley, and Halifax. Leading man J. L. Ashton was a former Saint John man whose real name was John J. Armstrong. Son of a schoolmaster, he had worked as a printer for George W. Day and commenced his theatrical work in the old Dramatic Lyceum. In 1873 he had left Saint John for a career in the professional theatre and had subsequently travelled all over the United States.[57] The company's popularity continued unabated into their third and last Saint John season in 1897; a standing-room-only audience again greeted the opening, a production on May 10 of the most recent play in the repertoire, Sims and Pettitt's *Master and Man* (1889). Prices in the three years remained constant at .25, .35, or .50 for a reserved seat, while the repertoire varied somewhat from year to year. In 1893 the company added Arnold's *Nobody's Child*, Stevens' *Passion's Slave*, and Courtney's *The Gambler's Wife*, and in 1897 Daly's *Divorce* and Sims' *Lights o' London*. Early in December 1897, Miss Mills disbanded her troupe in Fort William, plagued by small houses that barely covered expenses and by unfavourable publicity surrounding an actor's abortive attempt to commit suicide with strychine. This was the culmination of a series of troubles that year which included poor houses in Nova Scotia, the forcible removal of a nine-year-old actress to the United States, and an accusation in the *Dramatic Mirror* that she was pirating scripts.

Wallace Hopper, who had been born in Hillsboro, near Moncton, owed his favourable reception, at least in part, to his local connections. As a youth he had participated in amateur theatricals, later identifying himself with the professional stage. In the early 1890's he began to travel throughout New England with his own company, making his home in Truro, Nova Scotia. Wherever he went, he was "Canadian to the backbone".[58] Though his forte on tour was comedy, like most actor-managers he was versatile. In 1893 he delighted good-sized audiences in the Opera House for two weeks in April with a mixture of comedy and melodrama in which his own personations included Dustan Kirke in *Hazel Kirke*, Bob Brierly in *Ticket-of-Leave Man*, Peter Probity in *Chimney Corner*, Larry in *Reclaimed*, Budd Bunkum in *Nugget Nell*, Wool in *Capitola*, and Sam Swichel in *Ten Nights in a Bar-room*. In the fall of 1895 he engaged the Singer Rink during Exhibition week to provide specialty entertainment "of a high order" for only a dime.

Certainly Hopper's greatest triumph in Saint John was the seven-week season in the Mechanics' Institute from December 17, 1894, to February 2, 1895, which endured despite regular entertainment at the Opera House; it had not been Hopper's intention to stay so long, but an appreciative response justified an extension of his original engagement. Previous to this, the longest season of the 1890's had been T. D. Frawley's four-week occupation of the Opera House in 1892, and even that had been broken into two visits of a fortnight each to allow the company to appear also in Fredericton and Moncton. Frawley's company, engaged as Saint John's Summer Stock Company, had given "splendid" productions of Pinero's comedy *Sweet Lavender*, the farcical *Kleptomania*, Gillette's *All the Comforts of Home* and *The Legal Wreck*, and Sardou's *The Marquise*, resisting competition from *Peck's Bad Boy* and *Alvin Joslin* at the Mechanics' Institute and specialty acts at the Lyceum. The Opera House management had refused several liberal offers to transfer the company to Halifax, preferring "to test once for all whether the amusement loving people of this city would patronize a first-class dramatic entertainment".[59] At the company's testimonial benefit on July 7, no standing room was left and the extra chairs were filled; otherwise patronage was uneven, and the Opera House management did not again in the decade attempt to establish its own stock company. During his longer engagement in 1894/5, Hopper frequently offered up to 200 presents, including gold watches and tea sets, in an effort to attract an audience. His aim was to provide satisfactory performance of standard plays at reasonable prices of .25 and .35, changing the bill each night. Although he seldom packed the house and his earnings cannot have been high, he was, apparently, satisfied.

A great deal more fanfare and some disappointment accompanied the much briefer appearances of a considerably better known person of the theatre whom Saint John claimed as its own. In August 1897 Margaret Anglin made her first professional appearance in the city from which her parents came. Her father, Timothy Warren Anglin, had been for many years editor of the Roman Catholic *Morning Freeman* and a staunch opponent of Confederation. He had been elected to the Legislature in 1860, the first Roman Catholic to represent Saint John. Then, when he lost his seat in the second Confederation election which defeated the government, he accepted an invitation to represent the French-speaking and Catholic county of Gloucester. In 1876, the year of Margaret's birth, he was in the middle of a term as Speaker of the House and had his family in Ottawa with him for the session which lasted from February 8 to April 12. Consequently, when Margaret arrived on April 3, she was born in the Speaker's apartment of the House of Commons. Had the timing been just a little different, she might have entered life in the same substantial house on Waterloo Street in Saint John as her brothers did and where the Anglins spent three-quarters of their time until Mr. Anglin lost his seat again in 1882 and moved his family to Toronto.[60]

Margaret (or Mary, as she was christened) was educated at the Sacred Heart Convent in Montreal until the age of seventeen when, through the intercession of her mother, herself a talented amateur actress, she wrung permission from her angry father to enroll in Nelson Wheatcroft's Dramatic School in New York. There she came to the attention of Charles Frohman who engaged her for the Empire Theatre stock company with which she made her first professional appearance in 1894 as Madeline West in *Shenandoah*. Two years later she was playing opposite James O'Neill as Ophelia in *Hamlet*, Virginia in *Virginius*, Julie in *Richelieu*, and Mercedes in *Monte Cristo*. In 1898, after a season with E. A. Sothern, she organized her own company for a tour of Lower Canada and the At-

203

lantic Provinces, performing Rosalind in *As You Like It* and producing also *Christopher Jr.* and *The Mysterious Mr. Bugle.* Saint John's Opera House was, of course, included on the itinerary. This was her second professional appearance in her native city for, in 1897, while vacationing with her mother and sister Eileen at the home of the Misses Furlong on Coburg Street,[61] she had appeared at the Mechanics' Institute with a "Specially Selected Dramatic Company" which included Mr. and Mrs. Tom Wise, formerly of W. S. Harkins' Company. The performance of *Salt Cellar, Comedy and Tragedy,* and *Rough Diamond* on August 6 was "a society event of rare brilliancy".[62] Those who were able to acquire a ticket for .25, .50, .75, or $1.00 found the occasion "fully verified all anticipations"[63] and convinced the most critical of Miss Anglin's extraordinary ability. The same company performed in Calais on the 9th and in Moncton on the 11th and then, by special request presented *Pygmalion and Galatea* on Saturday the 14th — at 2 p.m. because the Wises had to leave the city to be in New York for Monday morning. Not so statuesque a Galatea as Rhea or Lily Langtry, Miss Anglin brought to the part an interpretation more suited to her years than the matronly interpretations of her distinguished predecessors.

In an interview prior to her stage appearances, *Progress* found her "very charming in manner and attractive in person, with a dainty, svelte figure, and a riante, sparkling face, brilliant conversational powers, and a very pleasing manner".[64] In fact, the reporter decided, "a more thoroughly bewitching and interesting young lady it would be hard to imagine". Present in the young actress were the graciousness and earnestness which would persist as her reputation as a modern emotional actress increased into the next century.[65] A woman who hated publicity but was always driven by some invisible force to express deep feeling in acting, she was skilled also as a stage director and producer. Her 1898 starring tour was the first of many occasions when she took her career into her own capable control. The Saint John Opera House's contribution to that tour must have been of considerable disappointment to her, for though she was greeted with rapturous applause, the audiences were not nearly as large as ought to have been expected.

In the second half of the last decade in the nineteenth century, when business at the Opera House was overall much improved from the opening half, several dramatic companies came there two years in succession. The Sawtelle Dramatic Company did an immense business from September 9-21, 1895, though the following autumn their reception was much poorer — "the less said about the work of the company the better", wrote *Progress* on October 3. A

Lewis Morrison as Mephistopheles in Fau (New York Public Library)

Margaret Anglin (Harvard Theatre Collection)

young company led by twenty-three-year-old Jessie Sawtelle and managed by her husband J. Al., it offered a familiar repertoire including *Rosedale, Streets of New York, East Lynne, Michael Strogoff*, and *Ten Nights in a Bar-room*.

Katherine Rober, Ethel Tucker, and Mora Williams had more flair and more success. All three were present in the Opera House in 1896 and 1897, Miss Rober for two weeks in January/February 1896 and in January 1897, Miss Tucker for two weeks in July/August 1896 and in June, November/December 1897, and Miss Williams in September and October 1896 and August 1897. Handsome and clever Katherine Rober, who could speak and write several languages fluently, was at the head of a company which appeared regularly in Boston, Providence, Worcester, Portland, and other large cities. She travelled with dozens of trunks for her costumes, elegant gowns of silk, satin, lace, and chiffon (one with 3,000 rhinestones) each carefully laid out in cheesecloth with layers of tissue paper between the folds.[66] With her went also her own brass band and orchestra. In 1896 she enjoyed a successful season in Saint John with mostly well-known pieces like *Banker's Daughter, East Lynne, Camille*, and *Moths of Society*. Her *Fanchon* filled the Opera House to capacity, its captivating shadow dance still the hit it had been for Caroline Lanergan and Maggie Mitchell. The next year her success, if anything, was greater. On January 8, the *Sun* enthusiastically anticipated the arrival of "THAT LITTLE FAVORITE" and added, "No star has won popular favor to a more pronounced degree with the patrons of the theatre than has this clever little lady". This time her repertoire was different, including a coquettish *Carmen*, a western comedy *Nobody's Claim* which, "unlike most westerns, had a plot",[67] an Irish comedy *O'Day the Alderman, Inez* written especially for Miss Rober, and *Clemenceau Case*, which the *Sun* thought the most entertaining of any play in the repertoire but *Progress* found vulgar. Whatever, even the normally slack Saturdays at the Opera House were full; the standing-room-only sign was up by 2:00, one-half hour before curtain time for *The Little Detective* on January 16, and the evening audience for *Pink Dominoes* was one of the largest on record for Saturday evening.

A still heartier reception was given Ethel Tucker, her manager H. P. Meldon, and company. At the end of her first week in 1896, the normally cool *Progress* sang her praises:

> Not a little surprise has been given theatregoers this week in the altogether full and superior programmes and performances . . . at the Opera House. . . . The startling fact is that St. John has seldom been visited by a higher priced company that puts

on better or stronger plays, that pays more attention to details, that gives more finished performances throughout than Miss Ethel Tucker and company. It is the merest act of justice to say that Miss Ethel Tucker is one of the cleverest emotional actresses that has ever visited this city and although in the plays produced at this writing, this lady's impersonations have been quite varied, yet the same strength, the same power and intensity is apparent in each. She has one attribute that is noticeable and that is a very distinct articulation, that is manifested whether she is speaking rapidly or slowly, whether forcibly or in subdued tones. Every word is heard distinctly and without any strain of listening on the part of her audiences.[68]

The crowning success that year was a matinee production of *The Pearl of Savoy* on Labour Day, for which over 2000 people crammed into the Opera House, leaving several hundred to be turned away, unable even to find standing room. Other particularly popular productions were *La Belle Marie* and *Queena* in a repertoire that included also *Alone in London*, *An Unequal Match*, and *Camille*.

A change of repertoire entertained audiences in Saint John, Moncton, Sackville, and other Maritime centres in 1897. This time reviews fastened on scenery, costumes, and special effects — the four special sets carried for *Sea of Ice*, the carload of nautical scenery for *A Legal Wreck*, the grand staircase for *A Broken Life*, the costumes for *Queena*. Appreciated also were Mr. Meldon's disguises in *Escaped From Sing Sing*, Miss Tucker's artistic portrayal of the emotional lead in *The Governess*, and the "up-to-date plot" of *Speculation*. As had by now become the custom, restless spectators had no waits between acts, for all spaces were filled with specialties or the new fad, cinephotograph. In November, Miss Tucker brought her sister Lillian as co-star and drew her support from Charles C. Vaught's Company. With a more traditional repertoire (*Pygmalion and Galatea*, *East Lynne*, and *Led Astray*), they again drew good business.

Mora Williams, star of the company that immediately followed Ethel Tucker in 1896, was a distinct contrast to the emotional actress. A soubrette known generally as "the Comedy Sunbeam", she received notices of commendation for her good voice, her clear articulation, her versatility, and her more than ordinary cleverness. The 'gods' were filled for light pieces such as *Pretty Poll*, *Velvet and Rags*, and *Pretty Hoyden*. Her *Dad's Girl* captured the sympathies of its patrons, several of whom were ready to weep with her in her troubles, and at *Her Husband's Friend* a skye terrior, equally caught up in the suspension of disbelief, raised its voice in concert with the applause around it and successfully eluded the efforts of a constable to evict it. Like Miss Tucker, Miss Williams presented other scripts in 1897, heavily staged with special scenery and mechanical effects. For the waits between the acts she too provided "new and novel" specialties, especially the "latest and greatest" moving picture machine, Edison's projectoscope.

All four of these women charged "popular prices" of only .10, .20, and .30 admission. This, as *Progress* pointed out on August 1, 1896, might suggest "inferiority of material and production". That this was certainly not the case with the Ethel Tucker company, the paper was careful to note, and the favourable notices attached to the other three suggest that they too provided excellent value for money.

As if to balance the ladies, four male dominated companies made two consecutive annual appearances. They were the Bennett-Moulton Comedy Company (October 1896 and 1897), the Miles Ideal Company (July & September 1897 and September 1898), Edward T. Spear's Comedy Company (April 1898 and February 1899), and Paul Cazeneuve and Company (December 1898 and January 1899). In typical fashion, the press pronounced all four among the best theatrical companies ever to play in Saint John. Nevertheless, neither Paul Cazeneuve nor Spear received the patronage the papers thought they deserved and, though the business accorded the Bennett-Moulton Company was reputedly large, by the Friday of its first week at the Opera House, the company found it necessary to reduce ticket prices from .50, .30, and .20 to the same .30, .20. and .10 as the other companies charged.

Paul Cazeneuve was a young French romantic actor whose real name was George Alba de Cazeneuve. He offered a limited repertoire featuring *Three Guardsmen*, *Two Orphans*, *The Three Gentlemen*, *The Strategists*, *Don Garrick*, and *Don Caesar de Bazan*. Much later, in 1917, the Brooklyn *Eagle* would wish that he had "just a little more magnetism or personality";[69] perhaps in this lies a clue to his less than enthusiastic reception and resulting financial losses in the Maritime provinces.

Spear, Miles, and Bennett-Moulton offered a change of bill nightly although, apart from *Monte Cristo* given by both Spear and Bennett-Moulton, the repertoires of all three companies were entirely different. Spear entertained with pieces like *Red Cross Nurse*, *Soldiers' Sweetheart*, and *The Bosom Friend of Bowser*, while Bennett-Moulton did *Mother and Son*, *Chimney Corner*, *Miss Columbia*, and *Mckenna's Flirtation*, and John Miles, with scripts that included *Michael Strogoff*, *Damon and Pythias*, *The Circus Girl*, and *Rosedale*, was commended for the better than average

208

quality of his choices. The best talent in the Bennett-Moulton Company was Justin Adams, a native of Worcester, Massachusetts, then in his mid-thirties and, in his lifetime, author of more than 100 plays, many of which were produced professionally and by amateurs.[70] Talent in the Miles company was more evenly spread. In important roles were the by now middle-aged Albert Tavernier and W. J. Butler. With the latter was his wife Emma Lathrop and daughter Kathleen Butler. John Miles, who was pronounced "more than ordinarily capable", possessed a dashing, pleasing style. He was "an ideal Elliott Grey" in *Rosedale*, and did "excellent" work in *Damon and Pythias*.[71] The company as a whole was commended for the careful, conscientious attention which characterized every aspect of each production and for its strong specialty work. Beset by some difficulties while in Saint John, including the sprained ankle of Mrs. Miles and the very serious illness of Frank Lee Miles in 1897, it invariably played to excellent houses. The audience at the Labour Day matinee in 1897 reportedly exceeded previous records at the Opera House. The reason for their success, the *Sun* suggested on July 10, 1897, was simply their "superiority over other companies".

There is not room to speak of all the dramatic companies who undertook single engagements at the Opera House in the last decade of the nineteenth century. They included J. C. Lewis and Company (1890), Harry LaMarr's Comedians and Louise Hamilton and Company (1892), J. S. Murphy and Company, George Timmons, and Nellie Ganthony (1893), the John E. Brennan Company (1896), Arnold Reeves and the Broadway Stock Company (1897), Frost's Dramatic Company, the Crowell-Emery-Mason Company, and Isham's Octoroons (1898) and the Morrison Comedy Company, Kennedy's Players, and the Edwin Maynard Company (1899). The Leighton Stock Company, in October 1894, was the first to introduce "living pictures" to Saint John. In July of the same year a company directed by George Frohman played *Jane* and *The Masked Ball* to light houses, and in December a company sent on tour by his more famous brother Charles did well with *Charley's Aunt*. The Bubb Comedy Company did exceedingly good business in two weeks in January and February 1895, whereas the Castle Square Theatre Company failed to make a profit in April.

Manager for the Bubb Company was the same John S. Moulton who had managed the Bennett-Moulton Opera Company and the Comedy Company of the same name. He claimed credit for inaugurating the ticket prices of .10, .20, and .30 that were then reigning on the North American stage. An interview with *Progress* conducted at Saint John's Victoria Hotel, in which he explained the reasoning behind this, gives insight into the attitudes of both managers and public of the period:

> The plan was to give the public many times in value for what they had paid for. They were not slow in responding, and with a bound the new venture was a gigantic success. The new departure was received by the profession and managers in general with derision. All were unanimous in predicting immediate failure for the audacious manager who had foresight enough to see that the middle classes were shut out from entertainments whose prices were 35 cents to $1, and usually where they paid the ruling high prices in the smaller cities they received very little as an equivalent. Most managers thought all that was necessary for success was to secure a star whose popularity was on the wane in the metropolitan cities, surround her with a mediocre company and create a grand flourish of trumpets. They thought the susceptible public was awaiting them with open pocket books. This was the case once, but the popular priced scheme has revolutionized the matter. Low prices have made thousands of theatre goers and they readily discovered they had been easily duped. Now only the leading standard attractions can draw anything at regular prices.[72]

Whether lured by the low prices or the high quality of the performances by the forty-member company and its twelve-piece orchestra, theatre-goers turned out in droves. At least 1500 people crowded into the Opera House and hundreds were turned away from the opening production of *A Kentucky Home*, 500 were reportedly turned away from *East Lynne* and 1000 from a repeat *Kentucky Home* to which 1673 ticket-holders gained admittance. According to the *Sun* of January 21, over 15,000 people attended during the first week, many of whom then eagerly anticipated the company's return from a fortnight at the Academy of Music in Halifax. Only *Progress* was not pleased. It accused the company of deceiving the public by advertising as *A Kentucky Home* a play whose proper name was *Lynwood* and accused Mr. Bubb of discrediting H. P. Webber from the stage, a charge Bubb denied in a letter to the *Sun* in which he noted that *Progress* had promised a roasting if he did not advertise there. Before leaving Saint John on February 9, Moulton booked the Opera House for a return engagement in November. This did not materialize, however, for the company disbanded because of disagreements among its members. Instead, Bubb's cornet virtuoso, E. E. Nickerson, brought a Comedy Company in his own name that included among its ranks W. D. Corbett, H. L. Webb, and Ethel Fuller, three members of the defunct company. Present also was Charles W. Burrill who would return with his own company in 1898.

The Opera House was packed from top to bottom for the performance of *The Octoroon* that began the much anticipated visit of the Castle Square Theatre Company from Boston. Advance publicity had announced the company, together with its "Celebrated Orchestral Band". *Progress* was suspicious and, sure enough, only an orchestra leader arrived to put together a local band. About the opening night the *Sun* on April 2 said kindly that it was a "fair performance", even though the cast seemed unfamiliar with parts of the script. *Progress* was more scathing on April 6: "They have organized to do the provinces at a cheap rate apparently"; not everything, it thought, could be blamed on the heavy cold contracted by some performers. Not surprisingly, business fell off, even though the press agreed that the company improved significantly during its fortnight engagement.

Excellent business was enjoyed by Rice's Comedians in July/August 1897. The eighteen member company with its sixteen sets of scenery and six specialty artists was managed and directed by George Peck, the man who, some years before, had been chosen by P. T. Barnum to manage the world tour of the midgets General and Mrs. Tom Thumb and who, as half of the firm of Peck and Fursman, had for years produced *Uncle Tom's Cabin* across the United States and Canada. Shortly after his association with Charles Rice finished, he was to open, with Fursman, a five-storey amusement palace in New York, to include curiosities, side shows, a circus, and a theatre.[73] He told the *Sun* that he had formed Rice's Comedians in 1893 "to avoid the common error of selecting a high priced 'star' and surrounding him with an inferior company". The company, he explained, was stock "in the fullest sense, each individual member contributing to the general excellence of the performance and nothing being sacrificed to show off the particular ability of any one".[74] There was a jam at the Opera House for Rice's own *All in the Family* and a good reception for *Danites*, in which the author's daughter Maud Miller played Billy Piper. The company extended its stay from one week to two because of good business.

Despite the increasing insistence of some on the merits of the evenly balanced stock company, there were throughout the 1890's, as has already been seen, a goodly number of companies designed to provide a showcase for a star. When Tyrone Power starred in his own play *The Texan* at the Opera House on June 7, 1893, people all kept their seats until the final curtain, something that had not to that point been known in the short history of that theatre. Power, an Englishman by birth, had begun his stage career in 1884 in St.

211

St. John. N.B.

Opera House,

FRIDAY NIGHT, SEPT. 13th *1895*

SAWTELLE'S DRAMATIC CO.

IN THE 6 ACT MILITARY DRAMA OF

MICHAEL STROGOFF

THE COURIER OF THE CZAR

CAST OF CHARACTERS:

MICHAEL STROGOFF	J. AL. SAWTELLE
NADIA FEDOR	JESSIE SAWTELLE
Ivan Ogareff	Jos. W. Girard
Benj. Franklin Blunt	Tony West
Bonaparte Laidlaw	Harry Bewley
Czar of Russsia	Lawrence Grattan
Emir Feofar, of Bakhara	Mr. Munroe
General Kissoff	Fred D. Munroe
Telegraph Operator	A. Walters
Grand Duke	G. W. Josephs
Tartar Chief	Lawrence Grattan
Passport Agent	J. R. Spackerman
Priest	V. E. Evans
Maria Strogoff	Margaret Tennant
Zangara	Maude Atchinson
Nidine Gogal	Winona Bridges

SCENERY AND INCIDENTS.

ACT I.—Scene 1. PALACE OF THE CZAR—the fete, the rival correspondents, the tale of trouble, important news from Siberia, the special passport, a courier must be despatched, arrival of Strogoff, the instructions. "I will go, sire." "For God, the Czar, and for my country."

ACT II.—Scene 1. POST HOUSE ON THE FRONTIER—arrival of Strogoff, meeting with Nadia. "No Russian to cross to Siberia." Ogareff's insult. "Come, my sister, we'll travel on foot to Irkutsk."

ACT III.—Scene 1. FRONTIER TELEGRAPH OFFICE—the rival correspondents. Maria Strogoff's heroic efforts to arouse the Siberians, Strogoff denies his mother. "Am I a coward now?" Zangara's discovery, triumph of Tartars.

ACT IV.—Scene 1. THE TARTAR CAMP—arrival of the Tartar general, the insult, "shoot the other one," "Never! Never! glory of the victorious foe, Zangara brings news." "I'll find a way to make her speak." "Is that man your son?" "My son is no spy—that traitor lies." The fatal Khoran, the fiery sword, "Death! Death?" "Let none molest this man." "On to Irkutsk."

ACT V.—BANKS OF THE ANGORA—the wanderers, arrival of Michael and Nadia, the Tartar hordes, the test of blindness, the assault, rescue by the correspondents, "Come Strogoff with us," "come mother," "come Nadia." "On to Irkutsk."

ACT VI.—ANTE-ROOM IN THE GRAND DUKE'S PALACE AT IRKUTSK. The traitor Ogareff. The attempted delay. Strogoff and Ogareff face to face. The hand to hand death struggle. The mission accomplished. Michael Strogoff's reward. The Grand Duke and Irkutsk saved. "For God, the Czar, and for my country."

Musical Selections by Sawtelle's Imperial Orchestra,
Under the direction of Prof. Geo. H. Miller.

1. OVERTURE, Light Cavalry .... Suppe
2. HARP SOLO, "Spring rejoicing," .... Spaulding.

Georgie Dean Spaulding.

3. SELECTION, Oolah .... Leocq
4. UNCLE EPH'S WEDDING .... Laupe
   The wedding march, wedding bells, in the church, the church, congratulations, Uncle Eph's favorite dance, the Essence, march to supper, ending with old plantation walk around.
5. PIPELAPHONE SOLO, "A Night Off" .... Geo. A. Parks
   DESCRIPTION—The first strains of a melody describing the honeymoon of a newly married couple, followed by the bridegroom accepting an invitation to go with the boys to the club for a good time, popping of champagne bottles, returning home at 4 o'clock in the morning, whistling, crowing roosters, finale.
6. MEDLEY OVERTURE, Gaiety Girls .... Sheppregell

Repertoire for the Week:

Saturday Afternoon	TEN NIGHTS IN A BAR-ROOM
Saturday Night	MIDNIGHT CALL
Monday Afternoon, Sept. 16th	MICHAEL STROGOFF
Monday Night, Sept. 16th	FAUST

E. J. Armstrong, Steam Printer.

J. K. Emmet
(New York Public Library)

(Harvard Theatre Collection)

212

Augustine, Florida, with a name already made famous by his grandfather "who was one of the most noted interpreters of Irish characters on the stage in the nineteenth century".[75] For two years he played with Mme. Janauschek and then joined Augustine Daly's company, to which he still belonged when he came north on a summer tour in 1893, having as his leading lady Edith Crane whom he eventually married in 1898, after the obstacles of his wealthy uncle's opposition and her first marriage were removed. A character actor with a heavy physique and a full voice, whose countenance and demeanor were those of a patrician, Power was called by dramatic critic William Winter "the chief hope of the American stage".[76] His week in Saint John must have been disappointing to him for, after *The Texan*, he drew only fair houses. The company then moved on to Montreal.

Sidney Drew, a Dubliner by birth and an adopted brother of the actor John Drew, toured with his first wife Gladys Rankin in comedy and vaudeville and later, during her illness, entered films. At his death in 1919 the Chicago *News* said of him: "No actor, however important, enjoyed wider popularity than this comedian who emitted sunshine to millions of cinema devotees, old and young, of every walk of life, through a series of clean and wholesome playlets."[77] The critic for the Halifax *Herald* who attacked his company's production of the *Oliver Twist* adaptation, *Nancy*, cannot have foreseen that reputation, nor can the people of Saint John who stayed away from his productions of *Still Waters Run Deep* and *The Wonderful Woman*. In the company were W. A. Whitecar, an old familiar face in the city, and the young Ethel Barrymore.

When James O'Neill, father of the famous playwright Eugene, brought *Monte Cristo* to the Opera House in September 1897, he had been starring as Dantes to the delight of theatre-goers all over the continent ever since he first played the role in 1883 at Booth's Theatre, New York, on the invitation of John Stetson. According to the Chicago *Chronicle*, in 1897 he was still as youthful looking as when he began, with an erect carriage, bright eye and vigorous voice.[78] Some years before he had tired of Dantes and had been trying, with little success, to ween the public away from it.[79] Thus he performed also in *Virginius, Hamlet, Richelieu, The Courier of Lyons*, and *The Dead Heart* — "a repertoire of unusual attraction", wrote *Progress*. His rendition of Dantes, at the Opera House, *Progress* believed, was a revelation to all who witnessed it, showing how meagre other productions were. This was not, however, sufficient to attract him further notice from the press. The *Sun*, though it carried advertisements prior to his arrival, had none during the actual week of his engagement and printed no reviews; the *Globe* carried advertisements but not reviews, though it contained full coverage of the variety entertainment offered in competition at the Palace.

Far more popular with the Saint John public and with the *Sun*, though not with the more serious-minded *Progress*, were J. K. Emmett Jr. and Lottie Gilson. Emmett had fallen heir, after his father's death in 1891, to the series of 'Fritz' plays which had made the senior Emmett the pioneer among successful German-dialect comedians and one of the wealthiest actors in the world. Charles Gaylor's *Fritz, Our German Cousin* was the first of a series of almost plotless plays that were excuses for the songs the star sang in his sweet voice to charm the ladies and children, his most loyal admirers. J. K. Jr. inherited his father's handsome looks, his graceful manner, his sweet voice, and his feminine admirers, though some critics thought his personal magnetism inferior to his father's, and he remained, despite his financial success and large following, essentially his father's son.[80] According to the *Dramatic Mirror* of December 24, 1898, Lottie Gilson, "The Little Magnet", was the most popular soubrette on the vaudeville stage and hence one of its highest salaried artistes. "Possessed of a pretty face, an attractive presence and that indefinable something called magnetism", she had steadily worked her way up from her debut in 1884 at the old National Theatre in the Bowery. For several years she toured as co-star with Emmett Jr., whom she took for her third husband in 1900.[81]

The pair presented *Fritz in a Madhouse* and *Jane* to large audiences, repeated curtain calls, and constant laughter at the Saint John Opera House in July 1899. Miss Gilson, the *Sun* said on July 25, captured the house with her songs, while Emmett's comic style caught the audience "with a vengeance". The only damper on an otherwise successful season was *Progress'* judgment, concurring with the New York *Spirit of the Times'* assessment of *Fritz in Love*, that *Fritz in a Madhouse* was a silly piece on which a pruning knife could be used to advantage. Emmett, it thought, did not shine very brilliantly; while Miss Gilson, admittedly bright, pretty, and possessed of a certain magnetism as well as a fair singing voice, cheapened herself and the company generally by the little "talks" in which she indulged.[82]

As the nineteenth century drew to a close and slipped easily into the twentieth, the Saint John Opera House at last reached firm financial ground. The Valentine Stock Company came there in December 1899 from twelve weeks at the Grand Theatre, Winnipeg, for what was expected to be a six-week engagement. But the six weeks stretched into four months, interrupted only by one night in

214

Calais while the Reverend Lindsay Parker gave an illustrated lecture on the Emerald Isle from the Opera House stage, by four nights in Fredericton when the Opera House was rented to the Father Mathew Association for a minstrel show and to the Saint John Amateurs for *Iolanthe*, and by two weeks at the Academy of Music in Halifax.

The company opened on December 25 with William Gillette's farcical comedy *All the Comforts of Home* in the afternoon and Bronson Howard's society drama *Young Mrs. Winthrop* in the evening. On the 26th, the *Sun* pronounced it "head and shoulders above any company seen in this city since T. D. Frawley's memorable engagement". In the evening "even standing room could not be had by late comers for love or money". The repertoire was a solid one and, with 100 plays at its command, the company had no need to repeat. During their nearly four months in residence at the Opera House, the actors presented Shakespeare's *Taming of the Shrew*, *Romeo and Juliet*, *The Merchant of Venice*, and *Othello* (the latter two in the Booth-Barrett version), Sheridan's *The Rivals* and *School for Scandal*, favourites from the Lanergan days in *Ingomar*, *Lady of Lyons*, *Richelieu*, and *Camille* (using Julia Marlow's promptbook), and standard scripts of the last two decades including *Little Lord Fauntleroy*, *Private Secretary*, *Lady Windermere's Fan*, *Moths*, *Lost Paradise*, *Monte Cristo*, and *The Jilt*.

The Valentine Stock Company was owned by two sisters, Anne and Kate Blancke. Its leading lady was Jessie Bonstelle, its leading man Edward Mawson. Other core members of the company included Jack Webster, "a manly and virile actor" whose stage presence delighted the eye; Robert A. Evans, a versatile character actor who had been with the company since its inception only three years previously in 1897; Charles Fleming, a native of Saint John and the son of the late novelist May Agnes Fleming; Edward N. Leonard, low comedian; Edmund Whitty; Frederick Haak; Mary Taylor; and Beulah Watson. Mawson, the most popular actor of the company, excelled in the heavy roles of Ingomar, Othello, Shylock, and Mercutio, leaving to handsome Jack Webster Romeo, Iago, and Bassanio. Miss Bonstelle was best as "a sweet, entrancing woman". Her Camille was idealized, showing all that was good and loveable in that unfortunate woman, her Portia full of "natural girlishness" and "charming naivete", her Desdemona "the very epitome of womanly grace and loveableness", and her Juliet "delicious" in the lighter scenes while possessed of "wonderful intensity and dramatic power" in the potion scene. Kate Blancke was splendid in the roles of older women like Mrs. Malaprop, Juliet's nurse, and Emilia. Repeatedly, the company as a whole was praised for its

Tyrone Power
(New York Public Library)

James O'Neill as
Count of Monte Cristo
(New York Public Library)

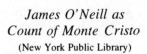

216

conscientious preparation, its attention to detail, its costumes, and its attractive and tasteful stage designs.

Not since the days of J. W. Lanergan had the citizens of Saint John entered so heartily into the entertainment provided for them. From week to week the house increased in size, easily supporting two plays a week and sometimes, as in the case of *The Merchant of Venice*, holding one for a full week. Typically, as people patronized the theatre more and more, they welcomed its actors into their lives. The *Sun* put into words what happened, on the occasion of the company's departure for Halifax on March 24:

> Three months ago last Thursday they arrived from Winnipeg, strangers in a strange land, not any of the company, with the exception of Messrs. Fleming and Whitty having a friend in the city. This state of affairs did not last long, and before many weeks, they numbered their friends by hundreds, and their admirers — the excellent business of the engagement attests to that point. During the last few weeks the doors of many of the most exclusive houses of the city have opened to the members and many of those little social functions which make life all the more pleasant, have been graced by the presence of the lady members of the company.[83]

It was with genuine regret, as at the loss of good friends, that Saint John finally said farewell to the Valentine Company at the end of April 1900, finding consolation in the assurance that the actors would return to the boards of the Opera House at the next Christmas season. The company could not remain past its April 28 closing date, for the Opera House was booked steadily through the rest of 1900 both by entertainers known to Saint John — Jere McAuliffe, Shipman's Lyceum Company, W. S. Harkins' Company, Frank Tannehill Jr. and Company, the Morrison Comedy Company, Yale's Forever Devil's Auction Company and the Evil Eye Company, and by companies that had not visited the city before — Jessie Harcourt Company, Richard's Stock Company, the Boston Stock Company, D. W. Truss Stock Company, Gorton's New Orleans Minstrels, the Black Patti Minstrels, the Alabama Troubadours, and the Ravel New Humpty Dumpty Pantomine and Specialty Company. So successful was the year that the slight net profits of $160 realized in 1899 turned into a cash credit of over $1,570 in 1900, even after paying all running expenses and adding considerably to the stage plant and house fixtures.[84] The Blancke sisters employed no gimmicks, either of script or staging; they stood outside the fads in theatre. The strength of their company lay in its reliability, in its ability to win the confidence of the people with good, solid,

217

consistent work. These were the qualities, as Lanergan had discovered forty years previously, that ultimately won the support of the sector of the population that understood and encouraged the arts.

» » » » » » » » » » » » » » » » »

They told the same old stories,
They sang the same old airs,
They sat in ancient costumes
On very modern chairs.

While paper snow was falling,
They cooked green ears of corn,
And 't wasn't fifteen seconds
Between the night and morn.

The same old villain plotted,
The same old lover sighed,
The same relentless parent
His eager suit denied.

They wrote in twenty seconds
A letter, or a will;
They waved in air their glasses,
Yet drank them brimming, still.

The thunder lacked an echo,
The moon was pale and weak,
And when the ghost was rising
The crank set forth a squeak.

Ah! yes, the same old people,
With nothing new to tell;
And yet, I must confess it,
Too soon the curtain fell.[85]

Notes

Chapter I

1. *Saint John Gazette*, March 31, 1789. The late date of publication of the response to the production might seem to indicate a performance date of March 28 rather than February 28. The evidence of Chipman's letter is strong, however. The dating of his letters is known to be reliable, whereas it was not unusual for a letter or prologue to appear in print some time after the event it described.

2. W.S. MacNutt, *New Brunswick, A History: 1784-1867* (Toronto: Macmillan, 1963), p. 85f.

3. W.O. Raymond, ed., *Winslow Papers* (Microfilm, reel 3 New Brunswick Museum), Ward Chipman to Winslow, March 3, 1789.

4. *Ibid.*

5. Allardyce Nicoll, *A History of English Drama* (Cambridge University Press, 1966), III, 88.

6. C. Leech and T.W. Craik, eds., *The Revels History of Drama in English* (London: Methuen, 1975), VI, 116f.

7. *Royal Gazette*, April 7, 1795.

8. Many details in this chapter can be supplemented by reference to Mary Elizabeth Smith, "Theatre in Saint John: The First Thirty Years", *Dalhousie Review*, LIX (Spring 1979), 5-27.

9. *Royal Gazette*, February 17, 1795.

10. *Ibid.*

11. Cited in H.H. Langton, ed., *Travels in the Interior Inhabited Parts of North America in the Years 1791 and 1792* (Toronto, 1937), p. 25.

12. *Royal Gazette*, February 3, 1795.

13. J.W. Lawrence, *Footprints: or Incidents in the Early History of New Brunswick* (Saint John: McMillan, 1883), p. 69.

14. McGill University Libraries, U.L.M. 74-573, "Characters of Different Plays As performed at the Theatre King Street". This handwritten manuscript belonged to Stephen Sewell, son of the Loyalist Jonathan Sewell, and was presented to McGill by his partner, F. Griffin, Esq.

15. Winslow Papers, Winslow to Ward Chipman, March 12, 1789.

16. *Saint John Gazette*, March 31, 1789.

17. *Royal Gazette*, January 20, 1795.

18. Public Archives of Canada, MG 23 D 1 series 1, vol. 6, Ward Chipman to Jonathan Odell, December 27, 1793.

19. *Saint John Gazette*, March 31, 1789.

20. Charles H. Shattuck, *Shakespeare on the American Stage* (Washington: Folger Shakespeare Library, 1976), p. xi.

21. *The Works of John Home Esq. now first collected, To which is prefixed an account of his life and writings by Herny MacKenzie* (Edinburgh: Constable, 1822), I, 38f.

22. *Saint John Gazette*, February 22 & March 15, 1799.

23. *Ibid.*, April 19, 1799.

24. *Ibid.*, April 26, 1799.

25. W.S. MacNutt, *The Atlantic Provinces: The Emergence of Colonial Society, 1712-1857* (Toronto: McClelland and Stewart, 1965), p. 112.

26. MacNutt, *New Brunswick*, p. 96.

27. *Saint John Gazette*, December 28, 1798.

28. Arthur Hornblow, *A History of the Theatre in America* (Benjamin Blom, reprint, 1965), I, 43.

29. Carleton County Historical Society. "Excerpts from the Diary of John S. Ellegood, Saint John, Jan. 4 – March 1801".

30. *Ibid.*, John S. Ellegood to Jacob Ellegood Jr., February 19, 1801.

31. New Brunswick Museum, Odell Papers.

32. Saint John Regional Library, Manuscript Accession No. 113. Discussion of Winslow's script is indebted to Ann Gorman Condon, "New Brunswick's First Play: A Political Satire by Edward Winslow" (unpublished manuscript).

33. W.G. MacFarlane, *New Brunswick Bibliography: The Books and Writers of the Province* (Saint John: Sun Printing Co., 1895), p. 2f.

34. Lt. Adam Allan, *The New Gentle Shepherd, A Pastoral Comedy* (London: W.J. and J. Richardson, c. 1798), A2.

35. *Royal Gazette*, February 6, 1809.

36. A "To Let" notice in the *City Gazette* and *N.B. Courier* on September 13, 1817, indicates that there were a number of rooms in the building.

37. *Royal Gazette*, February 6, 1809.

38. *Ibid.*, November 20, 1809. Other details regarding the disbanding of the company are in the *Royal Gazette* of October 23 & 30 and November 6 & 13.

39. James Hannay, *History of New Brunswick* (Saint John: John A. Bowes, 1909), I, 332.

40. Public Archives of Canada, MG 23 D 1 series 1, vol. 6, Ward Chipman to Jonathan Odell, May 16, 1814.

41. Saint John Regional Library, W.O. Raymond Scrapbook 2, 207, Clarence Ward, "Theatre, and Amateur Theatricals in St. John, from the Earliest Period".

42. In addition to the Marriotts and C.S. Powell, Saint John had had brief visits from professional showmen such as Messrs. MacGinnis, Hackley, and Rannie.

43. The playbill for the second night of *Tekeli* on September 17, 1817, is the oldest known extant playbill in Canada. It is in the Programme Collection, New Brunswick Museum Archives.

44. *Free Press*, January 28, 1817.

45. Cited in Y.S. Bains, "The Articulate Audience and the Fortunes of the Theatre in Halifax in 1816-1818", *Dalhousie Review*, LVII (Winter 1977/78), 726-735.

46. George C.D. Odell, *Annals of the New York Stage* (New York, 1927), I, 330.

47. Bains, p. 728.

48. *New Brunswick Courier*, August 2, 1817.

49. *Acadian Recorder*, June 6, 1818.

Chapter II

1. Esther Clark Wright, *Saint John Ships and Their Builders* (Wolfville, Nova Scotia, 1976), p. 12.
2. *Sketches of New Brunswick, Containing an Account of the First Settlement of the Province, with a Brief Description of the Country, Climate, Productions, Inhabitants, Government, Rivers, Towns, Settlements, Public Institutions, Trade, Revenue, Population, &c.* (Saint John: Chubb & Sons, 1825), p. 30.
3. *Letters from Nova Scotia and New Brunswick, Illustrative of Their Moral, Religious, and Physical Circumstances, During the Years 1826, 1827 and 1828* (Edinburgh: Waugh & Jones, 1829), p. 157f.
4. Wright, p. 11.
5. J. McGregor, *Historical and Descriptive Sketches of the Maritime Colonies of British America* (London: Longman, Rees, Orme, Browne & Green, 1828), p. 153.
6. *Courier*, July 17, 1819; *City Gazette*, June 14, 1820.
7. *City Gazette*, March 13, April 10, September 19 & November 28, 1822; *Courier*, August 30, 1823.
8. *Courier*, October 22, 1825.
9. This is the same reason given in *Sketches of New Brunswick*, p. 32, to explain why no attention had yet been given to beautifying the city.
10. The only member of the circus mentioned by name is Mr. Godeau.
11. Register of Voters, City of Saint John, 1785-1862, p. 44.
12. Saint John Registry Office, C2, 265-7 & 269f.
13. *Ibid.*, C2, 520f.
14. *New Brunswick Magazine*, III, iv (1879); cf. *Courier*, October 4, 1845.
15. *Courier*, July 25, 1829.
16. M.B. Leavitt, *Fifty Years in Theatrical Management* (New York: Broadway Publishing Co., 1912), p. 69.
17. *Times Star*, December 20, 1926.
18. *Courier*, May 2, 1829.
19. On these actors see Alston Brown, *History of the American Stage* (New York & London: Benjamin Blom, repr., 1969); W.W. Clapp, *A Record of the Boston Stage (Boston, 1853)*, George C. Odell, *Annals of the New York Stage* II (New York, 1927).
20. Clapp, p. 215.
21. *City Gazette*, June 18, 1828.
22. *Courier*, June 7, 1828.
23. *Ibid.*, June 28, 1828.
24. *British Colonist*, July 18 & 23, 1828; *Courier*, June 4 & 28, 1828.
25. Quoted in George Rowell, *The Victorian Theatre 1792-1914: A Survey* (Cambridge University Press, 2nd ed., 1978), p. 39.
26. *British Colonist*, June 27, 1828.
27. *Courier*, July 5, 1828, October 2, 1830.
28. Clapp, p. 113f.
29. *British Colonist*, July 18, 1828.
30. *City Gazette*, June 18, 1828. Cf. June 25, August 13, 20 & 27, 1828.
31. *British Colonist*, June 25, 1828; *Courier*, June 28, 1828.

32. *City Gazette*, June 10, 1829.

33. *Courier*, July 11, 1829.

34. Odell III, 410, shows Forbes at the Bowery in the spring of 1829, although Alston Brown, p. 129, says he made his New York debut in August 1835.

35. *Courier*, July 17, 1830.

36. Ralph Picard Bell Library, Stewart Scrapbook 27, Wilkie Collins, "Black-Eyed Susan".

37. Michael R. Booth, ed., *English Plays of the Nineteenth Century* (Oxford: Clarendon, 1969), I, 11.

38. *The British Theatre* (1808), xxiii.

39. New Brunswick Museum, W.O. Raymond Scrapbooks 5, 228.

40. H.J.M. Johnson, *British Immigration to British North America 1815-1860*, Canada's Visual History, Ser. I, vol. 8 (Ottawa: National Film Board, 1974), p. 2.

41. New Brunswick Museum, Moses Perley Letters.

42. *City Gazette*, June 18, 1828.

43. Reported users of the Theatre from 1831 to 1837 are: Mr. Black, manager of the Halifax Theatre (July 1832); "Aborigines of America" in an Indian dance (August 1833); equestrian performances (October 1832-February 1833); Boston circus (summer 1837).

44. For a full report of the incident, see M.E. Smith & A.E. McKim, "Death on the Saint John Stage", *Atlantic Advocate*, November 1978, pp. 86-88.

45. *Courier*, October 1, 8 & 15, 1831; Saint John Registry Office, L2,387; L2,542; S2,474.

46. Odell, IV, 159 & 246. Nickinson's career is sketched in Alston Brown, p. 265f. See also M.D. Edwards, *A Stage in our Past* (University of Toronto Press, 1968), pp. 12, 25, 27.

47. An article in *Progress*, September 19, 1891, entitled, "In an Old Playhouse", reproduces the tattered playbill of *Othello*. Since Deverna expresses his appreciation for "support already received from the inhabitants of St. John", this cannot have been the first programme.

48. *Weekly Observer*, August 14, 1838.

49. Odell, III, 624.

50. *Courier*, August 11, 1838.

51. *Courier*, September 29 & October 6, 1838.

52. Mrs. Charles had already played Hamlet in New York in 1836. See Odell, IV, 142.

53. *Commercial News and General Advertiser*, October 19, 1839.

54. Odell, IV, 287. *Courier*, August 17, 1839.

55. *Commercial News*, September 16, 1839.

56. *Ibid.*; *Courier*, July 27, 1839.

57. *Morning News*, June 19, 1840.

58. *Ibid.*; *Courier*, June 13, 1840.

59. *Morning News*, May 29, 1840.

60. *Ibid.*, June 19, 1840.

61. Odell, IV, 116.

62. *Morning News*, July 8, 1840.

63. *Ibid.*, July 6, 1840.

64. *Courier*, July 11, 1840; *Herald*, July 8, 1840.

65. *Morning News*, July 15, 1840.

66. *Ibid.*, July 27, 1840.

67. *Ibid.*, June 14, 22 & September 1, 1841; Odell, Brown, *et al.*

68. *Morning News*, June 21, 1841.
69. *Weekly Chronicle*, June 18, 1841.
70. *Ibid.*
71. *Morning News*, June 23, 1841.
72. *Ibid.*, September 26, 1842.
73. *Commercial News*, September 16, 1839.
74. Quoted in the *Weekly Observer*, January 12, 1841.
75. *New Brunswicker*, March 31, 1842; *Morning News*, May 3, 1844 & December 3, 1845.
76. *Morning News*, *Saint John Herald*, and *Loyalist* carry advertisements and reviews for the Histrionic Society.
77. *Herald*, April 4, 1845.
78. *Morning News*, April 4, 1845.
79. *Ibid.*, April 9, 1845.
80. *Herald*, April 11 and *Loyalist*, April 10, 1845.
81. *Courier*, June 21, 1845; cf. *Morning News*, June 30, 1845.
82. *Morning News*, September 8, 1845.
83. *Ibid.*, December 10, 1845; *Courier*, December 6, 1845; *Head Quarters*, December 10, 1845; *New Brunswick Reports*, December 12, 1845.

Chapter III

1. "Only Montreal and Quebec City had a larger population than the 31,174 in Saint John and Portland in 1851." C.M. Wallace, "Saint John Boosters and the Railroads in Mid-Nineteenth Century", *Acadiensis* VI,i (1976), 71-91.
2. Public Archives of Canada, M.G.9, A1, vol. 120. New Brunswick Executive Council, Local Government, Saint John, City and County: Correspondence, Petitions and Papers, 1819-1857.
3. *Reports on the Accounts of the Corporation of the City of Saint John for the year ending 31st December, 1864* (Saint John: Barnes & Company, 1865). See also Greg Marquis, "Crime in Saint John 1860-1870" (unpublished manuscript).
4. *Courier*, August 10, 1861. See also C.M. Wallace, "Saint John, New Brunswick (1800-1900)", *Urban History Review* No. 1-75 (1975), 12-21, and J.M. Careless, "Aspects of Metropolitanism in Atlantic Canada", *Regionalism in the Canadian Community* (Toronto, 1969), pp. 117-129. The population of Halifax in this period was 25,025.
5. (London, 1847), p. 331.
6. In 1846, 9,000 emigrants from Ireland landed in Saint John; of these one-half moved to the United States. See "Report of the Government Emigration Office – Saint John". *Journal of the Legislative Assembly* (Fredericton: S. Simpson, 1847), p. cxxi. The 1851 census notes that 12,872 of the 15,804 immigrants residing in the Saint John area were of Irish extraction.
7. 3rd edition (Edinburgh: Anderson & Bryce, 1844), p. 19.
8. *New Brunswick; with Notes for Emigrants*, p. 332.
9. "James W. Lanergan of the Globe Theatre, His Career as Actor and Manager", *Boston Times*, March 12, 1876.
10. "On the Stage", *Saint John Globe*, December 14, 1901.
11. In general, the legitimate drama included Shakespearean and other five-act plays. In the nineteenth century the term was used "as a defence against the en-

croachments of farce, musical comedy, and revue." *Oxford Companion to the Theatre*, 3rd ed. (Oxford University Press, 1967), p. 551.

12. *Boston Herald*, August 20, 1856, quoted in the *Morning News*, August 27, 1856.

13. *Boston Times*, March 12, 1876.

14. Saint John Registry Office, 14, 384-386, John Ansley to James West Lanergan.

15. *Courier*, March 21, 1857.

16. *St. John Chronicle*, May 15, 1857.

17. *Courier*, May 16, 1857.

18. *Morning News*, June 5, 1857. See also *Courier*, April 25, *Morning News*, May 11, and *Chronicle*, June 12, 1857.

19. *True Humorist*, June 24, 1865.

20. *Courier*, April 25, 1857.

21. *Ibid.*

22. New Brunswick Museum, Jarvis Papers. Armstrong to Jarvis, February 21, 1863.

23. *Morning News*, June 17, 1857.

24. *Courier*, June 20, 1857.

25. *Ibid.*, July 18, 1857. *Dred* was dramatized by John Brougham.

26. Harvard Theatre Collection, Marshall file.

27. *Morning News*, August 17, 1857.

28. *New York Express*, November 10, 1866.

29. *Courier*, August 7 & 21, 1858; *Morning News*, August 11, 1858; Halifax *Sun*, February 1, 1858.

30. *Boston Times*, March 12, 1876.

31. December 3, 1898. The New York *Dramatic Mirror* of the same date described how Couldock came by the role.

32. *New York Sun*, March 31, 1901.

33. *Morning Freeman*, July 21 & 30, 1859.

34. New York *Atlas* review, cited in *Gleason's Pictorial Drawing Room Companion* June 24, 1854, p. 416.

35. July 10, 1860.

36. M. Wilson Disher, *Melodrama* (London: Rockliff, 1954), p. 4.

37. The farce was localized from *Did You Ever Send Your Wife to Camberwell?*

38. Harvard Theatre Collection, Chanfrau file, "Early Struggles of Prominent Actors".

39. *Courier*, August 15, 1863.

40. *Ibid.*, August 8, 1863.

41. Programmes and advertisements spell this lady's name variously as Johnson and Johnston.

42. Harvard Theatre Collection.

43. *Courier*, August 2, 1862.

44. *Morning News*, August 8, 1862.

45. *Ibid.*, August 1, 1866.

46. *Courier*, June 13, 1863.

47. *Ibid.*, August 24, 1861.

48. New Brunswick Museum Playbill for June 20, 1866.

49. The following members of Lanergan's companies are mentioned in Eugene Tompkins, *The History of the Boston Theatre, 1854-1901* (New York: Houghton & Mifflin, 1908), as members of the Boston Theatre company: Messrs. Moses Fiske,

224

N.T. Davenport, H.R. Lampee, J.H. Browne, W.H. Whalley, Wm. Scallan, George Clair, Shirley France, C.H. Wilson, Wm. Collings, S.H. Forsberg, H.L. Bascomb, T.C. Howard, Frank Mayo, Louis Aldrich, D.R. Allen, Neil Warner, Frank Roche, Cowell Daymond, W.H. Danvers, and J. Taylor, and Misses Lizzie Emmons, Rachel Noah, Rachel Johnson, Susie Cluer, Louisa Morse, Annie Winslow, Helen Tracy, Belle Dudley, Mrs. E.M. Leslie, Mrs. D.R. Allen, Mrs. S. Flood, and Mrs. Sylvester.

50. *Courier*, June 14, 1862.

51. Harvard Theatre Collection, Lennox file, obituary notice dated March 25, 1905.

52. *Morning News*, July 26, 1861; *Courier*, August 16 & 23, 1862.

53. *Courier*, July 4, 1863.

54. *True Humorist*, June 24, 1865; *Morning News*, June 28, 1865.

55. *Daily News*, July 13, 1866.

56. *New Dominion and True Humorist*, July 13, 1867.

57. *Ibid.*

58. *True Humorist*, June 8, 1867.

59. *Ibid.*, June 22, 1867.

60. Among the plays repeated most frequently were *The Lady of Lyons, Still Waters Run Deep, The Honeymoon, Black-Eyed Susan, Money, Serious Family, The Marble Heart, London Assurance, The Willow Copse, Don Ceasar de Bazan, Richelieu, The Octoroon, Colleen Bawn, Toodles*, and the Shakespearean tragedies.

61. New Brunswick Museum, Playbill Collection.

62. Harvard Theatre Collection, Playbill for August 11, 1868; *Daily News*, July 20 & 22, 1868.

63. *New Dominion and True Humorist*, August 15, 1868.

64. *Courier*, July 19, 1862.

65. *Ibid.*, June 18, 1864. Cf. July 20, 1861.

66. H. Price Webber, "Fun at Lanergan's", *Progress*, 1891. Webber does not date the incident. Bock, however, played Achmet in 1864.

67. *Ibid.* In an article in the *Globe*, about 1922, Webber said that the stagehand fled to the paint bridge to escape the wrath of Mr. Couldock, who, just before curtain time, had found a warming pan not in its proper place on the set. (Saint John Regional Library, Willett Scrapbook 84).

68. *New Dominion and True Humorist*, May 16, 1868.

69. For more details on Lanergan's actors in Halifax see Janet Maybee, "Theatre in Halifax 1850-1880" (M.A. thesis, Dalhousie University, 1966).

70. *Boston Times*, March 12, 1876.

71. *New Dominion and True Humorist*, August 15, 1868.

Chapter IV

1. *New Dominion and True Humorist*, August 15, 1868.

2. *Halifax Herald*, November 11, 1909, quoted from the *Boston Post*, October 3, 1909.

3. *Morning News*, February 17, 1865.

4. *New Dominion*, March 6, 1869.

5. *Ibid.*, February 19, 1870.

6. *Ibid.*, February 13 & 15 and September 30, 1872. The evidence of the Saint John

newspapers does not always agree with the biographical details about Price Webber put forth by Fred Phillips in *The Atlantic Advocate* LIII, 6 (February 1963), 61-64 and *Canadian Theatre Review*, Spring 1979, pp. 102-105.

7. *Acts of the General Assembly of Her Majesty's Province of New Brunswick, 1870* (Fredericton: Fenety, 1870), 159f. A subsequent Act, passed on May 17, 1871, empowered the Company to raise the capital stock from $20,000 to $30,000.

8. *Daily Telegraph and Morning Journal*, December 19, 1870. Some details in the preliminary article are corrected by later information.

9. *Telegraph*, May 8, 1872. The paper says Beard resigned at the first annual meeting on May 1, 1871. The *Daily News*, May 6, 1872, omits his name from the list of original directors and names February 28, 1871 as the date of the organizational meeting. *Acts of the General Assembly*, 1872, p. 113, lists as directors in 1872 George E.S. Keator, Thomas W. Carritte, John Guthrie, Thomas B. Buxton, and Howard D. Troop.

10. Saint John Registry Office, 25, 16. Robinson's property was Lot 89 on Germain Street.

11. The source for construction details is *Daily News*, May 6, 1872; *Telegraph*, May 8, 1872.

12. *Daily News*, April 16, 1872.

13. *Ibid.*, May 2, 1872.

14. *Ibid.*

15. George Stewart's, *The Great Fire in St. John, N.B.* (Toronto, 1877), p. 51 gives the Academy's dimensions as 190 by 51 feet, while the *Telegraph* of May 8, 1872, says they were 200 feet by 50 feet 10 inches. According to the deed, the lot was only 50 feet wide. Stewart and the *Telegraph* give the height of the front of the building as 65 feet, whereas the *Daily News* of May 6, 1872 incorrectly says the front was 60 feet high and the rear 65. In addition, Stewart says there were 600 chairs in the parquet while the *News* says 546; the *Telegraph* says the theatre was designed to hold 1,200 persons overall. Though the *Daily News* and *Telegraph* give the most detailed descriptions of the interior, see also *New Dominion*, May 11, 1872, and *Morning Freeman*, May 9, 1872.

16. *Daily News*, May 6, 1872. Stewart says that the building, when finished, cost the company over $60,000. The *News* itemizes several of the costs. The *Telegraph* of May 8, 1872, gives the dimensions of the whole stage as 49 by 67 feet and of the area between the wings and from the rear flats to the footlights as 26 by 49 feet; it itemizes the scenery and lists the stockholders.

17. *Daily News*, April 24, 1872.

18. *Ibid.*, May 9 & 10, 1872.

19. *New Dominion*, May 11, 1872.

20. *Ibid.*, July 13, 1872.

21. *Ibid.*, June 3, 1872.

22. Saint John Registry Office, C6, 486-9. *Acts of the General Assembly*, 1872, 112-116, confirms the mortgage to Christie and Ferguson. It confirms also another mortgage to the directors of the Academy (C6, 34-36). The mortgage to Christie was cancelled on July 3, 1872, and that to the directors on December 22, 1873.

23. *Daily News*, September 30, 1872.

24. *Ibid.* See also September 27 and December 6.

25. *New Dominion*, October 6, 1872.

26. *Ibid.*

27. New Brunswick Museum, Quinton Papers. Besides the agreement with Quin-

ton and Tilley, bills of scantling and other documents pertaining to the construction of the building are contained in these papers.

28. *St. John and Its Business* (St. John: H. Chubb & Co., 1875), p. 42.

29. *Daily News*, May 6, 1872.

30. *New Dominion*, May 9, 1872.

31. For a demographic study of Saint John in 1871, see David Roberts, "Social Structure in a Commercial City: Saint John, 1871", *Urban History Review*, October 1974, pp. 15-18.

32. The Liberals were called Smashers because they were "allegedly the destroyers of the good old way of doing public business and the apostles of radical change." MacNutt, *New Brunswick*, p. 362.

33. See MacNutt, *New Brunswick*, pp. 423ff.; Hannay, *History of New Brunswick*, II, 233ff. for the political background of the satires.

34. See Hannay, II, 293ff; Katherine MacNaughton, *The Development of the Theory and Practice of Education in New Brunswick 1784-1900* (Fredericton, 1947); Peter M. Toner, "The New Brunswick Separate Schools Issue 1864-1876" (M.A. thesis, University of New Brunswick, 1967).

35. A fragment of a play that pokes fun at newspapers as well as at politicians is preserved in the New Brunswick Museum, Tufts Scrapbook 1, 150-152. Entitled "Land Ahead!" by "Loophole", it was written for the *Times*, a paper that was published for a short time in 1861.

36. The play is preserved in the New Brunswick Museum, Tufts Scrapbook 1, 63-65. Although it was written for the *New Dominion and True Humorist*, the papers are not extant. Dates of December 17 and 30, 1864, are pencilled on the play. Beside it in the scrapbook is a satirical article entitled, "The New Fire Brigade", which can be found in the *New Dominion and True Humorist*, December 10, 1864.

37. Scene 2 is missing.

38. St. Stephen, September 21, 1867.

39. On Murdoch see W.G. MacFarlane, *New Brunswick Bibliography* (Saint John: Sun Printing Co., 1895), p. 60 and *Telegraph Journal*, January 10, 1924.

40. *Daily News*, May 13, 20 & 26, 1872.

41. On August 24, 1872, Lanergan renewed his lease for five years from May 1, 1872 to May 1, 1877, at the yearly rent of £85. (Saint John Registry Office, B8, 393-396).

42. *New Dominion*, June 7, 1873.

43. *Daily News*, June 18, 1873.

44. *Telegraph*, May 8 & 9, 1874.

45. *New Dominion*, May 23, 1874.

46. *Ibid.*, July 11, 1874.

47. *Telegraph*, May 23, 1874.

48. T.C. Howard had been with Lanergan in 1866 and 1867 and received unfavourable reviews with his own company at the Institute in 1867.

49. *Morning News*, August 21, 1867; *New Dominion*, August 24, 1867. The company is not named.

50. *Telegraph*, December 1, 1874.

51. *McAlpine's Saint John City Directory, 1874-5* (Saint John: McAlpine). The gentlemen who rewarded Nannary with a complimentary bouquet are probably the same "merchants and professional gentlemen" who similarly rewarded Mr. Lanergan on July 18.

52. Small's Hall is next in the news in November 1875 as the Figaro. It had become a ballroom for the winter quadrille assemblies.

53. *Daily News*, June 15, 1875.

54. *New Dominion*, July 10, 1875. A review of the entire season, on September 11, expresses the same opinion.

55. Quoted in *Telegraph*, November 26, 1875.

56. *Telegraph*, December 28, 1875. A detailed description of the ornamentation is given.

57. A detailed account of the annual meeting of the Academy of Music is given in the *Daily News*, May 2, 1867.

58. *Watchman*, July 8, 1867, in Ralph Picard Bell Library, Stewart Scrapbooks. Cf. Chapter III, where Roche was praised as a 'natural actor'. The perception of what is 'natural' has obviously changed.

59. *Watchman*, probably June 3, 1876, in Ralph Picard Bell Library, Stewart Scrapbooks. *The Overland Route* was performed on May 29 & 30.

60. *New Dominion*, July 8, 1876.

61. *Daily News*, September 22, 1876.

62. Saint John Registry Office, B8,393-396. See also B8,4330435, and I1, 108f.

63. *Daily News*, May 24, 1877.

64. *Ibid.*, June 20, 1877.

Chapter V

1. Metropolitan Toronto Library, Taverner Collection, Box 8, "Address given about 1918 by Ida Van Cortland to the University Women's Club of Ottawa."

2. Annual Report (1877-1878), quoted in Evelyn Costello, "A Report on the Saint John Mechanics' Institute 1838-1890", M.A. report, University of New Brunswick, 1974, p. 30.

3. Journal of the House of Assembly of New Brunswick (1841), p. 189.

4. *Morning News*, September 17, November 12, 17 & 26, 1856.

5. *Telegraph*, May 7, 1881.

6. Jno. B. Jeffrey, *Guide and Directory to the Opera Houses, Theatres, Public Halls, Bill Posters, etc. of the Cities and Towns of America* (Chicago, 1887-8), p. 338.

7. *Telegraph*, May 7, 1881.

8. *Morning Freeman*, January 25, 1878.

9. *Daily News*, August 17, 1877.

10. *New Dominion*, September 1, 1877.

11. *Ibid.*, August 28, 1877.

12. *Daily News*, September 24, 1877.

13. *Ibid.*, October 15, 1877.

14. *Telegraph*, May 28, 1878.

15. *New York Dramatic Mirror*, May 14, 1898; New York Public Library, Locke Collection.

16. Metropolitan Toronto Library, Taverner Collection, Box 10.

17. New York Public Library, Locke Collection, Ser. 2; *New York Times*, May 6, 1924; *World*, May 11, 1924.

18. *Telegraph*, August 26, 1880.

19. New York Public Library, Locke Collection, Ser. 3.

20. A. Wagner & R. Plant, eds., *Canada's Lost Plays* (Toronto: CTR Publications, 1978), II, 158-193.

21. *Telegraph*, January 12, 1881.

22. *Ibid.*, February 9, 1981. The *Sun*, February 9, said that both gallery and parquet were filled and that people were sitting in the aisles.

23. *Telegraph*, July 21, 1881.

24. *Ibid.*, October 10, 1881.

25. *Minneapolis Journal*, January 17, 1916.

26. *Globe*, July 3 & 4, 1882; *Telegraph*, July 3 & 4, 1882.

27. *Telegraph*, July 25, 1882.

28. *Ibid.*, February 12, 1883.

29. *Ibid.*, April 28, 1883. On April 27, the *Sun* said that fewer than 180 people were present at *Patience* the previous evening. It agreed with the *Telegraph* that the company was excellent.

30. See David Goss, "When the Maritimes Met Jersey Lily", *Atlantic Advocate*, December 1979, pp. 57-62.

31. *Sun*, June 6, 1881; *Telegraph*, May 31, June 6 & 7.

32. The name is spelled variously Taverner, Taverney, Treverner, Teverner, and Tavernier. The spelling most frequently used on playbills and advertisements is Tavernier.

33. Metropolitan Toronto Library, Taverner Collection, Box 10.

34. *Ibid.*, Box 8, "Address given about 1918 by Ida Van Cortland".

35. *Telegraph*, September 11, 1883; *Globe*, September 15, 1883.

36. *Telegraph*, August 27, 1884; *Sun*, August 2, 1884.

37. Uncle Tom's Cabin Companies to perform in Saint John in the 1880's included the Double Boston Ideal Company, Peck and Fursman's Mammoth Spectacle Uncle Tom's Cabin Company, and Abbey's Double Mammoth Uncle Tom's Cabin Company.

38. *Harper's Monthly Magazine*, June 1912.

39. New York Public Library, Miln clipping file.

40. *Telegraph*, February 26, 1886.

41. *Sun*, January 3, 1887.

42. New York Public Library, Clay clipping file.

43. Interview in New York *Dramatic Mirror*, August 10, 1895.

44. *Telegraph*, August 24, 1886.

45. *Ibid.*, August 30, 1886.

46. Annual Report of the Mechanics' Institute (1886-1887).

47. *Telegraph*, April 19 & 20, 1887. The *Sun*'s evaluation of her acting was much more positive (April 19, 20 & 21).

48. VIII, 684.

49. *Acts of the General Assembly*, 1888, p. 78f.

50. *Telegraph*, August 21, 1889.

51. *Indianapolis News*, January 15, 1910.

52. *Telegraph*, September 11, 1888.

53. *Progress*, September 22, 1888.

54. New York Public Library, Locke Collection.

55. *Telegraph*, October 22, 1888. The *Sun*, June 22, 1889, described the Lansdowne as a "cosy theatre".

56. *Telegraph*, June 21, 1889.

57. *Ibid.*, June 25, 1889.

58. *Ibid.*, June 20, 1889.

59. *Sun*, July 20, 1889.

60. "Theatrical Stars in St. John", *Globe*, December 15, 1922.

61. The New York *Dramatic Mirror*, June 29, 1889, lists the future plans of company members.

62. New Brunswick Museum.

63. *Telegraph*, June 23, 1887; *Progress*, January 26, 1889.

64. *Progress*, March 2, 1889; *Telegraph*, March 1, 1889.

65. The Father Mathew Association was organized in Saint John on March 9, 1871. Its objects were to promote total abstinence among Catholic young men and to encourage its members in the practice of temperance and in intellectual advancement. See *Constitution and Rules of the Father Mathew Association* (Saint John: Lingley, 1901).

66. *Weekly Freeman*, March 22, 1884.

67. *Telegraph*, March 18, 1886.

68. New York: Dewitt, 1883.

69. Quoted in *Sun*, June 27, 1889.

70. *Weekly Freeman*, March 22, 1884.

71. For biographical details see New Brunswick Museum, Graves Papers, V, 107.

72. *Sun*, October 21 & November 20, 1893, and July 12 & 14, 1894.

73. *Coom-na-goppel* (Chicago: Dramatic Publishing Co., 1901); *A Medieval Hun* (Boston: Cornhill, 1921); *Crimson Wing* (Boston: Cornhill, 19–).

74. *Telegraph Journal*, May 29, 1936.

Chapter VI

1. *Telegraph*, October 29, 1878 has a detailed description of the proposed new theatre. See also December 4, 11, & 28, 1878.

2. New Brunswick Museum, "Prospectus and Stock List of New Academy of Music."

3. Details of the design are from "Prospectus and Stock List"; *Telegraph*, July 17, 1886; *Sun*, April 3, 1889.

4. The lease of the land from the Dockrills says it was actually back 64 feet. Saint John Registry Office, 37, 188-197.

5. *Julius Cahn's Official Theatrical Guide* (New York, 1906). Additional specifications in Cahn are these: "Distance between fly girders 39.6. No grooves. Height to rigging loft, 51 ft. Depth under stage, 9 ft. 5 traps. Height to fly gallery, 23 ft. 1 bridge, located in 4."

6. C.M. Wallace, "Saint John, New Brunswick (1800-1900)", *Urban History Review*, No. 1 – 75 (1975), 12-21; J.M. Careless, "Aspects of Metropolitanism in Atlantic Canada", *Regionalism in the Canadian Community* (Toronto, 1969), pp. 117-129; T.A. Acheson, "The National Policy and the Industrialization of the Maritimes, 1880-1910", *Acadiensis* I,ii (Spring 1972), 3-28.

7. *Telegraph*, September 6, 1887; *Progress*, November 3, 1888.

8. *Progress*, June 23, 1888.

9. *Telegraph*, August 11, 1886.

10. *Progress*, September 15 & 28, 1888, lists the new subscribers.

11. Saint John Registry Office, 37, 188-197. In a lengthy document, Richard H. Dockrill of Chicago and John F. Dockrill of Saint John leased the Union Street property to the Saint John Opera House Company for twenty-one years (renewable) at an annual rate of $1.00.

12. New Brunswick Museum, "Articles of Agreement . . . Between the Saint John Opera House Company of Saint John, N.B. of the First Part, and John B. Morri-

son of the same place Builder of the Second Part" and "Articles of Agreement . . . Between the Saint John Opera House Company of Saint John, N.B. of the First Part, and John Sharp and Richard Cassidy of the same place Builders of the Second Part."

13. Saint John Registry Office, 37, 199-205. Mary O'Connell, wife of David O'-Connell, Livery Stable Keeper, held the mortgage.

14. *Globe*, June 5, 1890; *Telegraph*, October 29, 1890.

15. *Telegraph*, October 22, 1890.

16. *Ibid.*, November 3, December 12 & 13, 1890, and January 27, 1891.

17. *Sun*, September 21, 1891.

18. *Julius Cahn's Official Theatrical Guide*; New Brunswick Museum, "Seating Plan St. John Opera House." The newspapers disagree as to the number of seats.

19. *Telegraph*, September 22, 1891. For a review of *Marble Heart* see *Globe*, September 22. The *Evening Gazette* of September 22 noted that many gentlemen showed their appreciation of the occasion by appearing in evening dress.

20. The *Sun*, November 5, 1894, reports fewer than 300 companies on the road — 125 dramatic, 47 comedy, 47 farce comedy, 14 comic opera, 12 minstrels, 11 variety, 7 burlesque, and 2 grand opera.

21. It is difficult to know what $5000 liability this was. The $5000 mortgage of October 17, 1890, to Mary O'Connell was not discharged until January 7, 1910 (Saint John Registry Office, 107, 553) and an additional mortgage of $5000 to Mrs. O'-Connell made on June 1, 1891 was not discharged until January 5, 1909 (Registry Office, 40, 485-496).

22. Philander Johnson, "Shakespeare Modernized", quoted in *Telegraph*, November 10, 1891.

23. *Telegraph*, January 9, 1893.

24. *Progress*, April 9, 1892.

25. New Brunswick Museum, Saint John Opera House Programme, Vol. 1, No. 57 (January 7 & 8, 1892).

26. *Telegraph*, December 2, 1890.

27. *Ibid.*, December 8, 1890.

28. *Halifax Herald*, November 11, 1909.

29. *Ibid.*

30. New Brunswick Museum, Tilley Papers, Three letters from L.H. Cronkhite to S.L. Tilley.

31. *Progress*, May 19, 1894.

32. *Sun*, July 2, 1894. See also *Sun*, July 4, 6 & 9; *Progress*, July 4; New Brunswick Museum, Tapley Scrapbook.

33. *Progress*, July 11, 1896.

34. New Brunswick Museum, Saint John Opera House Box Office Receipts. The ticket breakdown was as follows: 623 orchestra & 43 dress circle @ .50, 336 balcony@ .35, 485 gallery @ .15.

35. April 24, 1908.

36. *Sun*, May 30, 1898.

37. *Ibid.*

38. New York Public Library, Locke Collection, *The Green Book* (February, 1912); *New York Times*, September 23, 1949.

39. *Halifax Herald*, November 26, 1901.

40. *Telegraph*, December 5, 1891.

41. April 24 & May 22, 1875; April 6, 1878; May 20, 1882.

42. *Progress*, April 24, 1897.

43. *Sun*, January 20, 1894.

44. *Ibid.*, May 20, 1895.

45. *Ibid.*, August 20, 1899.

46. *Ibid.*, May 20, 1899.

47. New Brunswick Museum, Tapley Scrapbook 1.

48. New York Public Library, Locke Collection, Series 3, 343; Douglas L. Hunt, "Charles H. Hoyt: Playwright – Manager", *Theatre Annual* (1942), 42-50.

49. *Sun*, October 3, 1899.

50. *Boston Transcript*, October 20, 1898.

51. New York Public Library, undated programme.

52. *Ibid.*, Locke Collection.

53. *New York Dramatic Mirror*, July 4, 1896; *New York Herald Tribune*, May 30, 1933; *Telegraph*, September 7, 1892.

54. New Brunswick Museum, Saint John Opera House Box Office Receipts.

55. *Ibid.*, Tapley Scrapbook 1.

56. *Telegraph*, September 8, 1892. See J.F.L. Raschen, "Lewis Morrison's Production of Goethe's Faust," *Germanic Review*, IV (1929), 107-122.

57. *Sun*, March 30 & April 4, 1893.

58. *Progress*, January 5, 1895.

59. *Telegraph*, June 22, 1892.

60. Saint John Regional Library, Willet Scrapbook 7; William M. Baker, *Timothy Warren Anglin 1822-96* (U. of Toronto Press, 1977).

61. Young Monica Furlong made her stage debut with Miss Anglin at this time. She too later became a professional actress.

62. *Progress*, August 14, 1897.

63. *Sun*, August 11, 1897.

64. *Progress*, July 31, 1897.

65. Sarah Bernhardt was one of Margaret Anglin's admirers. After seeing Miss Anglin in *Zita*, Bernhardt "declared her the greatest English speaking actress and one of the few dramatic geniuses of the day." Saint John *Globe*, June 28, 1906, from the New York *World*.

66. *Dramatic Mirror*, April 30, 1892.

67. *Sun*, January 15, 1897.

68. *Progress*, August 1, 1896.

69. April 24, 1917.

70. *New York Times*, February 2, 1937; *New York Sun* and *New York Herald*, February 2, 1937.

71. *Sun*, July 6 & 17, 1897.

72. *Progress*, January 9, 1897.

73. *New York Herald Tribune*, April 6, 1937; *New York Times*, April 6, 1937.

74. *Sun*, July 26, 1897.

75. *New York Post*, December 30, 1931.

76. *New York Tribune*, January 10, 1932.

77. April 12, 1919.

78. February 28, 1897.

79. See interview in *New York Dramatic Mirror*, February 2, 1895.

80. *Dramatic News*, December 25, 1889 & December 25, 1892; *Dramatic Mirror*, February 13, 1892.

81. *Dramatic Mirror*, June 19, 1912.

82. *Progress*, July 29, 1899; *Spirit of the Times*, April 18, 1896.

83. *Sun*, March 26, 1900.

84. "Annual Meeting of the St. John Opera House Co. Shareholders", *Sun*, January 4, 1901.

85. A "Poem from Puck" entitled "At the Theatre", *Sun*, June 4, 1897. This poem effectively evokes the romance of the theatre at the end of the nineteenth century.

Index

234

236

239

240

Rogers, Katherine 150
Rollin Howard's Opera Bouffe Company 108
Roman Actor 35
Romeo and Juliet 35, 45, 73, 84, 115, 117, 126, 128, 139, 181, 215
Romp 32
Ronconi, Signor 165
Rose Michel 125
Rose of Castile 114, 136
Rose of Tyrol 124
Rosedale 123, 125, 147, 206, 208
Rossiter, Gabriel 40
Rosina 31
Rough Diamond 204
Rowe, George Fawcett 139, 147
Royal Dime Museum 135
Royal Museum 135
Royal Provincial Theatre 64
Roys, L. P. 73, 75, 85, 90
Russell, R. Fulton 128
Russell, Sol Smith 158
Russian Romance 148

Sackville x, 97, 150, 187, 207
Said Pashe 194
"Sailor's Return" 21
St. Andrew's Rink 175, 177, 180
St. Cecilia Society 173
St. John Amateur Athletic Club Minstrels 183
Saint John Amateurs 52, 183, 215
Saint John Amateur Minstrels 167
St. John Dramatic Club 98, 109, 114
St. John Fireman 149
St. John Gas Light Company 100
Saint John Histrionic Society 51, 52, 56, 223
St. John Hotel 61-63
Saint John Opera Company 165, 167
Saint John Oratorio Society 173, 174, 183
St. John Proscenium Club 183
St. John, Marguerite 162
St. John's 70, 140, 187, 201
St. Joseph Literary Club 109
St. Malachi's Hall 109, 168
St. Patrick's Hall 169
St. Stephen 187
St. Stephen's Hall 61
Salenki, Mrs. 9, 10
Salt Cellar 204
Sam 147
San Francisco 120, 158
Sands, Miss 42
Sanford, Edward 61-63
Santanella 184
Saratoga 123, 161
Sargent Aborn's Comic Opera Company 194
Savory, Miss 114
Sawtelle Dramatic Company 204, 212
Sawtelle, J. A. 206
Sawtelle, Jessie 206
Scallan, William 85, 225
Scammell, Fred E. 120
"Scene in the Bar Room of Barker House" 110
"Scenes in the Forecastle" 52
School for Scandal 56, 164, 215
Scribner Brothers Minstrel Troupe 97, 108
Scott, Claire 158

Sea of Ice 139, 207
Sergeants Amateur Dramatic Club 109
Serious Family 225
Seven Clerks 56
Sewell, Jonathan (Jr.) 6
Sewell, Jonathan (Sr.) 6, 219
Sewell, Stephen 6, 219
Shadows of a Great City 188
Shall He Forgive Her? 191
Sharp, John 174, 231
Shaughraun 122, 128, 137, 145, 164
Shaw, J. S. 48
Shea, Thomas 197, 199, 200
Shediac 108
She Stoops to Conquer 21, 28, 78, 84, 85, 148
Sheridan 73
Ship Ahoy 194
Shipman's Lyceum Company 217
Siddons, Sarah 6, 124
Side Tracked 196
"Sidewalks of Saint John" 111
Silver King 152, 200
Simonds, William 13
Singer Rink 202
Sinnott, W. Herbert 120
Siron Amateur Dramatic Club 167
"Sketches of St. John's Old Time's Rocks" 117
Skiff and Gaylord's Minstrels 108
Skinner, Alfred O. 174, 179
Skinner, Charles N. 174
Skinner, Professor 180
Slader 52
Slaves of Sin 199
Small's Hall 107, 110, 129, 227
Smith, A. Chipman 120
Smith, C. H. 147, 152
Smith, W. H. 35, 37, 42, 63
Smith, Mrs. W. H. 35, 37
Social Season 196
Soldier's Daughter 20, 22, 32, 40, 56
Soldiers Sweetheart 208
Solon Shingle 108
Sorcerer 167
Sothern, E. A. 70, 92
Sothern, Mrs. 70
Soudan 190, 191
Span of Life 196
Spear, Edward T. 208
Spectre Bridegroom 32
Speculation 207
Speed the Plough 17
Stafford, William 152
Standard English Opera Company 149
Standard Opera Company 180, 186, 194
Stanmore, Edith 153
Stanley 23
Star Company 61-63, 116-118, 122, 147
Sterne, Professor Max 165, 166
Sterner, Ernest 164
Stetson, E. T. 141
Stevens, James T. 120
Stevens, Sarah 70
Stewart & Hooper 28
Still Alarm 190
Still Waters Run Deep 62, 83, 139, 153, 213, 225
Stinson, Fred 141, 142